HISTORIES OF
THE IMMEDIATE PRESENT

THE MIT PRESS

CAMBRIDGE, MASSACHUSETTS

LONDON, ENGLAND

HISTORIES OF
THE IMMEDIATE PRESENT

INVENTING ARCHITECTURAL MODERNISM

ANTHONY VIDLER

© 2008 Massachusetts Institute of Technology

All rights reserved. No part of this book may be reproduced in any form by any electronic or mechanical means (including photocopying, recording, or information storage and retrieval) without permission in writing from the publisher.

MIT Press books may be purchased at special quantity discounts for business or sales promotional use. For information, please email special_sales@mitpress.mit.edu or write to Special Sales Department, The MIT Press, 55 Hayward Street, Cambridge, MA 02142.

This book was set in Filosofia by Graphic Composition, Inc. Printed and bound in the United States of America.

Library of Congress Cataloging-in-Publication Data

Vidler, Anthony.
Histories of the immediate present : inventing architectural modernism / Anthony Vidler.
  p. cm. — (Writing architecture)
Includes bibliographical references and index.
ISBN 978-0-262-72051-9 (pbk. : alk. paper)
1. Modern movement (Architecture) 2. Architecture—Historiography. 3. Architectural criticism—Europe—History—20th century. I. Title.
NA682.M63V53 2008
724'.6—dc22
                                                    2007020845

10 9 8 7 6 5 4 3 2 1

CONTENTS

FOREWORD: [BRACKET]ING HISTORY

Of all the terms in the architectural lexicon, or, for that matter, those of painting and sculpture, the one most laden with social and political opprobrium is *formalism.* To be a formalist is to be a target for everyone who feels that architecture is a social project full of rhetorical symbolism. Yet I was struck, while on a recent jury at a prestigious East Coast architecture school, by the pervasive influence of a new, perhaps more virulent breed of formalism, more virulent because it was posed under the banner of a neo-avant-garde technological determinism. The nexus of this formalism lay in advanced computer modeling techniques generated out of complex algorithms that produced parametric processes of enormous complexity and consistency, replete with their own variability and distortion. The range, variety, and energy of this work should have appealed to me personally, not only because of my memories of that particular institution as a bastion of intellectual conservatism, but also in part because this cutting-edge-process work was close to an idea of autonomy inherent in such authorless processes. Instead, I felt that something was radically wrong, something that speaks to a more general problem of architecture today. It was an autonomy freed from any passionate or firm ideological commitment. For the sake of argument, let us say that this lack of commitment lies squarely at the doorstep of such an empty formalism, one that internally determines how its products are to be read and interpreted. Both the lack of ideological commitment and the internally determined meanings link this new formalism with an idea of autonomy. But there is a second, more problematic idea of autonomy, a disciplinary one which is deceptively hidden, yet alluded to, in the chronological inversions of the title *Histories of the Immediate Present.*

Formalism, while seemingly emptied today of its critical and ideological power, nevertheless figured as a locus of resistance to postwar modernism. The repetitive or process-based sequencing of minimalist sculpture, of rationalist architecture, or of indexical, syntactic, linguistic analogies derived its formal bases from an internally generated system independent of social or functional concerns. In this context, the formal must be differentiated from formalism, the former having an internal value, the latter being the empty rhetoric of current shape-making. Any internally generated forms that are part of a critical system in one sense could be considered as autonomous, independent of social or market forces, while still offering a critique of these forces. It is a discussion of autonomy that animates one historian in particular in Anthony Vidler's text, and also might be said to animate the author himself. While autonomy is often understood as being implied by the formal, the distinction between the two is important, especially, today, between the terms *disciplinary autonomy* and *formal autonomy.* This difference seems important for Vidler, because it potentially allows him to confront and propose an answer to the Derridean claims against the possibility of a disciplinary autonomy.

In a first, sequential reading of this book, from the chapter on Emil Kaufmann to those on Colin Rowe, Reyner Banham, and Manfredo Tafuri, it appears that Vidler presents a narrative of architectural history-writing up to the third quarter of the last century. This in itself would be noteworthy, particularly since history today is so quickly consumed and forgotten. What is important, however, in this book is not the critical differences between these historians but how their differences reveal their arguments to be measures of the varied distances charted in architecture's disciplinary evolution, from circa 1920 until today.

Architecture's uncanny repetitions and recursions, from the formalism of Russian ideologues to that of today's expert renderers, for example, suggest that the distances mapped by such histories are anything but linear. This is revealed in a first reading of the book's title, as well as in its intellectual genealogy. However, while the sequence Rowe-Banham-Tafuri follows that genealogy, Kaufmann, positioned as originator, source, and starting point, does not. Why begin with Kaufmann, a historian of the Viennese school whose work is intellectually of another generation than that of the other three historians? Only on a close rereading of the chapter on Kaufmann does what appeared to be an anomalous inclusion (perhaps, as Vidler himself acknowledges, as a marker of the author's personal history) reveal itself to be the vehicle of a second, more important agenda. Whether Vidler intended this agenda is not at issue: rather, that it is possible to read this book in the following light.

Vidler's query is implicit in his very title: How is the history of modernism and its historians to be interpreted and written after Jacques Derrida's and other poststructuralists' critiques of disciplinary boundaries, given that it is these very boundaries that have traditionally made history's larger figures and minor movements visible? In the introduction to the chapter on Kaufmann, partial answers to the questions "why Kaufmann?" and "how, after Derrida?" are found; or, in other terms, how to see in the present moment the recursions to prior historical moments. In this sense, Vidler's *Histories* ultimately can be seen as a reply, no matter how schematic, to Derrida's critique of disciplinary boundaries.

In suggesting that the boundaries of disciplines such as architecture or history are primarily political, and therefore temporally bound if not at times even fictive, Derrida implicates the idea of disciplinary autonomy as one that relied on these fictive boundaries, and which is unsustainable in light of the contingency of meaning. Derrida's techniques for calling attention to such contingency involved placing a given term under erasure, or in other cases, bracketing the term, that is, calling attention to both its absence and presence, yet simultaneously avoiding a dialectical relationship between an absence and a presence. It is this undecidable nature that is the essence of the idea of the bracket. It could be argued that Vidler borrows a tool from Derrida's own arsenal by bracketing history, thereby suggesting that even the immediate present can be seen as the historical past. If "history" can be seen as a bracketed term here, then this bracketing offers an alternative to the disciplinary boundaries of history and architecture, and ultimately brackets any form of autonomy. To do this, Vidler purposely reintroduces the question of autonomy as a subject through the vehicle of Kaufmann.

Vidler begins the chapter on Kaufmann with a 1960 quotation from Clement Greenberg, who identified modernism with both a self-critical capacity and a disciplinary formalism: "To criticize the means itself of criticism" suggests the ability to erect an internal boundary, as it were, enabling the critic to view his own critique, which has been seen in the ensuing years to be an unrealizable goal. In his first paragraph, Vidler creates the link between any internal critique and an idea of autonomy, describing autonomy as an "internal exploration" and a way of transforming a discipline's "own specific language." For Kaufmann, architectural autonomy involved a range of large- and small-scale formal moves. For example, in articulating the difference between Renaissance and baroque architecture, he emphasized the formal aspects of massing and style. The breakdown of baroque part-to-whole hierarchies pointed toward the free association of entities, as in Ledoux's pavilion scheme for Chaux, whose independence of part-to-whole organizations embodied a type of formal autonomy. Kaufmann suggests that the isolation of parts in Chaux, which is a revision of the hierarchical, centralized massing of the baroque, continues even into the modernism of Le Corbusier. While modernism was thought to be a social project, Kaufmann argued that any definition of autonomy does not mean isolation from the social, but rather demonstrates the relations between the social and the formal.

It is necessary to turn to Kaufmann's predecessor and mentor in Vienna, Heinrich Wölfflin, for another distinction between a formal and a disciplinary autonomy, seen in the difference between the Renaissance and the baroque. Wölfflin argues that Renaissance architecture was autonomous because it was governed by an idea of a formal beauty internal to its discipline, one not deduced from the characteristics exhibited in the works of a particular style but that exists in its own right. On the other hand, for Wölfflin the baroque could not be considered autonomous because its forms were conditioned by the political factors of the Counter-Reformation rather than by any internal aesthetic concerns. Thus Wölfflin, unlike Kaufmann, locates autonomy squarely in the sights of a disciplinary autonomy.

If Wölfflin's and Kaufmann's attempts to articulate criteria for autonomy are to be accepted, and if Derrida is correct in pointing to the ways in which disciplinary boundaries are largely fictive, then it becomes clear that the concept of autonomy post-1968, and today, must be rethought. It is this problematic that Vidler would like to provoke, first by introducing Kaufmann and the idea of autonomy and then by proposing the concept of a posthistory in his conclusion. With the idea of a posthistory, Vidler addresses one of Derrida's most challenging critiques of disciplinary autonomy. The idea of a posthistory, in Vidler's terms, implies that there is a limit to every discipline. This concept would be applicable even to Derrida's deconstruction of disciplinary autonomy. If autonomy has been seen as the basis for architecture's capacity to enact a critical project, that is, a project that has the capacity to be critical of its own discipline, then deconstruction would hold that such a critical project remains in the realm of metaphysics, and in that sense, not autonomy. Thus, in proposing a posthistory, Vidler is himself bracketing Derrida's critique. Ultimately, this may be one way that the concept of a critical architecture can survive deconstruction.

Peter Eisenman

PREFACE

These essays on historians of architectural modernism represent my long-standing interest in the critical relations between architectural history and contemporary design. In this sense, the book is an introduction to the complex set of issues that have bound the history, criticism, and theory of architecture together in the assessment and influences of early twentieth-century modernism. It is a commonplace that history, whether written by architects or by art historians, has always been influenced by contemporary concerns, but this has been especially true in a profession that, since the end of the nineteenth century, has ostensibly jettisoned its relations to history and its "styles" in favor of abstract "form." The gradual historicization of this movement, not to mention its own characterization as "style," has resulted in a wide range of hypotheses as to its origins and consequences, all bound up with the critical reassessment of the effects of modernity and modernization since the 1940s. The early historians of the modern movement were open in their partisan espousal of one form or another of modernism and in their effort to trace its origins to particular historical moments in architecture, whether the baroque or the Arts and Crafts movement. The next generation—the protagonists of this book—coming to maturity after the catastrophe of the Second World War, were less inclined to such unabashed historicism and ostensibly more concerned with historical accuracy, but were, nevertheless, deeply complicit in different ways with architects' efforts to rethink modernism for the second half of the century. Most were equally committed to writing both history and criticism, and all were influential on the theory and practice of their contemporaries; all were inevitably marked by their own intellectual formation, in reaction to or continuity with their advisors and mentors.

In what follows I have looked at the contexts in which Emil Kaufmann, Colin Rowe, Reyner Banham, and Manfredo Tafuri forged their approaches to criticism and history, analyzing their more significant contributions and touching on specific instances of their contemporary influence. Despite the recent tendency of historians to join with Tafuri in the critique of what he called "operative" criticism, I take the position that such biases are inevitable and a part of the necessary intellectual equipment of the architectural writer. Kaufmann was open in his commitment to Enlightenment values, in the eighteenth century as in the twentieth; Rowe was never hesitant to apply the techniques of mannerist analysis to present design; Banham once wrote: "History is, of course, my academic discipline. Criticism is what I do for money," but it is evident throughout his writings in both fields that the two come together in his strongly held beliefs about technology, popular culture, and the new form of cities. Even Tafuri, turning to history and criticism after his training as an architect and planner, could not help but reveal his preferences, influencing a generation of designers through his theoretical choices and analytical strategies.

My interest in architectural history was stimulated in 1960, at my first (and quite terrifying) tutorial with Colin Rowe in his modernist apartment on Fen Causeway in Cambridge. Handing me a copy of Emil Kaufmann's then recently published *Architecture in the Age of Reason*, he asked, gesturing toward a folio of Colin Campbell's *Vitruvius Britannicus* lying open on the floor before him: "Well, and what do *you* make of *concatenation*?" This enigmatic question, over which I puzzled for many weeks, succeeded in stimulating my interest in the late eighteenth century and especially in Claude-Nicolas Ledoux. Rowe's subsequent desk critiques in Second Year studio, where *parti* was layered over *parti* on yellow tracing paper in thick soft-pencil with trembling hand, with his extraordinary visual recall of historic compositions as formal diagrams and potential inspiration, offered object lessons in the tradition of modernist art historical analysis from Heinrich Wölfflin and Paul Frankl to his own teacher, Rudolf Wittkower.

1960, the first year of my studies at Cambridge, also saw the publication of Reyner Banham's *Theory and Design in the First Machine Age*, a book immediately required by Colin St. John Wilson for his course on the history of modern theory. Banham's enthusiasm for futurism and Wilson's passion for the Dutch de Stijl movement created an excitement in the School of Architecture for research into the forgotten history of the avant-gardes, a history made more immediate by Professor Sir Leslie Martin's personal connection to the prewar *Circle* group, which included Naum Gabo and Ben Nicholson. Supporting this investigation into modernism's roots were visitors from the former Independent Group like Eduardo Paolozzi and Alison and Peter Smithson, together with others including Robert Maxwell, Neave Brown, and James Stirling, who was then occupied with the design of the History Faculty Library. The Smithsons' special issue of *Architectural Design* on the "Heroic Period of Modern Architecture (1917–1937)" in December 1965 summed up modernism for our generation—in some way as a sign of closure, but also of the need for competitive emulation. Against this, the unruly (from Cambridge's staid and strictly modernist point of view) incursions of Archigram, who with my willing help set up their "Living City" exhibit in the front lobby of Scroope Terrace in 1964, provided a healthy sense of utopianism and continuity with the early modern avant-gardes.

From 1960 to 1963, Peter Eisenman, an American doctoral student who taught me how to detail in wood "Japanese style" in the First Year design studio, was developing his own thesis on the formal analysis of modern architecture under the supervision of Martin and the intellectual stimulus of Rowe. It was Eisenman who, returning to a position at Princeton University, invited me to join him in a yearlong research project on the New Jersey Corridor in 1965, a year in the United States that has since stretched to the present. At Princeton I encountered another British exile, Kenneth Frampton, whose omnivorous and committed engagement with history and contemporary practice convinced me to dedicate myself to the teaching of history and theory. For several years the Analysis and Theory seminars were divided into two, one for the period 1650 to 1900, which I taught, the other from 1900 to the present taught by Kenneth. Such was my introduction to what became my first field of specialization in the eighteenth century.

It was also at Princeton that I first met Manfredo Tafuri, invited as a guest lecturer by Diana Agrest. Over the next several years in Venice, I came to know him as a colleague who, until his untimely death in 1994, stimulated and guided my work, offering his hospitality and introducing me to the group of his students and colleagues at the Institute of History, Istituto Universitario di Architettura in Venice, who have continued as lively interlocutors and friends to the present.

My selection of historians is thus obviously partial and avowedly personal: I have not attempted to treat the field of modernist historiography as a whole, nor do I consider in detail a number of significant contributors to the debates over the role of history—Vincent Scully in the United States and Leonardo Benevolo, Bruno Zevi, and Paolo Portoghesi in Italy would be notable examples of omission. Rather, as a historian and critic trained as an architect, I have been drawn to explore the complexities of my own relationship to the scholarly, critical, and professional disciplines of architecture—disciplines introduced to me by the four writers and teachers considered here. Nor has it escaped me, as an immigrant to the United States, that three out of the four scholars—Kaufmann, Rowe, and Banham—were to finish their careers here, the first in forced exile, the other two in voluntary emigration.

Acknowledgments

Those who have read, listened to, and discussed parts of this work include Carl Schorske, Kurt Forster, Reinhold Martin, Beatriz Colomina, Mark Wigley, Alan Colquhoun, Robert Maxwell, and Mark Cousins, who offered a stimulating critique in a seminar at the Architectural Association. My thinking on Kaufmann and Giedion was especially sharpened by discussion with Detlef Mertins as he developed his doctoral work at Princeton. I also thank those institutions that asked me to deliver portions of this work in progress, especially the schools of architecture at Yale, Columbia, Princeton, UCLA, and the TU Delft. Preliminary versions of parts of this book were written for the conferences and publications of Anyone Corporation, *Log*, *October*, *Representations*, *Perspecta*, and the University of California Press. I thank their respective editors for their advice. Finally, I want to thank those who read and commented on this book in its first draft as a doctoral thesis for TU Delft and the Berlage Institute, Rotterdam: Weil Arets, Arie Graafland, Michael Hays, Karsten Harries, Michael Müller, Jean-Louis Cohen, and Tony Fretton. I am indebted to Felicity Scott and Spyros Papapetros for their careful reading and comments, and to Cynthia Davidson for her editorial clarity. Unless otherwise noted, all translations are mine. The book is dedicated to the memory of Ignasi de Solà-Morales, whose critical mind was continually wrestling with these questions and whose friendship sustained my faith in architectural discourse for more than thirty years.

Anthony Vidler
New York
January 2007

HISTORIES OF
THE IMMEDIATE PRESENT

INTRODUCTION

What has been the influence of contemporary architectural historians on the history of contemporary architecture?
—Reyner Banham, "The New Brutalism"

In this book I am concerned with the various ways in which architectural historians in the decades after the Second World War began to assess the legacy of the avant-gardes in order to attempt a coherent narrative of the development of modernism. In the search for a unified vision of modernity following the heterogeneous experiments of the avant-gardes in the first quarter of the twentieth century, historians played a decisive role, defining early twentieth-century programs, forms, and styles in such a way as to imply possible continuities with the present. While there have been an increasing number of studies on the historiography of modernism in recent years, opening up fields of investigation into the value of viewing history as a participant in the history it recounts, I am interested in the ways in which histories of modernism themselves were constructed as more or less overt programs for the theory and practice of design in their contemporary context. That is, whether or not the "origins" of modernism were traced to earlier moments in the Renaissance, mannerist, baroque, or revivalist periods, each genealogy, itself based on art historical theories of style, society, space, and form, proposed a different way of looking at the present and its potential; each, that is, conceived within the dominant paradigms of abstraction, was susceptible to use by architects seeking a way to confront the social and cultural crises of the postwar period without losing sight of the principles that had inspired the early modernists.

Over the last few decades, architectural history has emerged as decidedly problematic for an architecture that, ostensibly at least, was from the beginning of the twentieth century dedicated to the suspension if not the eradication of historical references in favor of a universalized abstraction. What has been called "the return of historicism" by Nikolaus Pevsner, "postmodernism" by Charles Jencks, or "hypermodernism" by Manfredo Tafuri reveled in citations and renewed appeals to the authority of historical architecture, on the assumption that abstraction, the language of international modernism, had failed to gain popular acceptance, and was in any case essentially antihumanist.

Such a revivalism posed a problem for historians and critics. On the one hand, historians were again in demand, as much as they had been in the premodernist period, to provide authorization and depth to present practice. The idea of "type," to give one central example—an idea that stemmed from the need to rethink the tabula rasa planning strategies of the 1950s and to respect the internal formal and social structure of cities—was traced back to its theoretical roots in the eighteenth century.

This state of affairs modified what had been the dominant question for historians in the period of the high modern movement. Where, then, history was regarded with great suspicion as a potential harbinger of stylistic revival, now history was increasingly embedded in curricula and critical discourses. This history was no longer the "history" of the 1920s with its teleological vision of modern abstraction overcoming the "styles." It was both more academically correct according to the standards of art historical scholarship and more broadly based in interdisciplinary studies, linking it to the interpretative strategies of structuralism and poststructuralism. In the academy, the postmodernism of intellectual debates converged with the postmodernism detected in architectural practice; theory emerged as an almost separate discipline and, together with history in its most responsible forms, became more and more detached from design. For many historians and critics, like Manfredo Tafuri, this was as it should be: what Tafuri called "operative" criticism had been, in his terms, an obstacle since the seventeenth century to the dispassionate view of architecture demanded of the truly critical historian. In this ascription, historians should avoid espousing any particular tendency in contemporary architecture. But for others, this represented a dereliction of the social and political duty of the critic to engage the present with the full weight of past experience.

While more recently the acerbic debates between so-called modernists and postmodernists have softened a little, in favor of a generalized "late modern" position that joins technological expression to iconographic form, the question for history, and thereby for historians, remains. What, in short, does the architectural historian do, not qua historian, but for architects and architecture? Or, to put it more theoretically, What kind of work does or should architectural history perform for architecture, and especially for contemporary architecture? This of course is a version of the commonplace refrain, How is history "related" to design? Is it *useful*? And if so, in what ways?

This question is a relatively new one; for much of architectural history, history was not a problem for architecture—or rather, instead of being a "problem" per se, the questions surrounding history were a solution for the discipline. From the Renaissance to the mid-nineteenth century, that is, from the moment when medieval tradition was gradually but self-consciously replaced by the historical revival of antiquity, history supplied the very stuff of architecture. To that end, more or less without exception, the historian *was* the architect: from Alberti to Schinkel, it was the architect's responsibility to write the history that would authorize both precedent and innovation. Schinkel's unfinished lifework, *Das architektonische Lehrbuch*, was possibly the last in this long line of quasi-historical justifications of design. The emergence of the professional architectural historian, from James Fergusson, Jacob Burckhardt, Heinrich Wölfflin, Wilhelm Worringer, August Schmarsow, to Paul Frankl, marked the development of scholarly academic art history out of the scholarly revision of architectural history—until the sense of the "modern," allied with an emerging sense of "abstraction" and "form" guided by new structural imperatives, gave architects the sense of a break so complete with the "historical styles" that history itself became suspect.

Of course, history did not go away for modernism: rather, it became all the more essential on at least three levels—first, to demonstrate the fundamental antiquity of the old way of building; then, to tell the story of the prehistory of modernism as it emerged out of the old; and finally, with the help of abstract ideas of form and space, to be redrawn as a continuing process of invention and a repertory of formal and spatial moves.

To an extent, this condition held firm through the 1940s and 1950s, especially in academia, where historians like Bruno Zevi and Reyner Banham were appointed to chairs in architectural history in architecture schools. But it was also during this immediate post—World War II period that questions began to be asked about the continuing usefulness of history, traditional or modernist. For during these years the largely unselfconscious energies that had fueled the first- and second-generation modernists were themselves gradually subjected to the inevitable process of historicization. Indeed, as Fredric Jameson has pointed out, "modernism" itself as a concept and ideology—modernism as we tend to know it today—was largely a product of those postwar years, as critics and historians such as Clement Greenberg were building a coherent and systematized version of "modernism" founded on their interpretation of art from Manet to Pollock.[1] In the same way, in architecture, around the mid 1950s the status of history was thrown into doubt and its uses rendered questionable by the very history of the modern movement that had been written by its historians—Pevsner, Hitchcock and Johnson, and Giedion, to name just a few. Once relegated to the status of "history," modern architecture itself was susceptible to academicization, even to revival. And it was the revival of modern architecture as style in the 1950s and 1960s—what later critics were to see as the first instances of a "postmodernism"—that so disturbed the historians and critics who, like Sigfried Giedion and Nikolaus Pevsner in the 1930s and 1940s, had tried to write the history of modernism in a partisan, if not propagandistic, mode.

It is this moment that I want to examine, and through the lens of four of its most trenchant critics. For, in the debates about the effects of history on practice that enlivened the architectural scene in Europe and the United States in those decades, we can, I think, begin to set the groundwork for our own thinking about history, its uses and abuses, as Nietzsche once put it. Banham was one of the first to ask the question: "What has been the influence of contemporary architectural historians on the history of con-temporary architecture?" He answered it himself, noting, "They have created the idea of a Modern Movement. . . . And beyond that they have offered a rough classification of the 'isms' which are the thumb-print of Modernity."[2]

The first scholarly examinations of modern architecture began to appear in the late 1920s. Adolf Behne's *Der moderne Zweck-bau* (1926), Adolf Platz's *Die Baukunst der neuesten Zeit* (1927),

Sigfried Giedion's *Bauen in Frankreich* (1928), and Bruno Taut's *Modern Architecture* (1929), among many other collections, began the process of assembling the evidence and developing the criteria for "modernity," based on which Henry-Russell Hitchcock's *Modern Architecture: Romanticism and Reintegration* (1929), Walter Curt Behrendt's *Modern Building* (1937), Nikolaus Pevsner's *Pioneers of the Modern Movement* (1936), and Giedion's *Space, Time and Architecture: The Growth of a New Tradition* (1941) were able to construct more or less coherent narratives of origin and development.[3] Although almost all shared a common aversion to the word "history" as inimical to modern ideals, nevertheless, as Panayotis Tournikiotis has shown, these narratives shared a common concept of history as a determining, unfolding force, capable of articulating questions of the past, present, and future of architecture, as well as a belief in some form of sociocultural zeitgeist that, if correctly identified, equally determines the respective "modernity" or nonmodernity of the work.[4] History might lead architecture to modernity, but once there it was to be cast off, like the "styles" vilified by Le Corbusier in *Vers une architecture*.[5]

They were also extremely partial narratives, developing their genealogies from moments in the past that seemed to them starting points that would justify the specific contemporary practices they supported or admired. Thus Hitchcock, in *Romanticism and Reintegration*, sought the roots of his beloved "New Tradition" in the late eighteenth century, and was uneasy as well as excited by the work of the "New Pioneers," whom he saw as at once going beyond and disturbing the rationalism of Frank Lloyd Wright, Otto Wagner, Peter Behrens, and Auguste Perret. Pevsner, in *Pioneers of the Modern Movement*, focused on the relations between Britain and Germany, seeing the origins of Gropius's rational-functionalism in the Arts and Crafts movement and conveniently ignoring the French contribution, while Giedion failed to include more than a mention of Mies van der Rohe in his *Space, Time and Architecture*, preferring instead to leap from the baroque movement to that encapsulated in Le Corbusier's villas of the 1920s. But whatever their partialities, these pioneer works accomplished what the modernist architects themselves feared the most: the historicizing of modernism. Indeed, by 1940 modern architecture had become fully assimilated into the art historical canon and given its place in the history of the "styles." Where once Le Corbusier had declared the end of "The Styles" and Mies van der Rohe had rejected academic art history in favor of "building-art," now Hitchcock was rewriting the entire style history of architecture to define what he called an "International Style modeled on the spread of Gothic in the 12th century"; Pevsner was drawing a temporal line around something identifiable called the "Modern Movement"; and Giedion was articulating the relations and historical developments that tied together a modern vision and former styles.

Whether modern architecture was seen to begin with the baroque, classicism, neoclassicism, nineteenth-century eclecticism, or Arts and Crafts revivalism, the floodgates were now opened for a host of competing narratives, a variety of historically based modernisms, and several versions of a possible "unity" of style characterizing the "modern." Further, such a widening of historical reference and roots meant that the history of modern architecture was as dependent on the historians of other ages as it was on its own specialists: as modernity was defined, so its precedents were isolated—and vice versa, allowing historians of the Renaissance, the baroque, as well as those of the newly defined mannerist and neoclassical periods to refer to contemporary tendencies, if not define their own "styles" as a conscious or unconscious response to contemporary tendencies.

For what united all these historical assays of modernity with all other historical work in architecture was their common basis in a method that had emerged toward the end of the nineteenth century, a method that relied not so much on the identification of "stylistic" motifs as on the comparison of forms—masses, volumes, surfaces—in the abstract. Beginning with Alois Riegl's formal interpretation of ornament and his conceptual history of spatial vision, continuing with Heinrich Wölfflin's psychological analysis of form and studies of the Renaissance and baroque periods, and culminating in the spatial construction of history by August Schmarsow, the architecture of all periods was seen as a series of typical formal-spatial combinations, each tied to specific epochal "wills" or "drives," and each comparable to the next in a natural history of morphological transformation.[6] What the clues offered by the shapes of ears or drapery movements were to art historians like Bernard Berenson and Aby Warburg, so spatial form was to architectural historians.

Such a history, defining itself as more a history of space than a history of style, was not only commensurate with modernism's own aspirations but began to define an approach particular to an *architectural* history as it developed its disciplinary identity out of art history in general. Where, for Burckhardt and Wölfflin, architectural history formed an integral part of art history, if not a foundational and constructive object of its study, with the emergence of spatial analysis the three-dimensional characteristics of architecture began to set it apart, first from the visual and two-dimensional forms of painting, then from the equally visual but also empathetically haptic reception of sculpture as investigated by Adolf von Hildebrand.[7] Thus, Paul Frankl, in his 1914 study of the phases of development of modern building, set out to articulate a specific analytical method for architecture based on the identification of spatial form as it was inflected by structure, movement, and use.[8] His categories of spatial form (*Raumform*), corporeal form (*Körperform*), visible form (*Bildform*), and purposive intention (*Zweckgesinnung*) were then calibrated with each other in a chronology according to four phases of "development": Renaissance, baroque, rococo, and neoclassicism.

Perhaps most important to our argument, however, is Frankl's innovative attempt to develop diagrams of spatial organization. Whereas art historians had often described "virtual" diagrams of the temporal development of history, architectural historians like James Fergusson and César Daly had depicted temporal progress in diagram form, and historians of structure from Viollet-le-Duc to Auguste Choisy had adopted the axonometric projection to present plan, section, and volumetric form simultaneously, no historian until Frankl had conceived of a comparative taxonomy of diagrammed spaces, with their separate units, the rhythm of their bay structure, their interconnections, and potential movements between them joined in a single, simplified summary of the building.

This taxonomy differed from eighteenth- and nineteenth-century comparative presentations of type as in Julien-David Le Roy's comparative plans of religious buildings or Jean-Nicolas-Louis Durand's more complete historical "parallel," in that the notions of distribution and character that informed these earlier comparisons were directly related to plan form and effect. Frankl, by contrast, was working with an idea of spatial dynamics drawn from the psychology of Robert Vischer,[9] the baroque spatial studies of August Schmarsow, the psychological interpretations of Wölfflin, and later from the findings of gestalt psychologists. For Frankl, space has its own distinct relationships to movement, and the relations among spatial units have their rhythms and flows. Diagramming such relations would establish the essential formal characteristics of the object in its place in history and, through comparative analysis, trace the shifts between one phase of architectural development and the next. Through Frankl, architectural history gained its special form of representation, one that sought a diagram in each temporal moment and that was easily taken up by architects themselves as they attempted to incorporate history into their own more abstract designs.[10] In this process, which might be called the "diagramming" of history, it is possible to trace the reciprocal influence of abstraction as it emerges as a force in art and architecture and the exploration of more "scientific" methods in art history. Where modern architecture desires to shake off the stylistic eclecticism of the nineteenth century, modern art history obliges with a counterstylistic mode of analysis that emphasizes perception, experience, and psychological effect on the one hand, and basic formal attributes on the other. In this sense, Frankl's *Die Entwicklungsphasen der neueren Baukunst* (1914) appears as the architectural counterpart to Wölfflin's *Kunstgeschichtliche Grundbegriffe* (1915)—a relationship stressed by the title given to the later translation of Frankl's book: *Principles of Architectural History.*[11]

Given the preoccupation of the early generation of architectural historians with the Renaissance, it was no accident that the first histories of modernism were written by historians who had followed Riegl and Wölfflin in exploring the new territory of the baroque and its seeming extension into the modern period. Wölfflin had already shown his distaste for the baroque, seeing it as the first indication of the spatial dissemination characteristic of the modern period: "One can hardly fail to recognize the affinity that our own age in particular bears to the Italian Baroque. A *Richard Wagner* appeals to the same emotions."[12] Refusing Wölfflin's rejection of the baroque as "formless art," Giedion in his thesis *Spätbarocker und romantischer Klassicismus* (1922)—a work that relied methodologically on Riegl's *Spätrömische Kunstindustrie* (1901) even as it supplied the burthen of Hitchcock's *Romanticism and Reintegration*—began to fill the void left by Wölfflin between the baroque and the modern. Pevsner's first book, a detailed history of Leipzig baroque published in 1928 and based on his dissertation of 1924 (written at the University of Leipzig under Wilhelm Pinder), was explicitly indebted to Schmarsow's studies of baroque and rococo architecture.[13] His later studies in mannerism and the picturesque were directly tied to his belief that these styles prefigured modernism. Emil Kaufmann, student of Riegl and Dvořák, formed his conception of a "revolution" in architecture around 1800 out of his conviction that the generation of Ledoux and Boullée anticipated the modernism of Loos, Le Corbusier, and Neutra.

The enforced emigration of German and Austrian scholars in the 1930s brought these discussions to the attention of British and American audiences, giving a sense of historical legitimacy to a modern movement hitherto largely confined to the Continent. Emil Kaufmann, briefly in England and then taking up residence in the United States in 1940; Nikolaus Pevsner in England from 1933; Rudolf Wittkower moving to London in 1934 to join the Warburg Institute newly reestablished from Hamburg: these scholars and more, quickly integrated into the Anglo-Saxon intellectual culture of their hosts, were to provide the stimulus for a complete reevaluation of modernist history after 1945, as they gained an English-language readership hitherto denied them. Emil Kaufmann, hosted by Philip Johnson and the newly created Society of Architectural Historians in Boston, began ten years of research and publication on neoclassicism, its roots, and resonance to the present; Nikolaus Pevsner shifted his zeitgeist approach to national culture from Germany to England, and became a powerful force in contemporary architectural culture with his editorship of the *Architectural Review* after 1941; and Rudolf Wittkower, publishing his Palladian studies in the *Journal of the Warburg Institute* from 1946, began to attract the interest of a younger group of architects interested in reformulating the principles of a modernism distinct in its social and formal approach from prewar CIAM-dominated theory and practice.

The unsung progenitor of this reevaluation of modern history was Emil Kaufmann. By linking the pseudo-abstract designs of Ledoux and Boullée to the principles of the Enlightenment in his 1933 book *Von Ledoux bis Le Corbusier*, Kaufmann gave a depth to the idea of modernism that appealed to those wishing to sustain the inheritance of Le Corbusier, but needing to plumb new sources of rationalism in the face of its apparent betrayal in the postwar work at Ronchamp. Kaufmann's influence initially touched Philip Johnson in the early 1940s, endowing Johnson's own traduction of Mies with neoclassical overtones; later, with the posthumous (1954) publication of *Architecture in the Age of Reason*, Kaufmann won an audience in Britain and Italy, specifically with Colin Rowe and Aldo Rossi. Rowe himself was especially open to Kaufmann's thesis, having in 1947 followed his teacher Wittkower in pushing back the origins of modernism even further, to the mannerist period, stressing the continuity of tradition in mathematical order and mannerist composition. Rowe's influence on contemporaries, from Alan Colquhoun to James Stirling, was profound. At the same time, Reyner Banham, in an attempt to outdo his own teacher Pevsner, offered the first scholarly assessment of modern architecture in a kind of continuation of Pevsner's *Pioneers*, treating what he called the "zone of silence" between 1914 and 1939. It is paradoxical, in retrospect, that Rowe's modernized neo-Palladianism, at first taken up with enthusiasm by the "new brutalists," was to emerge as a foundation for Banham's own countermodern idea of the new brutalism, a stance later rejected in favor of his conclusion that the modern movement had failed in its technological aspirations.

The histories of modernism thus developed certainly rested on methodological, and often archival, bases that, from increased distance and primary research, were wider and deeper than those of their predecessors. However, their not-so-hidden agendas were, in different ways, still pointed toward contemporary practice. Kaufmann's Enlightenment was a clear moral fable for a renewed modern movement at a moment of serious social reaction in Germany and Austria; Rowe's modern mannerism opened the door to a variety of formal and semiotic experiments that gradually shifted the argument from new modern to postmodern; Banham's technological optimism and his call for "une architecture autre" supported brutalists, metabolists, and neofuturists. In this sense, the students of the first generation of modernist historians were as engaged in proselytizing as their teachers: from Pevsner and Giedion to Rowe and Banham, the objects of enthusiasm may have changed but not the message. History was at once source, verification, and authorization.

Among the first to criticize this "instrumental" use of history was Manfredo Tafuri, who, trained as an architect and planner, had begun his career as a historian by assessing the present state of modern historiography. Published in 1968, his essay *Teorie e storia dell'architettura* identified the profound "antihistoricism" of the modernist avant-gardes, and attempted to distinguish between the realms of criticism, theory, and history in such a way as to protect history from its complicity with practice.[14] His criticism was precisely aimed to those historians—Giedion, Zevi, Banham—who had seen history as instrumental in giving meaning to architecture, who had "read in late antique architecture the premises of Kahn or Wright, in mannerism those of expressionism or of the present moment, in prehistorical remains the premises of organicism or of a few 'nonformal' experiments."[15] Here, in his rigorous refusal of those who posed as the "Vestals" of the modern movement and his insistence on the historicization of the very instruments of criticism themselves, Tafuri attempted a demythologization of history, as complete as that assumed by his intellectual mentor Max Weber early in the twentieth century. And yet his ceaseless search for methods of analysis drawn from structuralism, psychoanalysis, semiology, and poststructuralism created a "theory effect" that proved for architects as powerful a lure as historical reference, one apparently shielded from the pitfalls of eclecticism by "scientific" authority.

In the following chapters, I examine the historical approaches of these four modernist historians and critics: Emil Kaufmann, Colin Rowe, Reyner Banham, and Manfredo Tafuri. Each is seen in the context of his intellectual formation, the specific nature of the "modernism" advanced by his historical narrative, and the influence of these models on practice. Rather than attempt a comprehensive review of the life and work of each historian, I have preferred to concentrate on a specific moment or group of writings that brings these issues sharply into focus and particularly on the period between 1945 and 1975, a period of especial intensity in the debates over the role of history in architectural practice and education. Each of these different histories imagined modernism in a form deeply complicit with the "origin" it proposed. Thus, the modernism conceived by Kaufmann was, like the late Enlightenment projects he selected, one of pure, geometrical forms and elemental composition; that of Rowe saw mannerist ambiguity and complexity in both spatial and surface conformations; that of Banham took its cue from the technological aspirations of the futurists, but with the added demand of successful realization; that of Tafuri found its source in the apparently fatal division between technical experiment and cultural nostalgia represented respectively by Brunelleschi and Alberti. Inevitably, each spawned its own version of the contemporary "modern," and each supported, often unwittingly, a selective list of approved architects.

In conclusion, I ask the more general question of whether the continued reliance on history by architects in the second half of the twentieth century should be seen as the apparently new phase commonly called "postmodernism"—or whether modernism as a whole, and from the outset, harbored its own spatio-entropic critique in what has become known since the 1860s as *posthistoire* thought, a sense of stasis and ending that matched the neofinalism of post-Darwinist biology.

In this investigation, then, I hope to demonstrate not the pernicious effect of history on design, nor the need radically to separate the two, but rather their inevitable collusion, one that pervades all modern architectural discourse, a collusion that has given rise to some of the more interesting architectural experiments of the postwar period, including Johnson's Glass House, Stirling's Staatsgalerie, Archigram's Living City, Rossi's Città Analogia, and, more recently, Koolhaas's Kunsthalle and Eisenman's Houses I–XI, to take only a very few examples.

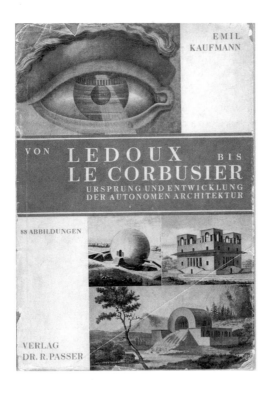

Emil Kaufmann, *Von Ledoux bis Le Corbusier* (1933), cover

1 NEOCLASSICAL MODERNISM
EMIL KAUFMANN

I identify Modernism with the intensification, almost the exacerbation, of this self-critical tendency that began with the philosopher Kant. Because he was the first to criticize the means itself of criticism, I conceive of Kant as the first real Modernist.
—Clement Greenberg, "Modernist Painting"

Autonomy

The idea of "architectural autonomy," the notion that architecture, together with the other arts, is bound to an internal exploration and transformation of its own specific language, has surfaced periodically in the modern period. Whether as a way of classifying the qualities of architectural "form" as opposed to "style," or as a way of defining the role of the architect in an increasingly specialized professional world, the assertion of autonomy has been a leitmotif of modernism since the end of the nineteenth century, if not earlier. Art historians beginning with Heinrich Wölfflin and continuing with Alois Riegl and their heirs; architects beginning with Adolf Loos and continuing with Le Corbusier and Ludwig Mies van der Rohe; critics beginning with Roger Fry and Adrian Stokes and continuing with Clement Greenberg and Rosalind Krauss, all in different ways and with differing agendas, have established their grounds of debate on the autonomy of modernist practices. In architecture, Aldo Rossi, Robert Venturi, and Peter Eisenman, among many others and in very different ways, have laid claim to the autonomy of architectural language.

Of all the writers and architects who have contributed over a century or more to the debate over autonomy, the Viennese historian Emil Kaufmann stands out as a consistent reference point for all subsequent discussions. For while, in retrospect, Wölfflin's development of a formal method for characterizing architectural periods, and Riegl's proposition of a historical and cultural specificity to the interplay of vision and space, could be seen as setting up the grounds for a modernist idea of autonomy in architecture and the other arts, it was Kaufmann who first joined the analysis of historical architecture to a philosophical position, derived from Kant, and who coined the phrase "autonomen Architektur," drawing on Kant's philosophical concept of the "autonomy" of the will. And it was Kaufmann who served to introduce the twin ideas of autonomy and modernism to successive generations of architects and critics, from Philip Johnson in the 1940s to Colin Rowe in the 1950s and Aldo Rossi in the 1950s and 1960s. More recently his work was at the center of a historical reassessment of autonomy and the avant-garde in the United States.[1]

Yet Kaufmann's thesis that modernism emerged in the work of Claude-Nicolas Ledoux in the 1770s and culminated in Le Corbusier has also had many art historical detractors since the publication of his polemically titled *Von Ledoux bis Le Corbusier* in 1933.[2] Since then the Viennese historian's view of architectural progress has been dismissed as simplistic by contemporaries like Edoardo Persico and Meyer Schapiro, cited as a pathological symptom of the decadence of modernism by conservative historians like Hans Sedlmayr, and deemed a travesty of historical scholarship by researchers from Michel Gallet to Robin Middleton.[3] Castigated as having "suffered from an excess of generalization," blamed for his "obsessive search for underlying principles . . . pursued to an extreme degree," and "undermined," in David Watkin's words, by a host of researchers following the lead of Wolfgang Herrmann's debunking of the traditional Ledoux chronology in 1960, Kaufmann's achievement is now largely forgotten.[4] He is perhaps the only important member of the so-called Vienna school of the 1920s whose work has not been reassessed in the last decade for its scholarly or methodological qualities. Hans Sedlmayr and Otto Pächt, even Guido Kaschnitz von Weinberg and Fritz Novotny, have been translated and their work analyzed in its historiographical and theoretical context.[5] Yet, in Christopher Wood's recent and important introductory study to his *Vienna School Reader*, Kaufmann is relegated to a footnote.[6]

His work has not always been denigrated, however. Kaufmann made significant contributions to the history of French eighteenth-century architecture throughout the 1920s, redefining traditional "classicism" by introducing the idea of "neoclassicism," and publishing the first major assessment of the architecture of Ledoux in the second volume of Sedlmayr and Pächt's flagship journal of Viennese *Strukturanalyse*. Schapiro, despite his measured social critique of the formal approach, dedicated a large portion of his 1936 review of the Vienna school's methods to Kaufmann's writing on Ledoux. And in his notes for the unfinished *Das Passagen-Werk*, Walter Benjamin also cited liberally from Kaufmann's brief but trenchant treatment of Ledoux's life and work in *Von Ledoux bis Le Corbusier*—the first comprehensive monographic treatment of the French architect by any architectural historian.[7]

Further, Kaufmann's discoveries have inspired generations of scholars to work on the architecture of the revolutionary period, whether or not they agree with Kaufmann that something "revolutionary" was to be detected in the prerevolutionary and monarchical Ledoux. His work posed questions about the historiographical treatment of the "origins" of modernism and, by implication, about the entire construction of historicist history from Nikolaus Pevsner to Sigfried Giedion. It interrogated the nature of abstraction in relation to the geometrical forms employed by the Enlightenment and the modernist avant-gardes, and thereby challenged the premises of anachronism in history and criticism. It opened up the imbricated problems of form and politics, architecture and society, in a way that directly challenged the cultural ideology of National Socialism in the 1930s. His sobriquet "revolutionary architect," as applied in his 1952 book *Three Revolutionary Architects* to the trio Ledoux, Boullée, and Lequeu (a trio he had largely discovered and, so to speak, invented), while much misunderstood, nevertheless succeeded in gaining these three the attention of serious scholars.[8] For at least a decade, his posthumously published *Architecture in the Age of Reason* was considered the last word on eighteenth-century European architecture.[9] Finally, Kaufmann's work set all these questions within a philosophical framework that has not ceased to inform critical theory: Kant's insistence on the "autonomy" of the will as a fundamental premise of bourgeois freedom. Whether or not it is historically "verifiable," the link Kaufmann established between Ledoux and Kant, as Hubert Damisch notes in his introductory essay to the French translation of *Von Ledoux bis Le Corbusier*, remains challenging to all interrogations of the nature of architectural language and of the place of the discipline in modern society.[10]

Beyond this, Kaufmann's work had a direct influence on architectural practice, and especially on the way that the modernism of the 1920s and 1930s was received in the United States immediately after the Second World War. Emigrating to the United States in 1940, Kaufmann was taken up by Philip Johnson, who hosted his lecture to the newly formed Society of Architectural Historians in his Harvard apartment. Johnson's Glass House of

1949 was, according to the architect, deeply indebted to his reading of *Von Ledoux bis Le Corbusier*.[11] The translation of Kaufmann's
Architecture in the Age of Reason strongly influenced the theories
of architectural "autonomy" characteristic of the neorationalist
school in Italy after 1971, and especially the theory and design of
Aldo Rossi, who reviewed Kaufmann's books in detail.[12]
    Read today in the context of the detailed monographic re-
search that has modified his once seemingly oversimplified conclusions, research that has brought other themes and architects
to the fore to counterbalance the image of the "three revolutionaries," Kaufmann's analysis regains much of its original force, as
grasping the phenomenon of an "architectural enlightenment"
in its intellectual and formal dimensions. At the very least, his
theses bear reexamination as representing a critical stage in
the development of the discipline of architectural history—as
important in their own way as those of Riegl, Paul Frankl, and
Giedion—at the same time as they pose challenging questions
to our contemporary conceptions of architectural form and our
preconceptions of its political and social significance.

Neoclassicism and Autonomy
Emil Kaufmann was born on March 28, 1891, in Vienna; he stud-
ied at Innsbruck with the celebrated papal historian Ludwig von
Pastor (1854–1928), and then at Vienna with the Renaissance
specialist Hans Semper, the Byzantinist architectural historian
Josef Strzygowski (1862–1941), and the archaeologist Emanuel
Loewy (1857–1938), a friend of Freud and later a teacher of Ernst
Gombrich.[13] From Loewy, Kaufmann no doubt derived his interest in the perception of form and its relation to typical images,
but he was particularly drawn to the teaching of Max Dvořák
(1874–1921), with whom he formed a close friendship and from
whom he derived many of his analytical insights. Dvořák was a
student of Alois Riegl and Franz Wickhoff, and while he is better

known as a scholar of the baroque, and credited with the expansion of the concept of mannerism with reference to the work of El Greco, his concern for architecture, both historical and contemporary, was equally strong. As Riegl's successor in the post of curator of public monuments, he formulated policies for historic conservation; a supporter of modernism, he was a friend of Adolf Loos, who designed a tomb for him, to be decorated by Oskar Kokoschka, another friend for whose 1921 album he had written a foreword.[14]

Kaufmann was awarded his doctorate in Vienna in 1920, and went on to forge an entirely new field by his "rediscovery" of three generations of French architectural theorists and designers from the 1750s to the 1820s. However, as Schapiro noted in his brief obituary in 1953, Kaufmann was unable to obtain a regular academic post (no doubt a result of Viennese anti-Semitism) and was obliged to work in a bank for much of his early career.

His first major article, written in 1920 and published in the *Repertorium für Kunstwissenschaft* in 1924 (alongside another ground-breaking architectural study by Paul Zucker, "Der Begriff der Zeit in der Architektur"), outlined the bases for his study of late eighteenth-century architecture by dividing a period generically known as "classic," albeit in a late moment, into two. As explicated by Georges Teyssot, Kaufmann's essay, titled "Die Architekturtheorie der französischen Klassik und der Klassizismus" (The architectural theory of French classicism and neoclassicism), established a difference between what had been called *Klassik* (classic) and a period that he called *Klassizismus* ("classicism," or what we now call "neoclassicism"), which he described as having a formal expression, or rather a structure, of its own.[15] Here Kaufmann was underlining what he saw as a distinct variation between French developments and those in other "baroque" countries. Between "classicism" in the mid-seventeenth century and "neoclassicism" after 1750, Kaufmann found certain continuities of "clarity and truth" but sharp differences in composition, which seemed to him to shift from a principle of harmony inherent to the work toward a principle of expression or communication provoking sensations beyond the work.[16]

After 1925, save for a slim book on the architecture of the city of Baden,[17] Kaufmann concentrated his researches on the architects of the late eighteenth century, and most importantly Ledoux; he contributed the entry on Ledoux to the Thieme-Becker encyclopedia, and an article on the German painter Ferdinand Georg Walmueller.[18] The concept of autonomous architecture was present in none of these early studies, except perhaps by implication, as when, in 1929, Kaufmann characterized Ledoux's architecture, with its geometrical play of masses, as "anti-baroque."[19]

. Kaufmann's first direct reference to "autonomen Baukunst" occurred in a short study in 1931 of Ledoux's church architecture, centered on the project for the Church of Chaux, probably designed in 1785, and published in Ledoux's *L'architecture considérée sous le rapport de l'art, des moeurs et de la législation* (Architecture considered in relation to art, mores, and legislation) in 1804.[20] Contrasting Ledoux's scheme with Soufflot's design for Sainte-Geneviève, to which it obviously was a response, Kaufmann identifies it with the qualities of the new "neoclassicism" he saw emerging with Ledoux's generation. Unlike the baroque church, the neoclassical church was organized as a solid geometrical block with reduced decoration and a distinct separation and identity of its functional parts. To Kaufmann, "In place of the conception of architectural form as living, organic nature, there enters the feeling for strict geometry."[21]

Kaufmann developed this theme two years later in the book-length article on "The city of the architect Ledoux," published in the second volume of the Vienna art history school's journal *Kunstwissenschaftliche Forschungen.*[22] In this first sketch of what was to become his second book, Kaufmann gives the idea of autonomy a fundamental place, with the subtitle "On the discovery of autonomous architecture" (*Zur Erkenntnis der autonomen Architektur*). In this detailed study, Kaufmann, his critics notwithstanding, builds the argument for autonomy both historically and with deliberate recognition of the complexity of architectural practice.

For Kaufmann, Ledoux is a transitional and pivotal figure in the shift from what he calls "baroque" to what he characterizes as "neoclassicism." According to Kaufmann, it is precisely this "mixed" nature of transitional work that allows the historian to understand this shift as an organic and slow process of internalization and cognition on the part of the architect as he confronted the problem of architecture during the Enlightenment and its proper means of expression in an epoch itself undergoing radical shifts in its intellectual, social, and political forms. Thus, Kaufmann's argument moves slowly toward the "Erkenntnis" or "discovery" of autonomy, through a number of stages represented by detailed analyses of Ledoux's designs in roughly chronological order and culminating in a long section devoted to "The autonomous solution" (*Die autonome Lösung*).

First Kaufmann analyzes the dramatic change in plans for the Saltworks of Chaux between the initial project of 1771 and the final project of 1774. Ledoux transformed his original plan for a unified, square courtyard to a number of separate pavilions grouped around a semicircle, a change that Kaufmann reads as a sign of the move from "baroque unity" (*barocken Verband*) to the pavilion system of the nineteenth century (*Pavillonsystem*).[23] The breakup of the project into functionally defined and formally expressed units was for Kaufmann an indication of the "principle of isolation," the emergence of an "architecture of isolation" (*isolierenden Architektur*) that paralleled the emergence of the modern "individual" consciousness (*Individualbewusstsein*).[24]

Once Ledoux had accomplished this, Kaufmann proposes, the architect finally effected the transition from baroque "dynamic" composition to neoclassical "static" composition in the project for the Church of Chaux. Here, the flattened, low dome and the horizontal lines of the block reinforce a sense of calm meditation, as opposed to the emotive upward movement of baroque churches. Further, the articulation of the different altars—one for festivals and marriages on the upper level, and one for burials and memorial services below in the crypt, with its own entrances and exits—enunciates for Kaufmann a "principle of isolation" (*Prinzip der Isolierung*) corresponding to the sense of "distance" (*Distanzierung*) necessary for the communication of sublime effects.[25]

Kaufmann next analyzes two symbolic monuments, the Panarèthéon and the Pacifère, citing Ledoux's statements that "The form of a cube is the symbol of immutability," and "The form of a cube is the symbol of Justice," as a way of introducing the concept of "architecture parlante," or "speaking architecture."[26] Kaufmann had discovered this term, not itself of eighteenth-century origin, in a mid-nineteenth-century article satirizing Ledoux's attempts to communicate ideas through buildings, and immediately saw it as both positive and apt in its characterization of the aspirations of late eighteenth-century architects to develop a truly social language of forms.[27] The "symbolic system" that Ledoux wished to deploy was, of course, itself dependent on the separation of individual buildings as identifiable masses and their shaping as readable signs. Here, for Kaufmann, the pavilion system, the isolation of parts, and the articulation of the appropriate "character" of each structure led naturally to what, in reference to Ledoux's design for the Maison d'Education, he finally named "the new concept of the *autonomous* treatment of the materials."[28]

In this way, Kaufmann establishes the complex development of Ledoux's design practice as leading to the "autonomous solution" evinced in the series of nine-square-plan houses deployed in the landscape of the Ideal City of Chaux, "all varied, all isolated," as Ledoux stated.[29] Such isolation, Kaufmann avers, marked the end of baroque compositional practice, that of "concatenation" (*Verband*), and the beginning of the new building form (*die neue Bauform*) characterized by the Enlightenment pressure for "clarification" (*Abklärung*).[30] Kaufmann thus prepared the analytical ground for the systematic comparison of Ledoux's architectural method with the general method of the Enlightenment—that developed by Kant: "At the time when Kant rejects all the moral philosophies of the past and decrees the autonomy of the will as the supreme principle of ethics, an analogous transformation takes place in architecture. In the sketches of Ledoux these new objectives appear for the first time in all their clarity. His work marks the birth of autonomous architecture."[31]

The theory of autonomy was given its fullest development in Kaufmann's second book, a slim treatise polemically titled *Von Ledoux bis Le Corbusier*, published in 1933 and summarizing and developing the arguments put forward in "Die Stadt des Architekten Ledoux." In the preface, dated "Vienna, May 1933," Kaufmann outlines his methodological premise. This was to be, he writes, "something more than a monograph, and different from the mosaic of an artistic life." Rather it was to be seen as "a part of the history of architecture which, through the interpretation of the work of Ledoux, appears in a new light" while simultaneously demonstrating "the importance of the great movement of ideas around 1800 for the domain of art."[32] This theoretical aim was expressed in the subtitle to the book, no longer "Zur Erkenntnis der autonomen Architektur" but now the more dynamic "Ursprung und Entwicklung der autonomen Architektur." The substitution of "Origin and Development" for "Discovery" represented both a firmer conviction in his own "discovery" and a sense of its historical implications for later developments.

From the outset, Kaufmann makes it clear that he sees the French architecture of the Enlightenment and Revolution as of equal or greater importance to the already well-established tradition of German neoclassicism represented by Schinkel. His title, in fact, refers directly to the earlier study by Paul Klopfer, *Von Palladio bis Schinkel*, an argument for the primacy of German architecture as it received the Renaissance tradition from Italy.[33] By contrast, Kaufmann emphasizes the role of the French and Latin traditions in the continuation of Palladio's legacy to the present. His work in Paris had convinced him that the Latin countries were the ones that counted in the development of modernism. While philosophy under the aegis of Kant and poetry following Hölderlin could be seen to have constructed the intellectual and literary foundations of romantic modernism, it was in France and Italy that the work of enlightenment entered fundamentally into the visual arts, and especially architecture. This was accomplished, Kaufmann argues, by the final break with baroque modes of composition ("heteronomous," as he called them) and the introduction in their place of modern forms of disposition ("autonomous" or "free-standing"). Once ratified by the Revolution, and despite attempts to veil the radical nature of the shift by means of historical styles, autonomy survived to establish the abstraction of modernism as the apotheosis of Enlightenment reason. Kaufmann explains:

> If we are well-informed about the historic role of Italy as the initiatory land of modern times in the domains of art and society, we remain, by contrast, ignorant of the role of France as pioneer of a new art and creator of a new architecture. Towards 1800, as during the Gothic period, the decisive innovations come from the French architects.

In the following work, I am first concerned to render justice to the artist who was the first, not with a vague intuition of distant goals but with a clear and full self-consciousness, to traverse the long route from the baroque to modern architecture: Claude-Nicolas Ledoux. Placed at the frontier of two epochs, before and after the Revolution, his work is the first to announce the new artistic aims; it is the tangible witness to the appearance of a new world. But it is also my concern to show how his ideas and those of his epoch are transmitted to us, and how, in a way, the unity of the last hundred and fifty years is reflected in architectural activity.[34]

Kaufmann thus announces that he is concerned with the "revolutionary" period *as a whole*—1770 to 1790. Precise dates (which for Ledoux were hard to come by before the meticulous archival research of Michel Gallet in the 1960s) were less important than a sense of the signification of the global shift in art and philosophy, as in the social and political realm. The years that saw the preparation of the "great revolution that was completely to transform the social system of the west" were "the same years in which the work of Kant matured": "Globally, there was a profound (we could say today, definitive) denial of the past; a clear and self-conscious rupture, a decisive step toward a new *autonomy.*" Kaufmann believed the interconnection between these movements and the work of Ledoux was not accidental, and was established by Kant's and Ledoux's common respect for and indebtedness to Rousseau: "At the moment when, with the Declaration of the Rights of Man, the rights of the individual are affirmed, at the moment when, in place of the old heteronomous morality, Kant instituted the autonomous ethic, Ledoux laid the foundations of an autonomous architecture."[35] The correspondence was direct: if for Kant the *Critique of Pure Reason* had accomplished "what numerous centuries had been unable to realize," for Ledoux "the moment in which we live has broken the chains that shackle architecture."[36] From a study of Ledoux, Kaufmann asserts, would emerge the answer to three critical questions: the reasons for the "abandoning of the aesthetics of baroque classicism," the "relations between the Revolution and architecture," and the "profound signification of neoclassicism and the architecture of the end of the nineteenth century."[37]

The general concept of architectural autonomy for Kaufmann was represented by a wide range of large- and small-scale formal moves. The first and most fundamental, because it was the most radical shift from baroque modes of composition, was the separation of buildings according to a quasi-functional identification, rather than their unified and hierarchical massing to include all functions. This step, taken by Ledoux at the beginning of his career when he jettisoned the preliminary square courtyard scheme for the Saltworks of Chaux in favor of a semicircular grouping of pavilions, was decisive: "The passage from the first to the second project reflects no less than one of the most important events in the history of architecture: *the dismembering of baroque concatenation*. . . . In a remarkable parallelism with the general historic evolution, concatenation is replaced by *the system of pavilionnate composition*, which, after that moment, becomes predominant: this is the free association of autonomous entities."[38]

In this transformation of compositional techniques, the instrumental force, both for the production of the buildings and their historical analysis, was the rational plan. As Kaufmann notes, the plan "allows us to discover the fundamental reasons for the determination of forms"—no doubt a first step that enabled Kaufmann's historical connection of Ledoux with Le Corbusier and his principle of "the plan as generator." This plan and the three-dimensional form of the pavilions are constructed not by any reference to a baroque observer, but purely geometrically. Geometry operates as a calculated control of form for use; not only does the "rationality of the plan" (*die Ratio des Planes*) exercise "absolute sovereignty," but it offers a neutral system of order, entirely abstracted from the personal experience of a perspectival observer. Where "all baroque architecture was conceived as a function of the observer," now "the center of the new buildings is no longer the heart of the whole. . . . It is no more than a geometrical point to which all the parts relate. The new buildings are assembled and not intimately linked" (*Zusammengesetzt, nicht zusammengewachsen*).[39] In accordance with the spirit of autonomy, the new pavilions are entirely self-sufficient. As opposed to the classical and baroque system, inherited from Renaissance aesthetics, where "to detach a part is to destroy the whole," the pavilion rejects parts and becomes "an association of independent elements": "If one wishes to characterize the architectural systems by formulae as reduced as possible, one could define baroque association in these terms: one part dominates all the others and nevertheless all the parts form a whole; the deep sense of the pavilion system can be translated thus: *the part is independent within the frame of the totality* [*Der Teil ist frei im Rahmen des Ganzen*]. Between the two systems lies a Revolution."[40] Kaufmann is far from claiming that Ledoux ever entirely threw off the baroque sensibility—in different ways, all of Ledoux's work exhibited its transitional character. Indeed, in his analysis of buildings from the 1770s (the Hôtel Montmorency, the pavilion at Louveciennes for the Comtesse du Barry) and the 1780s (the Hôtel Thélusson), Kaufmann stresses that "the opposed principles were living *at the same time* in the artist," but he discerns in Ledoux's "fanaticism" for geometry and rigorous planning an anticipation of the architect's later, more abstract projects.[41]

Here Kaufmann detects the influence of the Enlightenment desire for "clarification," or *Abklärung*, which when applied to architecture called for the use of "massive blocks" superimposed

in compositions that, rather than relying on a central, principal motif, gained effect through the simple strength of masses
themselves. And while Ledoux was still free in his use of baroque
motifs that gave his buildings character—the upturned urns and
grotto in the Saltworks, for example—his preference was for the
architecture to "speak" by means of its own stereometric forms,
as in the designs for the House of the Surveyors (a vast elliptical
tube), or the Coopers' Workshop (with its concentric rings and
intersecting barrel-shaped form). As Kaufmann describes this
tendency:

> Experiments with forms themselves *count among the*
> *most astonishing initiatives of this epoch. The preference*
> *for the simplest stereometric configurations is indicative*
> *of the gravity of the spirit of the age.* Thus one finds in the
> projects of Ledoux, severe cubes (as one sees for example
> in the Country House of Jarnac or the House for a Man
> of Letters), the House of the Woodcutters in the form of
> a pyramid, the cylindrical Country House (also the Bar-
> rière of the Boulevard of La Villette, still standing, and the
> cylindrical House of M. De Witt) and finally the Spherical
> House of the Agricultural Guards.* [42]

Building up his argument for Ledoux as an originator of modernism, Kaufmann remarks that "our own epoch, linked to that of
Ledoux, is open to experiments of the same kind which, even if
they are without issue from an architectural point of view, are no
less very significant of the indefatigable research for new forms"
(*neuer Gestalt*).[43]

Bringing together all these compositional innovations was,
as Kaufmann had intimated in his earlier writings, the seminal project for the Church of Chaux. Combining the demand
for a single, horizontal and static freestanding mass with the

separation of functional elements, it also construed a new kind of neoclassical "sublime." This was a sublime of "calm meditation in a solemn immobility," a sublime of individual self-absorption and contemplation, opposed to the medieval "sanctuary of unworldliness" or the baroque "spiritual elevation." It was also a sublime of "distance," reflecting the idea that objectivity and rationality required "keeping one's distance" (*distanzhalten*).[44] Finally, the entire effect of the church, its own enlightened form of spirituality, was achieved not by the introduction of painting, sculpture, images, or symbols but by "the autonomous means of architecture" (*die autonomen Mittel der Architektur*).[45]

From Kant to Le Corbusier

Autonomy *of the will is the sole principle of all moral laws and of duties in keeping with them;* heteronomy *of choice, on the other hand, not only does not ground any obligation at all but is instead opposed to the principle of obligation and to the morality of the will.*

—Immanuel Kant, *Critique of Practical Reason*

The connection that Kaufmann sought between architecture and philosophy, and ultimately between Ledoux and Kant, was provided and historically grounded by Ledoux's reading of Rousseau. Rousseau is evoked explicitly and implicitly in many passages of *L'architecture:* the obvious interpretation of "l'homme primitif" embodied in the plate illustrating the shelter of the poor ("L'abri du pauvre"); the enthusiasm for natural settings throughout the descriptions of the City of Chaux; the constant references to "le pacte social"; and finally the overall adherence to a "return to origins" exhibited in Ledoux's theory and design. The key passage for Kaufmann joining this "return" to "autonomy" was again that in which Ledoux justified the separation of each function in pavilions in the second project for the Saltworks: "Return to the principle. . . . Consult nature; everywhere man is isolated" (*Remontez au principe. . . . Consultez la nature; partout l'homme est isolé*).[46] Kaufmann further draws parallels between Rousseau's social thought and the institutions designed by Ledoux for his ideal "natural" society. The strange phallic-plan brothel, or "Oikéma," masquerading as a "Fragment of a Greek Monument," resonated for Kaufmann with all the romantic sensibility of the "autonomy of the pleasure of the senses" typical of the epoch. He cites the author F. Gundolf who had characterized Friedrich Schlegel's *Lucinde* (1799) as "an important witness to a historical tendency: the first expression of the profound demand for an autonomy of sensual pleasures" in "the series of philosophical petitions in favor of the independence of the strengths and instincts of human nature, a series which is opened with Kant's affirmation of the autonomy of morals."[47] For Kaufmann, Rousseau was behind Ledoux's emphasis on hygiene, physical exercise, education, communal living, and his more general preoccupation with the citizenry of his new ideal state as a whole—a "universal citizenry" or *Weltbürgerlichkeit*. If Ledoux was by no means an egalitarian along the lines of later revolutionaries such as Gracchus Babeuf, he certainly believed in a "pacte social" that endowed the poorest member of society with architecture. This characteristic would later appeal to the socialism of Hannes Meyer, who in 1942 would praise Ledoux for having endowed the masses with a pyramid, a form previously reserved for the elite.[48]

While the connection between Ledoux and Rousseau may be obvious, that between Ledoux and Kant seems less so. For, at first glance, the question of "autonomy" posited by Kant as the basis for moral principles, and taken up throughout the nineteenth and twentieth centuries as the watchword of bourgeois liberal politics, does not easily relate to architecture, either in theory or practice. First advanced in the *Critique of Pure Reason* as a "call to reason" to gain "self-knowledge," the question of autonomy presented the paradox between law and self-will that has haunted political reasoning ever since. In Kant the "critique of pure reason" presupposes what he calls a "court of justice" that will ensure the claims of reason and operate "not by despotic decrees" but "in accordance with its own eternal and unalterable laws."[49] As parsed by Theodor Adorno, this strange double imperative—the freedom to give oneself laws—represents the "supreme concept in Kant's moral philosophy," whereby "acting in accordance with laws appears as a function of freedom—or, conversely, freedom manifests itself as a function of the law."[50] Such a principle might seem distant from any instrumental concept in architecture, save perhaps for a vague analogy between freedom and order in aesthetics.

For the generation of the 1920s, however, Kant's principle of autonomy represented far more than a simple appeal to reason or a century-old claim in the philosophy of knowledge. It was historically and conceptually the founding principle of bourgeois society, a product, as Adorno had it, of "the enthusiasm of the youthful bourgeoisie which has not yet started its never-ending complaints that reason cannot solve anything, but which still feels confident of its ability to achieve things by virtue of the powers of its own reason."[51] Thus understood, the interrogation of autonomy was joined to the interrogation of bourgeois liberal democracy, under severe threat in the interwar period. Inspired by the researches of the Marburg school, under the leadership of Hermann Cohen, many philosophers in the early twentieth century, including Ernst Cassirer who studied at Marburg, were returning to Kant as the initiator of modern critical philosophy, and in particular the philosophy of autonomy. "The basic concept of Kantian ethics: the concept of autonomy. Autonomy signifies that binding together of theoretical and practical reason alike, in which the latter is conscious of itself as the binding agent," wrote Cassirer in 1918 in his intellectual biography of Kant.[52] Cassirer's two studies *Freiheit und Form* (1916) and *Kants Leben und Lehre* (1918), the latter the first modern comprehensive philosophical biography, became the reference point for a new generation, including Kracauer, Adorno, and Walter Benjamin, who saw Kant, for better or worse, as the beginning point of an investigation necessary for the development of a truly "critical" theory. Adorno, in particular, saw Kantian autonomy as a double-edged sword, much in the way that contemporary thinkers were characterizing Rousseau's social contract as implicitly totalitarian. Questioning the implications of appeals to "reason" that had, under the impetus of science and technology, already begun to exhibit their "dark side," Adorno believed that autonomy in Kant—the "kernel of his philosophy"—articulated "a very dark secret of bourgeois society": "This secret is the reality that the formal freedom of juridical subjects is actually the foundation of the dependency of all upon all, that is to say, it is the foundation of the coercive character of society, its conformity with law. That is what lies behind the very strange theory that in Kant reason is a tribunal which has to sit in judgment over reason as the accused."[53] It was, of course, the paradoxical nature of this dichotomy that led many humanists in the interwar period to interrogate their own objects of study from philosophy to art history, at a moment when bourgeois autonomy, and its supposed links to reason and liberalism if not social democracy, was challenged by the movement from the "freedom" of law to totalitarian "coercion."

Kaufmann, in Vienna, was equally exposed to this neo-Kantian revival, but in taking up Kant as the founding father of modern bourgeois society in 1933, he was making a very different point from that of the German theorists. Where the Frankfurt school sociologists were already looking at the paradoxes and problematics of Kantian idealism, and Cassirer himself was struggling with the difficulties of reconciling Rousseau and Kant in an essay published in 1932,[54] Kaufmann preferred a generalized appeal to "Rousseau/Kant" as signifying an Enlightenment unified enough to provide an intellectual base, both for Ledoux and his interpretation. Such apparent simplification is explicable on two grounds.

First, Kaufmann was concerned with sketching the intellectual grounds for an architect who himself was anything but a systematic thinker, one who readily appealed to a wide range of authorities in his attempt to justify new forms. Kaufmann's seeming confusion, in these terms, was historically accurate in delineating the discursive breadth of Ledoux's sources and its impact on design. Certainly Cassirer's *The Philosophy of the Enlightenment*, also published in 1932, had the aim of constructing such a unity of thought. Second, and equally important, Kaufmann's own intellectual agenda reached beyond a purely historical interpretation. Embedded in the title of *Von Ledoux bis Le Corbusier* and in Kaufmann's appeal to Kantian thought was an implicit challenge to the emerging cultural politics of Austria and Germany, and a covert appeal to a "united" front using the rule of law and reason as the basis for the restatement of the ideal of a liberal, social democratic state.

Published in May 1933, just three months after the Reichstag fire and Hitler's assumption of extraordinary powers, Kaufmann's little book seems calculated to assert the social democratic values of Enlightenment, republicanism, and modernism, values under severe attack not only from Nazi ideologues who had denounced them as degenerate and bolshevik, but also from conservative Viennese art historians like Strzygowski and Sedlmayr. The latter, a member of the National Socialist party and then a loyal supporter, was to wait until Kaufmann's flight to the United States before developing his own thesis of the "loss of center," using Kaufmann's material to set out a despairing thesis of decline and fall where Kaufmann had seen only progress and justice. Returning to 1933, however, it was an act of real intellectual, if not physical, courage, as Damisch has pointed out, to delineate the continuities between the French Revolution and modernism, at a moment when Albert Speer and his cohorts were finding solace in the gigantesque revival of German neoclassicism. In this context, Ledoux was, more than a historical subject, a cover or metaphor for the explication of liberal bourgeois society, if not a kind of utopian socialism in historical guise. The real subject of the treatise would then be the architecture of Loos, Gropius, Richard Neutra, and Le Corbusier—the architecture of modernism developed between 1900 and 1929. Kaufmann wrote: "The continuity of the development of post-revolutionary architecture can in a way be traced through to the beginning of our own period, which opens around 1900 with the Dutch Berlage and the Viennese Adolf Loos, a period one can usefully designate by naming its most self-conscious protagonist, the leader of the young French school: Le Corbusier" (*den Führer des jungen Frankreich Le Corbusier*).[55]

The first mention of Le Corbusier in Kaufmann's writings is in a footnote to the article "Die Stadt" that points to the similarities between three statements by Ledoux and the text of *Vers une architecture*.[56] Kaufmann cites Ledoux's descriptions of "the appreciable feeling of a plan" that stems from the subject, the site, and the needs of the building; of the destructive effect of details on surfaces; and of the "forms described with a single stroke of the compass," the square and the circle as the "alphabetical letters used by authors in the text of their best works."[57]

Two years later, *Von Ledoux bis Le Corbusier* was to elaborate these analogies as systematically and historically grounded. Ledoux, Kaufmann argued in the last section of the book, was the progenitor of a modernism that was in no way formalist ("he did not confine his attention only to formal details, as did the Secession a hundred years later"; rather, "in his research he envisaged the totality of the *reorganization of the body of the building itself* and of the *systems of large complexes of buildings*").[58] Considering Ledoux's later works, and especially his group of town houses designed after the Revolution for the sugar planter Jean-Baptiste Hosten, Kaufmann introduced his first modernist comparison, not to Le Corbusier but to Gropius: referring to Ledoux's late works, he notes, "The principal artistic quality of these projects is the 'play of masses' that Ledoux looked for above all. The formal principle on which these realizations were based corresponds to the leitmotif of our present architecture, as Walter Gropius has expressed it in the first volume of the Bauhaus books: 'a variety starting with the same fundamental type obtained by the alternate juxtaposition and superimposition of repetitive spatial cells.'"[59] In tracing the development of autonomous architecture after Ledoux, and through the nineteenth century, Kaufmann is clearly aware of the deterioration in aesthetic content and of the deleterious effects of the incessant repetition of the "pavilion system." Thus, he analyzes the teaching method and influence of Jean-Nicolas-Louis Durand, who systematized Ledoux's own system for the École Polytechnique, repeating the fundamental elements of architecture as if they were so many geometrical points, lines, and planes on graph paper, and traces its effects on architects like Louis-Ambroise Dubut. But it is obvious that Kaufmann is here only attempting to demonstrate that, despite the overt historicist "clothing" of the pavilions in question, varied according to taste and stylistic revival through the century, the survival of the pavilion and its fundamentally geometrical/functional foundation allowed the principles of modernism to survive.

Kaufmann's assessment of the effects of autonomy on urbanism, for example, is bleak enough, and parallel to that of Camillo Sitte at the end of the nineteenth century. He castigates the pavilion structures around the Place de l'Étoile, the Place Royale in Munich, or the Ringstrasse in Vienna, whose buildings are set up like isolated blocks:

In its isolation each one could, without hindering its attractiveness, be displaced to another site. It is of little importance that the parts have been realized, one after the other, and of different appearance, as in Munich, or contemporary and fit amongst themselves, as in Vienna. The double aspect of the past century which, like Janus, looks at once forward and backward, appears even more clearly in that portion of the Ringstrasse with the monumental buildings of the Parliament, the City Hall, the University, and the Theater. Conceived according to an absolutely heteronomous inspiration, the buildings are destined for show. In this intention, each of them carries an old suit, passing for Greek, Gothic, or late Renaissance. But in this diversity there is also a new trait: the total indifference to the effect of the whole. Each building remains in a total isolation, none is linked in an ensemble.[60]

Yet, despite the moribund, half-heteronomous, half-autonomous aspect of the style revival buildings of the Ringstrasse, the principle of autonomy survived to triumph in the younger generation of modernists following Berlage. Kaufmann is not inclined to enter into a detailed analysis of twentieth-century modernism as a conclusion to his Ledoux monograph; the "evidence" of Le Corbusier and his contemporaries is enough to make the point. Interestingly enough, it is Neutra, the Viennese exile in California whose *Wie baut Amerika?* had been published in 1927, whom Kaufmann selects as the spokesman for modernism's continuity with the past, Roman and baroque. Kaufmann quotes Neutra:

"It is a long way from the plastic formalism of the Greek world to the twisted facades of the baroque, but this route is not illogical, it always crosses so to speak the same region: that of a certain spiritual attitude towards

architectural creation. " *The general principle the development of which we have wanted to demonstrate here in
architecture is defined by Neutra in these terms: "Disso-
ciation, juxtaposition, the strict delimitation of concepts,
of the domains of thought and action, such seem to be the
fundamental tendencies of this development.*[61]

It is, however, with Le Corbusier that Kaufmann concludes his
little book: a Le Corbusier represented not only by *Vers une architecture* but by the version of *Urbanisme*, translated into German as
Städtebau, and by the first volume of the *Oeuvres complètes*, published in 1930. Kaufmann is thus able to refer to the Corbusian
commonplaces of the "'fascination for the straight line,'" or the
"return to the 'fundamental realities of the sphere, the cube and
the cylinder in great architecture,'" as well as to extend his comparison with Ledoux to the layout and projected monuments of
the Mundaneum, with its already contentious pyramidal scheme
for a World Museum, reminiscent of the pyramids of Ledoux and
Boullée.[62] As opposed to the trenchant critiques of the Marxist
Karel Teige, Kaufmann lauds the "idealism" of this utopia as directly relating to, if not influenced by, that of Ledoux:

> *The resemblance between the epoch of Ledoux and our
> own is not limited (this will be one of our conclusions)
> to formal and thematic aspects. This resemblance does
> not only rest in the fact that in his epoch as our own one
> sees the new and important problem of the masses emerge
> as the powerful motive of solutions. Independently of the
> new demands of the real, one discerns now as at that
> epoch a new idealism. It appears in* L'architecture *of
> Ledoux as in the writings of Le Corbusier, in the project
> for the Ideal City as in the Cité Mondiale. It is in this ide-
> alism, founded on the new ideals of ethics and law, in*

*which is, in the end, rooted, it seems to us, before 1800
even as today, the renewal of architecture.*[63]

Kaufmann concludes: "Because Le Corbusier has no less faith in
these than Ledoux, because in the one and in the other the intimate link between art and life is as strong, one must cite side
by side the master whose work crowns the triumph of the new
principles and he whose activity has opened the way for these
principles."[64]

Structural Analysis

Kaufmann's methods of analysis, and those of the Vienna school
with which he was loosely associated, have often been criticized
for their incipient "formalism," and especially from the left in
the 1930s. Meyer Schapiro, responding in an incisive review to
the confused and contradictory "formalism" of the Viennese
school, tried to redress the historical problem in terms of a less
reductive political position.[65] Assessing Kaufmann's article "Die
Stadt des Architekten Ledoux" and the later *Von Ledoux bis Le
Corbusier*, Schapiro, while recognizing the merit of Kaufmann's
rescue of Ledoux, points to the limitations of the formal approach
in relating architecture to its social context. Kaufmann had attempted to join what he called Ledoux's principle of architectural
"autonomy"—the derivation of an architectural aesthetic from
internal requirements of construction and use rather than from
any external, imposed artistic conception—to a similar characteristic of emerging bourgeois society "which thinks of itself
as composed of isolated, equally free individuals."[66] Schapiro
argues that Kaufmann, in fact, had succeeded only in joining an
architectural principle to a social principle, one found indeed in
Ledoux's writings: "The correlation," Schapiro writes, "is with
bourgeois ideology, not with the actual class structure and conditions of bourgeois society, and depends more on quotations than

on a study of social and economic history. "[67] In light of our analysis of Kaufmann's theses of autonomy, we would have to conclude that Kaufmann might readily have agreed with Schapiro's critique: far from trying to develop a materialist history assuming the fundamental relations between base and superstructure, society and culture, Kaufmann had a more modest goal, confined to demonstrating the relations between thought about social form and thought about architectural form.

But Kaufmann's method was not attacked only from the left; like many social-democratic theses, it was equally subject to criticism from the right. Indeed, Kaufmann did not have to look so far for his enemies as the Berlin of Hitler's putsch. Hans Sedlmayr, another distinguished student of Dvořák and an editor of *Kunstwissenschaftliche Forschungen*, in which Kaufmann had published his breakthrough article, had disagreed sharply with Kaufmann's democratic and idealistic reading of the architecture of 1800. Sedlmayr, who had joined the Nazi Party as early as 1932, when it was still illegal in Austria, remained for the rest of his life a committed opponent of Kaufmann, of modernism, and of all who espoused democratic-socialist ideals.[68]

It had been Sedlmayr, of all the Vienna school historians, who took seriously the lessons of Riegl, in opposition to his dissertation advisor Julius Schlosser. He conceptualized a method of art history that completely integrated architecture, developing Riegl's concept of *Kunstwollen*, as reinterpreted by his contemporary Panofsky, into what he termed a *Strukturanalyse*, or analysis of structural principles. These were not, however, the principles of "structure" as an architect might understand them. Sedlmayr's treatise on Borromini's church San Carlo alle Quattro Fontane found its "structural" principle not in the physical structure per se, nor even in the "structural" organization of its intersecting spaces and volumes, but rather in the decorative treatment of the wall. As Christopher Wood notes, "In other words, structure may reveal itself in apparently marginal or meaningless features."[69] Here Sedlmayr relied on gestalt theory to introduce the notion of "shaped vision," which in his terms formed an objective and rational way of looking beneath appearances, of seeking out principles of form and organization not apparent in normal characterizations of function, style, and the like.

Wood and Meyer Schapiro before him have pointed out the "specious" nature of this "rationalism," criticizing its intuitionist and implicitly racist undertones. In Sedlmayr's view, while Kaufmann had analyzed the formal shifts correctly, he had entirely misdiagnosed the symptoms. Where Kaufmann saw renewal in revolutionary and modern architecture, Sedlmayr saw decay and decline; where Kaufmann saw increasing health in society and architecture, Sedlmayr saw decadence and death. Architecture was but a sign of the "huge inner catastrophe" set off by the Revolution, a "loss of center" and stability imaged by what for Sedlmayr was the most characteristic motif of 1800, the sphere, with all its implications of destabilization—the literal deracination of traditional architecture. Kaufmann's heroes were Sedlmayr's devils: as the latter observed of Goya, "The more we study the art of Goya, the more intense grows our conviction that, like Kant in philosophy and Ledoux's architecture, he is one of the great pulverizing forces that bring a new age into being."[70] Sensing an ally in his fight against the demon of modernism, Sedlmayr cites Ernst Jünger approvingly in characterizing the *musealen Trieb*, the "face turned towards the things of death," of the contemporary epoch.

More specifically, explaining his so-called "Method of Critical Forms," which he claims is "capable of separating the true from the false," of "concentrating on that unconscious sphere of instinctive receptivity and of 'possession' in which the soul of the age stands naked before us"—a method that is common to the pathologist and the psychologist—Sedlmayr finds in Ledoux's architecture one such apparently bizarre but fundamentally symptomatic form that describes the folly of the modern age: the Sphere House of the Agricultural Guards, which Kaufmann had seen as a brave innovation, a harbinger of modernist abstraction. Sedlmayr argues,

> Such a radical new form, for instance, is inherent in the idea of using a sphere as the basic form of an entire house. Most people have treated this notion as nothing more than a bad joke or a very ordinary piece of lunacy, while the more charitable have looked upon it as an "experiment with form." The thing is certainly insane enough, but if it were no more than that, we should hardly be justified in wasting much time over it. A nonsensical idea, however, need by no means be wholly without significance . . . such abnormalities reveal very specific characteristics—"ce sont les abus qui charactérisent le mieux les tendances." Thus the sphere when used as the shape of a building is a critical form which . . . is a symptom of a profound crisis both in architecture and in the whole life of the human spirit. Here we are beginning to deal with the zone of the unconscious.[71]

Sedlmayr viewed this nonarchitectural form as the fatal symptom of an abstraction that, with Le Corbusier, had reached its most nonsensical and anti-architectural end. Agreeing with Kaufmann that autonomy was the key (it "implies that architecture under Ledoux had as it were become conscious of its own true nature—it was the same idea that animated Loos and Le Corbusier"), Sedlmayr denigrates the Maison Savoye at Poissy—the epitome of Corbusian modernism for Sigfried Giedion and perhaps for Kaufmann too—as resembling "a spaceship that has just landed."[72] Le Corbusier's pictures, Sedlmayr comments with disgust, "are full of floating transparent things."[73]

Sedlmayr is here opposed to the "autonomous" nature of this geometrical architecture—the apparent repulsion for the earth of an architecture wishing to float in the air, transparent, and thereby no longer holding to its tectonic foundations and dangerously open to the deleterious effects of what he calls "paper architecture." It is no coincidence that Sedlmayr uses Kaufmann as the scholarly source of every one of his critical descriptions of the dreams, unhappy visions, and "shadow values" of Boullée's and Ledoux's architecture. Indeed, Kaufmann is acknowledged as the source of Sedlmayr's whole study, as, in his postscript, he admits: "The very beginnings of this work were inspired by the research of Emil Kaufmann on Ledoux, which came to my notice in 1930. I saw at once that Kaufmann had succeeded in making a discovery of the utmost importance towards the understanding of our age, but that at the same time he had not wholly recognized the true significance of his own discovery, and that the phenomena so clearly perceived by him were not correctly evaluated."[74] Of course, this acknowledgment did not prevent Sedlmayr from claiming almost equal credit, as he recounts that he expounded the "thoughts . . . developed here" in *Verluste der Mitte*, in a lecture given in 1934, and again in 1937 in an unpublished essay, finally to set them down in 1941, delivering them "in university lectures in 1941 and 1944."

Paranoia seems to have been the common disease of both Sedlmayr and Kaufmann. Sedlmayr concludes his study of the loss of center in sullen resentment that *his* formulation of Kaufmann's Ledoux had not been received as authoritative: "Whoever upholds the doctrine of 'the lost center' can be certain from the outset to perceive the consequences of doing so personally. He will have against him not only those people who reject what is new because it is unaccustomed, but also those who only propagate what is new because it is 'contemporary,' 'modern,' and therefore 'interest-ing,' 'worshippers of the past and futurists' united against him."[75] Kaufmann's footnotes in *Architecture in the Age of Reason* are no less bitter:

> Hans Sedlmayr, Verlust der Mitte (Salzburg, 1948), p. 98. Having myself pointed out the extraordinary signifi-cance of the revolutionary designs and interpreted them as symptoms of their period (Von Ledoux, pp. 11, 25, etc.), I certainly do not underrate what Sedlmayr terms kri-tische Formen. However the large number of original and yet "normal" inventions reveals that the complex period with all its excitement was sound enough to bring about a true regeneration of architecture. In the Epilogue to his book, Sedlmayr points out that my rediscovery of Ledoux became the starting point of his investigation into the formative forces of our era. Though he does not fully agree with my interpretation, he nonetheless adopts most of my concepts and observations, especially those of the new decentralization in composition—Verlust der Mitte! . . . the abolition of the old aesthetic canons . . . the increasing hostility to decoration . . . , the new "mobility" of furni-ture . . . , the altered relationship between structure and environment . . . , the ideal of equality in architecture . . . the triumph of elementary geometry . . . , the parallel phenomena in the graphic arts, particularly the fashion of the silhouette . . . , the end of the Baroque anthropo-morphisms and the new attitude towards matter . . . , the coming up of new architectural tasks . . . , the new sense of commodiousness . . . , the presentation of new forms long before new materials fitting them were found . . . , the continuity of the development after 1800 . . . , the struggle of antagonistic tendencies in the nineteenth century . . . ,

*the appearance of a new structural order behind the masks
of the various styles . . . , and the typically nineteenth-
century thought that perfect solutions of the past should
be the standards for all the future.*[76]

A few years earlier Kaufmann had been no less irritated when
reviewing the book *Claude-Nicolas Ledoux* by Marcel Raval and
J.-Ch. Moreux (Paris, 1945); he summarized his "serious charge
of plagiarism" in a long note.[77] And he was no less charitable to
Helen Rosenau, who had written on Lequeu and Boullée, following up the leads provided by the Viennese scholar.[78]

The debate between Kaufmann and Sedlmayr has generally
been seen by art historians as the starting point for the reevaluation of Revolutionary architecture, as well as the origin of many
myths only recently dispelled by less formalistic and more historically dispassionate research. But its significance in the late
1930s and 1940s was definitively political. It posed the Nazi Party
member Sedlmayr, who had collaborated throughout the war,
against the emigré Kaufmann, forced into the position of "private scholar," itinerant and dependent on small grants. When, in
1949, Sedlmayr was allowed once more to teach, his position was
ostensibly transformed from the political to the religious; yet this
change did not prevent the stormy reception of his speech "On
the Dangers of Modern Art" at the Darmstaedter Sezession, with
shouts of "Heil Hitler" and boos arising from the audience. Nevertheless, as a reviewer recalled, "Only once was Sedlmayr's position seriously challenged . . . in a dadaist speech by the painter
Willy Baumeister," who compared his own persecution under the
Nazis with Sedlmayr's "black record of collaboration."[79]

In this context, the fundamental distinction drawn by Damisch between what semiologists and their heirs have spoken of
as the "meaning of architecture," which considers architecture as
a system of communication, and the question he posed as to what

architecture means in a specific moment gains in significance. According to these distinctions, when Kaufmann wrote in 1924 that classicism demands a "harmony" that confines "signification . . . to the intrinsic qualities of the subject and their expression," and that neoclassicism sees form as having "no other function than to be the support for thought, to transmit impressions, to provoke sensations," he was perhaps not stating that these two architectures accomplish this goal within their particular societies and cultures, as much as arguing that they aspire to that goal in their theories and ideals. Similarly, when he speaks of Ledoux in the same breath as Kant and Rousseau, he was perhaps claiming not that there is an inner essence in Ledoux's architecture that is Kantian—nor, certainly, that Ledoux had read Kant or wished to be a Kantian architect—but more simply that there seemed to be a homology between, in their different realms, Ledoux's use of separate, independent, geometric forms and, say, Kant's desire for principles of independent critical judgment, and Rousseau's return to the principle of "natural man." I say "more simply," but in fact such relations introduce a complexity in the interpretative structure that is belied by the crude juxtaposition, and that goes well beyond the equally crude "social/economic/formal" postulations of Marxist art historians of the period.

Admittedly, Kaufmann has been cast as a reductive systematizer because of his attempt to construct an interpretative scheme derived from Riegl's *Kunstwollen* that corresponded to architecture. And yet, in his view, his notion of an "architectural system" offered a far more precise tool of analysis. As he defined it, "attention is focused not so much on problems of style, nor on descriptions of single features, nor even on the investigation into general form, but rather upon the interrelation of the several parts of the composition, and especially the relationship between the several components and the whole architectural composition itself."[80] Here we have moved beyond a generic "will to form," and even beyond Sedlmayr's static "structural analysis," to a flexible model that approximates not only to similar types in music, literature, and painting, but also, in this case, to the architect's own design procedures. Such analysis allowed Kaufmann to distinguish between architectural systems of different periods: "The architecture of the late eighteenth and nineteenth centuries has much in common with classical and baroque art. But these common traits concern only the surface. The continued use of classical features creates a certain superficial resemblance between these periods preceding and following the Revolution. Only by an analysis based on the concept of an 'architectural system,' can we appreciate how fundamentally the mode of architectural composition was transformed."[81] In this analysis, the notion of architectural autonomy might be isolated as a systematic structure. In his review of Raval and Moreux's book on Ledoux, Kaufmann explained that "autonomy" did not mean isolation: "What I attempted to demonstrate was that the architect passed from the traditional unification of the parts to the modern isolation of the elements, both within the single structures and within the groups of buildings, or . . . to the *system* of architectural *autonomy.*"[82]

Once identified with similar structures in thought and social life, the comparison and matching of such a structure was entirely flexible and always shifting:

> In the relationship between forms and system, each epoch establishes its own basic ideas of disposition and interrelation of parts. Either older forms are remodeled until they are perfectly adjusted to the new system of arrangement; or new forms proffered by new constructional methods are adopted if they accord with the new system; or natural forms are reinterpreted in keeping with the changed ideal of general disposition. The search for new forms is, therefore, a necessary consequence of the desire

for a new system. Forms themselves are secondary factors;
the system is the primary consideration. [83]

We might characterize this method, in contrast to the more psychological and teleological "structural analysis" of Sedlmayr, as not so much structural as "structuralist," paralleling similar contemporary attempts to identify systems of relationships in linguistics and symbols by, say, Cassirer and Panofsky in other domains.

But for all his reliance on the formal method, Kaufmann grounded his "structuralism" in a historical narrative. Even though his history fell short of Schapiro's desired social and economic inquiries, it was, for its time, rigorously enough based in intellectual developments. Indeed, it is clear that Kaufmann intends us to see his "architectural system" as commensurate with intellectual developments, as the manifestation, in other words, of the architect's thought processes. This is what he means when he speaks of "peering behind the facade of architectural development" to "discover the metaphysical background of building" in a particular era. [84] This notion of the particular era was fundamental to Kaufmann's view of the specificity of history. As he noted in a review of Nils G. Wollin's study of the work of Louis-Jean Desprez, "each epoch requires specific categories of treatment." New material should be interpreted not within the categories "derived, originally, from the production of another (as a rule prior) period," but rather according to "some new approach adequate to their novel ways." He concluded, "The idea of all-embracing categories is a chimera. Still worse, of course, is the sterile application of categories formed on the accomplishments of a different period." [85]

Kaufmann was keenly aware of the limitations of art historical method, both categorical and empirical. Writing in exile, in 1946, he noted:

We live in a time in which the gathering and recording of factual data are often considered the unique end of art history. No doubt such activity is indispensable. Yet one should not overlook the fact that it does not require much originality to transform a card file into a book, after having added just a few details to the findings of many predecessors in a field labored, perhaps, through centuries. One should rate higher the biographer who ventures out into unmapped territory, who discovers a forgotten artist, or proffers a new picture of a personality, and an era. Such a biographer is more likely to err in his evaluations and comments than the simple compiler, although the latter is by no means infallible in his attributions. Art history should not care less about the epiphenomenon than the phenomenon. The biographer who struggles to grasp the meaning of artistic production will become a source of stimulus and progress for the discipline even when he errs. Needless to say, these remarks apply still better to those rare historians who, gifted with a keen vision, rediscover or reinterpret a whole epoch as, e.g., did the scholars who about 1900 inaugurated the study of the Baroque, or those who somewhat later brought Mannerism to light. Interpretative history alone is constructive history.[86]

In this quasi-autobiographical justification, we sense not only the pathos of the lonely explorer, the destitute scholar searching for his "California," but also his consciousness of the role of scholarship itself when, building on its formative achievements, it has the courage to invent its own future.

More or less penniless after 1942, Kaufmann eked out a living on grants from the Fulbright Committee and the American Philosophical Society. In the Avery Library and numerous other collections he found more general material for his expanding studies of Enlightenment and Renaissance architecture, including an unfinished translation of Filarete's fifteenth-century text describing the ideal city of Sforzinda, a text that Kaufmann considered the true antecedent to Ledoux's Chaux. In 1953 he died in Cheyenne, Wyoming, while on his second journey to Los Angeles. It was with characteristic humility that Kaufmann admitted in his posthumously published book: "I do not believe that I have solved the momentous problem of how the architectural transformation of about 1800 came to pass."[87]

From Kaufmann to Johnson and Rossi

The cubic, "absolute" form of my glass house and the separation of functional units into two absolute shapes rather than a major or minor massing of parts comes directly from Ledoux, the Eighteenth Century father of modern architecture (see Emil Kaufmann's excellent study Von Ledoux bis Le Corbusier*). The cube and the sphere, the pure mathematical shapes, were dear to the hearts of those intellectual revolutionaries from the Baroque, and we are their descendants.*
—Philip Johnson, "House at New Canaan, Connecticut"

In retrospect, it seems neither accidental nor totally ironic that Kaufmann's belief that architecture's autonomy paralleled the emerging "autonomy" of the bourgeois (modern) individual would appeal so strongly to that paradigm of the high bourgeois, architect Philip Johnson.[88] In 1940 Kaufmann had fled Austria for the United States; in August 1942 he was asked to present his work to the newly constituted American Society of Architectural Historians at the Cambridge home of Philip Johnson, whose visits to Germany with Henry-Russell Hitchcock had alerted him to the growing interest in eighteenth-century neoclassicism. The text of this talk, Kaufmann's first English-language article, was published the next year in the new *Journal of the American Society of Architectural Historians.* [89]

In this talk, prepared to introduce Ledoux and his protomodernism to an American audience for the first time, Kaufmann opened by linking the profound changes that took place in late eighteenth-century "philosophy, literature, social life and economics" to an architecture in which "even a number of twentieth century features were revealed."[90] He compared Ledoux's Panarèthéon to Le Corbusier's Mundaneum; described the residence of the River Surveyors as a representation of "man's mastery of the flood . . . presented so vividly that one might easily suppose some present-day expressionist had devised it for a hydraulic power plant"; and claimed the spherical Shelter for the Rural Guards as a model "only recently . . . revived to dominate New York's World Fair." In sum, this "early cubism" was created by Ledoux as an "architecture parlante" that pointed to the future more than to its sources in the past: "Important as it is to explain works of art by comparison and by analogies with predecessors, it is more important . . . to ask not whence they come, but whither they lead."[91]

Based on Johnson's own encounter with German history and theory, Kaufmann provided the convenient link between the neoclassicism of Schinkel, admired by both National Socialists and the then sympathetic Johnson, and the modernism of Le Corbusier and Mies. Johnson had read Kaufmann's 1933 book *Von Ledoux bis Le Corbusier,* and was easily able to reconcile Kaufmann's formal linkage of Ledoux and Le Corbusier with his own predilection for Schinkel and Mies—"von Schinkel bis Mies" seemed a natural corollary to Kaufmann's "Von Ledoux bis Le Corbusier," as was the implied extension: from Schinkel, Ledoux, Le Corbusier, Mies, to Johnson.

Writing about his Glass House in New Canaan, Connecticut, in the *Architectural Review* of 1950, Johnson specifically cited

Kaufmann's book in order to link the geometrical forms of Ledoux to his own cubic design. Indeed, the article provides an unabashed collage of Kaufmann, Le Corbusier, and Mies van der Rohe, in eight easy stages, as a justification and as authorizing sources for Johnson's design. First, Johnson illustrates Le Corbusier's 1933 plan for a village farm in order to describe the approach to his own house: "The footpath pattern between the two houses I copied from the spiderweb-like forms of Le Corbusier, who delicately runs his communications without regard for the axis of his buildings or seemingly any kind of pattern."[92] Secondly, Mies's 1939 plan for IIT is adduced as precedent for the formal layout of the two pavilions in New Canaan. This is followed quickly by Theo van Doesburg's painting (the origin of Johnson's "asymmetric sliding rectangles"); Auguste Choisy's plan and perspective of the Athenian Acropolis (an image already commandeered by Le Corbusier to illustrate the dynamic force of nonrectilinear plans in *Vers une architecture*); Schinkel's Casino in Glienecke; and, as a prelude to Mies's glass house idea, Ledoux's spherical House of the Agricultural Guards, so loved by Kaufmann and hated by Sedlmayr. Thence Johnson passes to Kazimir Malevich and the suprematist painting that prefigured the plan of the Glass House with its circle in a rectangle, and finally returns to Mies, who concluded the eight points of Johnson's new architecture with the Farnsworth House of 1947–50.

The paradox, of course, is that Johnson, often criticized for "betraying Mies" in the obviously boxlike and nonuniversal counterhorizontal space of the Glass House, was there following Kaufmann's principles of autonomy almost to the letter. Revealing his deeper affinities with German neoclassicism and Schinkel, but disguising them by an intellectual detour to France and a liberal, idealized classicist modernism, Johnson in fact produces a transparent "Ledoux" box, that "proves" Kaufmann's thesis even more powerfully than Le Corbusier's horizontally open Domino diagram. This was the fate of many so-called late modernisms: they authorized already written history rather than making it for themselves. Certainly the rewriting of history in reverse, against the progressive movement described by the historians of Kaufmann's generation, was to be a leitmotif of "postmodernism," or what Pevsner would call a "new historicism," from the 1960s on. The "Kantian" autonomy of architecture descried by Kaufmann would here be reduced to a justification for stylistic nostalgia and the endless play of apparently signifying motifs drawn from the past.

Thirty years after Johnson completed his Glass House, the architect Aldo Rossi, also working with concepts he derived from Kaufmann's analysis of Enlightenment architecture, saw autonomy as a means of saving architecture from an increasingly disseminated field of aesthetic, social, and political authorizations. Rossi understood the word to refer to the internal structure of architectural typologies and forms, as they composed part of the sedimented structure of the historical city.

For Rossi, the idea of an *autonomous* architecture was joined to that of a *rational* architecture. Thus in 1973, when he was curator of the international section of the Milan Triennale, Rossi sought to identify those architects who, in Manfredo Tafuri's words, espoused an "autonomy of language," and collected them together under the banner of "Rational Architecture." In this Triennale, the premises of "neorationalism" became evident in the beliefs of many Italian and French designers, from Aldo Rossi to Bernard Huet and Leon Krier: that architecture was in some sense a discipline of its own, that its "language" was derived from former architectures, and that its form and role in the city were as much a product of a historical urban structure as of social or political concerns. That is, whereas in the politicized climate of the 1960s society had been seen as the generator of space and shelter, in the 1970s, perhaps in reaction to the evident loss of architecture this implied, architecture asserted its own determinism. Fueled by Rossi's *Architecture of the City*, a kind of structuralism in urban analysis and a semiotics of architectural analysis emerged in parallel to the revival of Russian formalism, so-called Cartesian linguistics, and deconstruction in literary studies. "Autonomy" of the text and autonomy of the building were seen as complementary facets of the refusal of sociopolitical determinism, the vagaries of urban development planning, and what Pevsner had already identified in 1960 as "the return of historicism."

For Rossi, however, as evinced by his reviews and critical writings from the late 1950s on, autonomy also represented the purest heritage of the Enlightenment, and thence the modern movement, for an age that had lost its sense of roots in the eclecticism and, more to the point, in the adjustments required by the postfascist political struggles of the immediate postwar period. In this context, Rossi's fascination with the geometrical forms of late Enlightenment architecture was more than a simple attempt to recuperate the sources of modernist minimalism; it was grounded in his reading of Kaufmann, not only of *Von Ledoux bis Le Corbusier* but also of his postwar books, *Three Revolutionary Architects: Boullée, Ledoux, Lequeu* (1953) and the more general, posthumously published *Architecture in the Age of Reason: Baroque and Post-Baroque in England, Italy, and France* (1955). Rossi reviewed these books for *Casabella*, taking note of the earlier 1930s essays, and found in them a programmatic source for his "neo" rationalism, joining Ledoux and Boullée (whose *Essai sur l'architecture* Rossi translated and introduced in Italian) not only with Le Corbusier, but equally with his own modernist hero, Adolf Loos. The early critical writings of Rossi include ample evidence of his study of Enlightenment theory by way of Kaufmann, which he then translated into research on specifically Italian examples (Milizia to Antonelli) and modernist parallels (Loos).

Hubert Damisch, in his preface to the first (1981) French translation of *Von Ledoux bis le Corbusier* entitled "Ledoux avec Kant" (a title with echoes of Lacan's own aleatory preface to the Marquis de Sade's *La philosophie dans le boudoir*, "Kant avec Sade"), notes that this peculiar fascination of the 1970s with the idea of autonomy is directly linked to the continuity of Kantian thought. Damisch asks what would happen if Kant's analysis of the origins of geometry in the *Critique of Pure Reason* were coupled with the autonomous geometry of Ledoux in order to meditate on the special autonomy of architecture from Ledoux, to Le Corbusier, to Loos, and thence to the autonomies claimed by the new neorationalism of the late 1970s:

> *At our present moment, when the history of architecture hesitates between a renewed form of the history of styles and a form of institutional analysis which ignores everything that comprises the proper material of architecture, the idea of autonomy, to take it in the philosophical sense, takes on the value of a regulating concept. To think Ledoux with Kant is to recognize that in architecture understanding does not proceed solely from history, or in other words, with Kant, that an understanding which* subjectively *presents itself as history with respect to the way in which it has been acquired, can participate,* objectively, *in one form or another of rationality.*[93]

To think of Ledoux with Kant, Damisch concludes, is to ask what constitutes architecture as an object, not only of history, but also of thought, and thought that is constrained by conditions that are a priori formal, or in another sense, internal to the discipline of architecture.

Autonomy Revived

At the 1998 conference honoring the career of Philip Johnson, the theme of autonomy was resurrected, but in a more distant, historical sense, as one that neatly joined the trajectory of Johnson's work to a newly aroused interest in the various "modernisms" of the 1940s, 1950s, and 1960s, and to a renewed preoccupation with the *discipline* of architecture.[94] The Johnsonian saga was presented at the conference as fundamentally reliant on autonomy, making its first appearance in the Glass House projects and building of 1948–49. This desired return to disciplinary roots, following similar calls in the humanities and social sciences in the wake of poststructuralism's interdisciplinary experiments and critical innovations, seemed to answer a number of concerns held by a generation unconvinced by the pluralism of postmodernism. A return to the fundamentals of architecture, generally represented in the modern tradition by abstraction, would, it was thought, counter the pluralism of postmodernism and architecture's always suspect relations to the "society of the spectacle" and its consumerist aftermath.

As evidenced by the papers given at the conference, historians, critics, and architects agreed generally that "modernism" in some form—whether classic "high" modernism or the less polemical but more socially present modernism of the immediate postwar period (corporate modernism, domestic modernism, suburban modernism), or even "countermodernism" of the kind posed by Kiesler—was decidedly preferable to postmodernism, and even more desirable than the "deconstructivism" that, in the Johnson itinerary, had supplanted it in the 1980s. Thus, the conference proposed to satisfy a number of problems at once: Johnson was endowed with an overarching theme that, superficially at least, made historical and critical sense of his otherwise eclectic work; postmodernism and the relativizing theories that seemed to support it were definitively abandoned; and, in a nice turn of intellectual agenda, a new post-theory, pragmatic era implicitly opened up.

Beneath this often self-contradictory trajectory of the idea of autonomy in architecture, we can trace through the twentieth century all the tensions evoked by the history of the concept of "Enlightenment." From the general assumption of "progress" and "reason" common to the Third Republic and its liberal interpretation of the Revolution, to the contested domain of social democracy after the First World War, to the defensive promodernist posture of the idealist avant-garde and its Popular Front allies in the 1930s, to the despairing and negative critique of the Enlightenment developed by Adorno and Horkheimer in exile, to the reassertion of democratic values in the postwar Frankfurt school against the pessimism of a withdrawn and posthistorical conservatism, and thence to the return of "form" and "structure" as renewal tactics for architecture in the 1970s, and finally to the quasi-nostalgic revival of the idea of autonomy itself in the 1990s; all this attests to the power of Kant's idea of autonomy, both formal and political, implying at once freedom and order, collective reason and expressed individuality.[95]

It seems to be no accident that from Jürgen Habermas's attack on postmodernism in his dramatic lecture at the Venice Biennale of 1980 entitled "Modernity: An Unfinished Project" to Fredric Jameson's studies of Adorno's "late" Marxism, Kant—and by implication, Kaufmann—have been seen as central, not only in defining the trajectory of modernity in theory and practice, but also in critically redefining the status of modernity in the present.

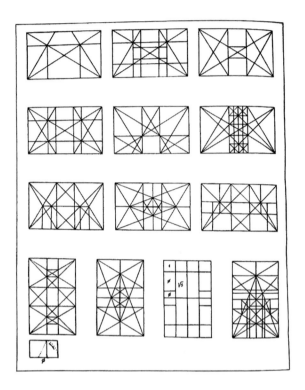

Matila Ghyka, "Harmonic decompositions of the φ rectangle," in Ghyka, *The Geometry of Art and Life* (1946), reprinted in **Colin Rowe,** "The Mathematics of the Ideal Villa" (1949)

2 MANNERIST MODERNISM
COLIN ROWE

A criticism which begins with approximate configurations and which then proceeds to identify differences, which seeks to establish how the same general motif can be transformed according to the logic (or the compulsion) of specific analytical (or stylistic) strategies, is presumably Wölfflinian in origin.
—Colin Rowe, "Addendum 1973"

In 1973 Colin Rowe wrote an addendum to his first published article, "The Mathematics of the Ideal Villa" (1947), admitting the "limitations" to what he terms its "Wölfflinian" approach—its difficulty with iconographical content and its demanding (for both reader and author) "close analysis."[1] However accurate it might be to characterize the method of "The Mathematics of the Ideal Villa" as Wölfflinian (and we shall find other, more powerful influences at work in its argument), the assumption of such a paternity indicates the still pervasive force of the late nineteenth-century German school of architectural history in England in the years after the Second World War.

The formal analysis of architecture, as developed out of Heinrich Wölfflin's work and advanced by the Vienna school, emerged in Britain with a slightly different history from that of the Kaufmann-inspired influences in the United States and

Italy. In the 1920s, the force of Wölfflin's typologies of form were joined to the postcubist analyses of Roger Fry and Clive Bell and the psychological interpretations of Adrian Stokes. The English translation of Wölfflin's early work, *Klassische Kunst* (1899), had been introduced into British circles by Fry as early as 1903; and Wölfflin's influence had been reinforced by Geoffrey Scott's *Architecture of Humanism* in 1914 and the translation of Wölfflin's methodological treatise *Kunstgeschichtliche Grundbegriffe* (1915) as *The Principles of Art History* in 1932. Yet the real impact of the German formal method on professional art history arrived with the art historical emigration, albeit in a fundamentally transformed guise, of the Warburg historians Fritz Saxl and Rudolf Wittkower, who had both studied under Wölfflin. The combined impact of these multiple but overlapping traditions formed a generation of architectural historians, critics, and architects, including Colin Rowe, Robert Maxwell, and James Stirling in Liverpool; Alan Colquhoun and Sam Stephens at the Architectural Association School in London; and the London-based architects Alison and Peter Smithson, John Voelcker, and Ruth Olitsky.

Among these, Rowe in particular would develop a coherent and powerful model of modern architectural history that was to influence generations of architects and subsequent historians and critics. Fundamentally opposed to the technological and progressive vision of his contemporary Reyner Banham, Rowe's interpretation of modernism was self-reflexive and sought formal precedents in history. But rather than proposing sources that were, in some post-Hegelian sense, genetic or formative, as Giedion saw the baroque and cubist traditions, Rowe understood them as in some way homologous, structural, and parallel—paradigmatic formal *procedures* allowing for deeper interpretation of difference and similarity. As he understood Wölfflin, the method involved a study of "configurations," or what he was fond of calling *partis*, that were then to be compared (like the side-by-side images from Wölfflin's lantern projector) to discover difference, and thus to trace transformations in the organizations, seen as impelled by cultural or stylistic force. Despite his later reservations, Rowe deployed such an approach for much of his career, convinced of the efficacy of an immediate *visual* analysis that was primary to perception and any iconographic or historical framing. "If normal intuition might suggest so much," he concluded his "Addendum," "a Wölfflinian style of critical exercise (though painfully belonging to a period *c.* 1900) might still possess the merit of appealing primarily to what is visible, and of, thereby, making the minimum of pretences to erudition and the least possible number of references outside itself."[2] Such a claim for accessibility, cultivated by the English school and championed by Bernard Berenson, perhaps indicates from the outset Rowe's ambiguous relationship to "professional" art history, as represented by Wittkower and the Warburgians, and his fondness for a more "amateur," if not "gentleman amateur," stance, characteristic of Fry and Bell and Evelyn Waugh (another favorite author of Rowe). It was also a clear statement of his insider approach to architecture as a trained designer, and of his desire to reconstrue the formal method with three-dimensional specificity. As he noted somewhat ruefully, his two years with Wittkower made of him an "architect manqué."[3]

   For after completing his architectural degree at Liverpool University in 1945, Rowe had enrolled as a master's student at the University of London under the direction of Rudolf Wittkower. Wittkower had joined the newly established Warburg Institute in 1934, and had become a founder-editor of the *Journal of the Warburg Institute* in 1937 (to become the *Journal of the Warburg and Courtauld Institutes* in 1940). Ten years later, he was appointed a Reader when the Institute was officially incorporated into the

University. Rowe's thesis subject, "The Theoretical Drawings of Inigo Jones," was in his own words "just what those Warburgians wished to receive."[4]

An English Palladio

The immediate impetus for Rowe's master's thesis came from Wittkower himself, who noted this fact later in his 1953 article "Inigo Jones, Architect and Man of Letters." Wittkower's essay studies Jones's intellectual development through such a close analysis of his extant drawings that the author claims he takes "a leaf out of Scotland Yard's book" in his recognition of the importance of the almost invisible pinpricks of the dividers. Wittkower posits that the architect had been preparing a theoretical treatise, along the lines of his Renaissance predecessors Palladio and Scamozzi, left unfinished at his death: "We know that there exist about 200 theoretical drawings coming from Inigo's office and mainly drawn by John Webb, probably during the 1640s. For a good many years I believed that the puzzle of these drawings becomes intelligible if one assumes that they were made in preparation for an architectural thesis. Now a pupil of mine, Colin Rowe, has substantiated this assumption in a brilliant but not yet published thesis."[5] This "brilliant" thesis, 330 pages long, had been submitted by Rowe in November 1947 to the University of London for a master's degree in the history of art, awarded in 1948.[6] There was no preface or acknowledgments, but we know that in 1945 he was "Wittkower's only student," and that Saxl and Gertrude Bing were also involved. Saxl and Bing were, in Rowe's own words, "highly impressed by it."[7] From the evidence of Rowe's footnotes, he had also discussed aspects of the thesis with Frances Yates, another member of the Warburg Institute.

Wittkower himself had laid the groundwork for such a cross-national study in an exhibition of photographs he had curated in 1941 with Saxl, then director of the Warburg Institute. In the accompanying catalog, *England and the Mediterranean Tradition* (1945), Wittkower published his article "Pseudo-Palladian Elements in English Neoclassicism," raising the question of transmission and transformation as a legitimate field.[8] Although Wittkower did not publish his studies on Inigo Jones until after Rowe's thesis was complete, it is clear from this exhibition that, influenced by Saxl's work on the migration of classical symbols, his inquiry had already begun, utilizing the comparative method to study the influence of Italian works on English examples of painting, sculpture, and architecture from early times to the present.

Given its title, "The Theoretical Drawings of Inigo Jones: Their Sources and Scope," the structure of Rowe's thesis appears simple enough. After a brief introduction to Jones, his biography, architectural formation, and "stylistic development," it is divided into three main parts: an essay on the "English Architectural Treatise" in relation to its Italian and English antecedents; a central section on what Rowe considers to be Jones's own treatise; and a third, which catalogs Jones's and Webb's drawings "arranged," as Rowe puts it, "as a Treatise."

This was the "architectural treatise" referred to by Wittkower, one that Jones himself did not write—indeed, Jones left little writing besides his marginal annotations to his copy of Palladio's *Quattro libri* and his posthumously published examination of Stonehenge reconstructed as an antique Roman temple. But the burden of Rowe's thesis is "that there exists a corpus of drawings, some by Jones himself, some by John Webb in Jones's office, that represent the work in preparation for the publication of a major theoretical treatise on architecture, along the lines of those previously written and drawn by Serlio, Scamozzi, Palladio, et al.," a treatise left incomplete and unpublished at Jones's death: "The content and schematic feeling of the drawings [of this group] recall irresistibly the characteristics of the Renaissance architectural treatise," Rowe claimed, and "it is the object of this thesis to establish that these drawings represent the preliminary studies for such a theoretical work on architecture."[9]

In other words, Rowe's own master's thesis consists of a theoretical argument for a theoretical treatise for which no written evidence exists, the planned existence of which relies on visual identification alone. It is, he allows, visual inspection that "suggests a preconceived system" comparable to those already developed by earlier architects of the Renaissance. Rowe, who was never to sustain the writing of a complete and fully developed treatise of his own, thus began his career as "a didactic exponent of architectural education" (as he characterized Jones) by completing (if not inventing) Inigo's own treatise for him. Such an exercise, however, went far beyond the Scotland Yard detective work of his supervisor.

Completed in 1947, the same year that Rowe published his first and seminal article, "The Mathematics of the Ideal Villa," and three years before "Mannerism and Modern Architecture," the thesis gives us a precise understanding of the development of his idea of modern "Palladianism" in its first iteration.[10] Indeed, the true subject of the thesis might be seen as Palladio rather than Jones, or more specifically, Jones as the eponymous hero of English "Palladianism," heir to the mannerism of the late Renaissance, precursor of Burlington and Kent, and perhaps even the first "neoclassicist."

The thesis, though hardly acknowledged by Rowe in his later career, was an extraordinary synthesis of historical interpretation derived from Wittkower and formal analysis derived from Wölfflin. It still remains one of the most succinct studies of the nature and role of the Renaissance treatise in Italy and England. Two aspects of the work, however, stand out as informing the two articles published by Rowe shortly after. The first is his construction of Palladio—Jones's model and standard—as a theoretician and, above all, as a systematizer of the Renaissance tradition: "In the school of Palladio the diverse elements [of Renaissance architecture] become classicized, and absorbed into an academic repertoire, which was to provide a European model."[11] In his "architectural conservatism" and his Neoplatonic sympathies, Palladio "prolonged the Renaissance urge toward scientific clarity, reinforced his archeological preoccupations with a persuasive emotional depth, and a serious reserve of looseness and flexibility."[12] More interested in ideal harmonies than antique remains, Palladio found in the printed treatise a perfect vehicle for his own project. According to Rowe, the *Quattro libri dell'architettura* was the most influential of all treatises, as "those accurate, and austerely programmatic pages" provided an "intelligible architecture, and the apparatus of artistic judgment for the Protestant world":[13] "It [Palladio's treatise] is a methodical conception of the ancient world, which combines the dramatic qualities of Mannerism, with that voluntary sense of abstraction and balance, which Alberti had shown. . . . Palladio always proceeds by way of the specific, to his generalization; and it is in this quality of rational embodiment that his compelling power seems always to lie. The particular admirations of Mannerism are reduced to a scheme analogous to that order which the Renaissance had postulated."[14] Here we might note a formulation of the general and the particular, the idiosyncratic embedded in the universal, that would act for Rowe as a theoretical bridge to the language of Le Corbusier. Each work of Palladio represents "a fragment of the universal order," at the same time encapsulating an "emotional suggestiveness" of the antique world that invites the viewer to reflect on the "consonance and measure," the "stoicism and control" of a synthesized classicism.[15]

Second, if Palladio was the synthesizer, Jones emerges as the transmitter and historicizer of Palladio for an English audience. Eclectic in the face of what Rowe characterizes as the "ambiguous inheritance of Rome and Venice," Jones used his edition of the *Quattro libri* as model, standard, and commonplace book, jotting in the margins his observations of Palladio's buildings as he visited them, as well as daily notes and notes on his own projects. For Jones, "the Palladian villa system offered a focus for the development of a whole complex of outside ideas." References to the antique and its mannerist reconstructions, to Scamozzi's classicism, to the restrained expansion of early baroque, were all "regulated by a continual reference to Palladian ideals of scale and intelligibility."[16] For this, "Palladio's treatise seems to have provided Inigo, less with a model, than with a standard, around which his own impressions could cohere."[17]

By a careful formal analysis of Jones's designs beginning with the Banqueting House, Rowe demonstrates the emergence of a gradual academicism, tracing the appearance of Inigo's developed style of historicism, intellectualism, and academic correctness: "An eclectic with a natural restraint and classical bias, he evolved from a decorative and graceful early style, through a period of historicism, in which a Mannerist element is implicit, to a final period, where a classicism is imposed upon this Mannerist basis."[18] We are thus presented with a thesis that construes Jones, systematizer of the systematizer, as he builds up a collection of more than 200 plates in readiness for their publication as the first English equivalent of Palladio's *Quattro libri*.

Modern Palladianism

That the immediate postwar period, especially in England, saw a revival of interest in what was called Palladianism is now a commonplace of intellectual history—indeed, the phenomenon itself was almost immediately historicized. Banham's 1955 article "The New Brutalism" is usually cited as a reference. Here he pointed not only to the prevailing tendency for naming movements along the lines of art historical styles ("The New Empiricism," "The

New Humanism," "The New Brutalism"), but also to the recent interest in Palladio and Palladianism stimulated by Wittkower's *Architectural Principles in the Age of Humanism*, published in 1949, and informing the Smithsons' entry for the Coventry Cathedral competition.[19] Looking back on this period ten years later, Banham wrote:

> *One can safely posit the interference of historical studies again, for, though the exact priority of date as between the Smithsons' design and the publication of Professor Wittkower's* Architectural Principles of *[sic]* the Age of Humanism *is disputed (by the Smithsons) it cannot be denied that they were in touch with Wittkowerian studies at the time, and were as excited by them as anybody else.*

> *The general impact of Professor Wittkower's book on a whole generation of post-war architectural students is one of the phenomena of our time. Its exposition of a body of architectural theory in which function and form were significantly linked by the objective laws governing the Cosmos (as Alberti and Palladio understood them) suddenly offered a way out of the doldrum of routine-functionalist abdications, and neo-Palladianism became the order of the day. The effect of* Architectural Principles *has made it by far the most important contribution—for evil as well as good—by any historian to English architecture since* Pioneers of the Modern Movement, *and it precipitated a nice disputation on the proper uses of history. The question became: Humanist principles to be followed? or Humanist principles as an example of the kind of principles to look for? Many students opted for the former alternative, and Routine-Palladians soon became as thick on the ground as Routine-Functionalists.*

The Brutalists, observing the inherent risk of a return to
pure academicism—more pronounced at Liverpool than
at the AA—sheered off abruptly in the other direction and
were soon involved in the organization of Parallel of Life
and Art.[20]

Banham was well aware that by 1955 any "Palladianism" in
British modern architecture had already been cast aside. As he
noted, Peter Smithson had introduced an AA student debate with
the words, "We are not going to talk about proportion and symmetry"—what Banham described as the architect's "declaration
of war on the inherent academicism of the neo-Palladians" and
"crypto-academicism" in general.[21] Banham's own purpose in
his "New Brutalism" essay was similar, as he worked to identify a
new "aformalism" emerging in the Hunstanton School, Sheffield
University, and the Golden Lane project, all departing from the
"formalism" of Palladian reference. Banham described this as
a movement from modernist/structuralist "typology" to a new
modernist/visual "topology." In retrospect, Banham summarized the mood of this period:

> *What this generation sought was historical justification*
> *for its own attitudes, and it sought them in two main*
> *areas of history—the traditions of Modern Architecture*
> *itself, and the far longer traditions of classicism. . . .*
> *Their degree of sophistication about the history of Modern*
> *Architecture was remarkable by world standards at the*
> *time; their sophistication about classicism was remark-*
> *able for its peculiar interests rather than its extent. Most*
> *of this generation had passed through some form of run-*
> *down Beaux-Arts training . . . all had had their interest*
> *in classicism confirmed by their readings in Le Corbusier,*
> *but all came under the influence of the brilliant revival of*

Palladian studies in England in the late Forties, either directly through Rudolf Wittkower and his book "Architectural Principles in the Age of Humanism," or through the teaching of his outstanding pupil, Colin Rowe. Like many others among them, Colin Rowe believed that there was a direct architectural relevance between the classical past and the work of twentieth-century masters. . . . Somewhere in this amalgamation of ancient and modern exemplars of architectural order, there was thought to lie the one real and true architecture implied in the title of Le Corbusier's first book "Vers une architecture," the image of a convincing and coherent architecture that their elders had lost, and their teachers could no longer find.[22]

In *Architectural Design* of October 1954, Banham had called this movement "New Formalism," mentioning John Voelcker and Ruth Olitsky; in 1966 he delineated its principles: "In the British view, the importance of that tradition ['Classical'] lay in its abstract intellectual disciplines (proportion, symmetry) and habits of mind (clarity, rationalism) far more than matters of detailed style. . . . The Palladianism was restricted [in Voelcker's plans for electrical engineering stations] to an abstract planning diagram, and did not involve even room-shapes, let alone the detailing of the elevations."[23]

But the historicization of neo-Palladianism had in fact been accomplished in 1957 in a debate at the RIBA around the motion "that Systems of Proportion make good design easier and bad design more difficult." Nikolaus Pevsner's defense of the motion had been countered by Misha Black and Peter Smithson himself. Certainly, Smithson conceded, the issue "was important to architects as a matter of tooth and claw debate, in 1947 and 1948," when Palladian buildings were understood as "something to believe in . . . something that stood above what they were doing themselves," but in 1957 the issue was "passé": "The right time for the Palladian revival was 1948." All the rest was no more than an "academic post-mortem" of the European postwar impulse, "as is also this debate at the RIBA."[24]

Smithson's suggestion that 1948 signaled the *high* point of English neo-Palladianism is interesting, for the often cited source of such principled Palladianism, Wittkower's *Architectural Principles in the Age of Humanism*, had not yet been published.[25] It appeared in 1949, to decidedly negative reviews. A. G. Butler, for example, writing in the *RIBA Journal* in 1951, found Wittkower's book "exhausting," "unintelligible," and "almost a bore." Yet a group of young architects were already prepared for its arguments: the Smithsons, Colquhoun, Banham, and Rowe were enthusiastic. In protest against Butler, Smithson attested: "Dr. Wittkower is regarded by the younger architects as the *only* art historian working in England capable of describing and analyzing buildings in spatial and plastic terms and not in terms of derivation and dates." For them, Smithson stated, *Architectural Principles* was "the most important work on architecture published in England since the War."[26] This response, however, was written in 1951. Although Wittkower's central essay, "Principles of Palladio's Architecture," had been published in two parts in the *Journal of the Warburg and Courtauld Institutes* in 1944 and 1945, these articles were not generally circulated to the architectural public; thus another catalyst for the young architects' interest in Palladian principles must be sought. It was not the publication of Wittkower's book that started the trend, nor the earlier publication of its chapters, but rather the enormous impact of his student Colin Rowe in the circle around Banham. It was Rowe who had, in 1947, coopted Wittkower's historical analysis for a sweeping comparison of form and principle with the modern movement, and, by implication, with the demand for "principles" in the extension of a truly modernist architecture for the present.

Thence came Smithson's sense of 1948 as the year of Palladianism, poised between Rowe's publication of his first article and
his teacher's publication of *Architectural Principles*, between 1947
and 1949.

Diagramming Palladio

Wittkower's analysis of Palladio did not, at least initially, imply
any such relationship to contemporary design. As he writes in
his conclusion, his aim was to provide an account of Renaissance
proportional systems that, "though limited in scope, aims at
being less speculative than some previous writings." This was,
he noted, a "subject which had become historical."[27] But from
Wittkower's two articles on Palladio's principles, Rowe was able
to seize on three concepts that, while apparently innocent of
modernity in Wittkower, took on an entirely new significance
in juxtaposition with those of Le Corbusier. First was the idea of
architectural principles in itself. Wittkower had made it clear that
his thesis was directly opposed to those of writers in the British
historical tradition who associated the Renaissance with individual taste and inspiration, rather than with systematic thought and
proportional theory. His critiques of Ruskin and Geoffrey Scott
resonated for a postwar generation seeking what Alina Payne,
speaking of Wittkower's intentions, has termed "a conscious
intellect-driven will to form aimed at conveying meaning, and
hence, aimed at the mind rather than the senses."[28] Second was
the detailed analysis of proportion and geometry as it revealed a
constructive principle in Palladio's work. The third, and perhaps
most important, concept was derived from a page of diagrammatic plans of Palladio's villas demonstrating their reliance on a
common schema of spatial distribution, modified and elaborated
in each example.

The section in which this last diagram appeared, "Palladio's Geometry: The Villas," is barely three pages long, but its

influence would be formidable. Wittkower's purpose was to demonstrate Palladio's adherence to the "precepts of art," to "that which reason dictates," to "some universal and necessary rules of art."[29] One example that carried out these precepts was "a hall in the central axis and absolute symmetry of the lesser rooms on both sides," the insistence on which showed Palladio creating a "complete break with the older tradition" through the "systematization of the ground plan."[30] Thus, Wittkower argues, Palladio had adhered to a typical plan, with "loggias and a large hall in the central axis, two or three living-rooms or bedrooms of various sizes at the sides, and, between them and the hall, space for small spare rooms and the staircases." Wittkower ranges some eleven "schematized plans" of villas built after the late 1540s, finding that they were "all different statements of the same geometrical formula," "all generated from the same fundamental principle," and concludes his geometrical summary with a typical plan incorporating the fundamental "Geometrical Pattern of Palladio's Villas."[31] Beginning with the Villa Godi Porto at Lonedo, and continuing with the Villa Thiene at Cicogna, the Villa Sarego at Miega, the Villa Pojana, the Villa Badoer at Fratta, the Villa Zeno at Cesalto, and the Villa Cornaro at Piombino, the variations of this plan circulated, so to speak, around the "type" of the Villa Malcontenta, and found their ultimate model in the Villa Rotonda, "the most perfect realization of the fundamental geometrical skeleton."[32] In sum, Wittkower considers the villas as "archetypes," "variations on a basic geometric theme, different realizations, as it were, of the Platonic idea of the villa." As Wittkower reconstructs Palladio's design method: "What was in Palladio's mind when he experimented over and over again with the same elements? Once he had found the basic geometric pattern for the problem 'villa,' he adopted it as clearly and as simply as possible to the special requirements of each commission. He reconciled the task at hand with the 'certain truth' or mathematics which is final and unchangeable. This geometrical keynote is, subconsciously rather than consciously, perceptible to everyone who visits Palladio's villas and it is this that gives his buildings their convincing quality."[33] Such an approach, Wittkower advances, similarly informed the composition of Palladio's villa facades. Again Wittkower treats the three dimensions of the villas as a geometrical abstraction—solid three-dimensional blocks, they take the form of cubes. These, in turn, "had to be given a facade" that was "grafted" onto its front—most notably, in Palladio's innovative move, as a temple front. Wittkower describes the process:

> *The facades of Palladio's villas present us with a problem essentially similar to that of the plans. In contrast to French and English, most Italian monumental architecture is cubic and conceived in terms of a solid three-dimensional block. Italian architects always strove for an easily perceptible ratio between length, height, and depth of a building, and all villas by Palladio have that block-like quality. The cube had to be given a facade. He found his motive in the classical temple front. . . . The idea that the temple is a magnified house throws an interesting light on Palladio's own crystalline conception of architecture. He cannot think in terms of evolution, but envisages ready-made units which may be extended or contracted.* [34]

These themes, not unnaturally, formed the foundation of Rowe's master's thesis. In the bibliography he lists the three articles that Wittkower published in the *Journal of the Warburg and Courtauld Institutes* on Palladio's "principles" and English neoclassical architecture; further, he notes that his "resumé of Barbaro's theory" is indebted to Wittkower, quoting Barbaro from "Principles," and cites his teacher again "for Palladio's conception of the temple springing from the forms of the ancient house." But beyond this, the qualities of Rowe's own formal analysis indicate that the debt between advisor and student might well have been reciprocal. Wittkower had closed "Principles of Palladio's Architecture" with a purely historical statement—"While thus the harmonic mathematical conception of architecture was philosophically overthrown in the age of 'nature and feeling' and disappeared from the practical handling of proportion, scholars began investigating a subject which had become historical"[35]—but his conclusion to *Architectural Principles* four years later ended in the present: "Les proportions c'est l'infini:—this terse statement [of Julien Guadet] is still indicative of our approach. That is the reason why we view researches into the theory of proportion with suspicion and awe. But the subject is again very much alive in the minds of young architects today, and they may well evolve new and unexpected solutions to this ancient problem."[36]

The double inheritance of the Renaissance from Palladio through Jones would be of simply academic interest if it did not form the basis of Rowe's own historical view of architecture in general, and of the modern movement in particular. For as Rowe elaborated in the London essays "Mathematics" and "Mannerism" (1947–50) and later reinforced in articles of his Texas period (1954–56), "modernism" for him referred directly to the "Palladianism" of this first iteration in two fundamental respects: its crystallization in the work of a single "systematizer," in this case Le Corbusier; and its propagation through a central written treatise, *Vers une architecture*. Rowe's modernism relied on the initial experiments of two generations of multiple innovators from the Arts and Crafts movement to expressionism, and on the completion of a few synthetic, paradigmatic works that encapsulated its ideals and their formal representation—the villas Stein and Savoye. For its assumptions of coherence and periodization, it also relied, apparently paradoxically for one opposed to the very notion of "progress" in history, on a coherent theory of the historical zeitgeist. Rowe expressed this view in comments he drafted in 1954 for the use of Harwell Harris, chair of the department of architecture at the University of Texas: "It cannot be assumed that the present day is without an overt artistic urge, will, volition. No earlier time has been without one and there is no reason to believe that we are exempted from what has so far been universal. That modern architecture is not merely a negative rationalism, that it embodies a positive will, is proved by evidences which are daily before our eyes."[37] This, then, was the basis for Rowe's incisive, brief (only four of the celebrated "blue" pages, dedicated to theory and sometimes to history, of the *Architectural Review*), but extraordinarily influential, first essay.

The publication of "Mathematics of the Ideal Villa: Palladio and Le Corbusier Compared" had been to some extent prepared by the growing interest of the *Architectural Review* in the relation of proportional geometries to design. Wittkower himself, in a review of a "primer of proportion" the year before, had been less than enthusiastic for the contemporary fate of proportion, concluding, "In the last hundred years we have seen too many systems of proportion from which their authors expected salvation. They have all been passed by by the artists. The old universality has irrevocably gone, and Ruskin's conviction that it must be left to the inspiration of the artist to invent beautiful proportions is for better or for worse still our own."[38] But Rowe's article captured the cover of the journal, represented by a black-and-white reverse drawing from a 1920 treatise on historical proportions, illustrating the west elevation of Notre Dame in Paris, superimposed with lines indicating the supposed use of the Golden Section rectangle. The editors noted that whether or not the Gothic use of this system could be proved, "it is certain that in more modern times a great many architects have consciously employed the science; on pages 101–104 in this issue Colin Rowe compares

Palladio's Villa Malcontenta and Le Corbusier's Villa at Garches, showing that both are based on the belief that right proportions may be expressed in mathematical terms."[39]

Mathematics

There are two causes of beauty—natural and customary. Natural is from geometry, consisting in uniformity, that is equality, and proportion. Customary beauty is begotten by the use, as familiarity breeds a love to things not in themselves lovely. Here lies the great occasion of errors, but always the test is natural or geometrical beauty. Geometrical figures are naturally more beautiful than irregular figures; the square, the circle are the most beautiful, next the parallelogram and the oval. There are only two positions of straight lines, perpendicular and horizontal; this is from Nature, and consequently necessity, no other than upright being firm.

These words, attributed to Christopher Wren and published in the mid-eighteenth century in his posthumous fragments titled *Parentalia*, appear as an epigraph to Rowe's "The Mathematics of the Ideal Villa," framing a discussion of the comparative uses of geometry and associative form in Palladio and Le Corbusier.[40] Wren's lapidary formulation—which paralleled a similar distinction drawn between "absolute" and "arbitrary" beauty by Claude Perrault at almost the same moment—was developed in relation to a social and historical approach emerging from the comparative study of languages that attempted to explain shifts in style, even within the classical (antique) and revived classical (Renaissance) periods. This formulation allowed Wren to postulate a fundamental order for all architecture based on pure geometry and a changing outer form dependent on social and cultural custom, and enabled his calibration of the appropriate style for different, historically meaningful institutions. Thus, his projects in quasi-Gothic style for St. Paul's, both before and after the fire, and his neo-Gothic entry gate for Christ Church, Oxford, were designed following a "judgment" of architecture's "political Use," its role as "Ornament" of a country.[41]

For Rowe, Wren's didactic statement implied an opposition between a radical "autonomous" architecture internally considered to derive its formal condition *as* architecture from geometry, whether typological or topological, and an architecture deriving its authority from an evaluation of its social and cultural symbolism, drawn back from the Arts and Crafts to the classical. In purely visual terms, this opposition manifested itself as between abstract and realist; in historical terms, it might be seen as between an architecture that extended the abstract formalism of the 1920s avant-gardes and one that returned to a restatement of the literal forms of classical tradition. On an ideological plane, we might say it stood as a contest between posthumanist modernism and retrohumanist postmodernism; between an assumption of a humanist subjectivity disseminated and perhaps irrevocably lost, and one precariously surviving, perhaps to be regained.

Out of Wittkower's observations on Palladio, Rowe derives a founding concept—the ideal villa—and its principles of form— geometry—joining them to a comparison of Palladio's villas and Le Corbusier's modernist counterparts. In the formal tradition of Wölfflin, the argument works more by juxtaposition and comparison than by derivation. Rowe was not proposing any direct filiation between the late Renaissance architect and the modernist architect; he admits that the villas of Palladio and Le Corbusier were "in different worlds," and insists that "the world of classical Mediterranean culture, on which Palladio drew so expressively, is closed for Le Corbusier."[42]

The structure of this short essay is simple enough. Rowe begins with a comparison of Palladio's Villa Capra or Rotonda with Le Corbusier's Maison Savoye at Poissy, based on Palladio's eloquent description of his villa's rural surroundings and Le Corbusier's similar description of his villa's site as "un rêve virgilien": "It would have been, perhaps, the landscape of Poussin that Palladio would have longed to penetrate, to roam among the portentous apparitions of the antique . . . and if the contemporary pastoral is not yet sanctified by conventional usage, apparently the Virgilian nostalgia is still present."[43] Rowe's evocation of arcadia as the imaginary site of Palladio's Villa Rotonda and his connection of the villa to Poussin's arcadian landscapes echo another Warburgian influence: Erwin Panofsky's essay "'Et in Arcadia Ego.'" Panofsky cited Virgil as the originator of the myth of Arcadia, a region formerly understood as wild and inhospitable but endowed by Virgil with the bucolic landscape of Sicily in a utopian myth of elegiac force, later to be adopted by the Renaissance as "an enchanting vision" and studied by Saxl, among many others.[44]

Whereas this reference to the Warburgian version of arcadia might represent a progressive, modernizing side of Rowe's analysis, the same reference, employed as the title of Book I of Evelyn Waugh's *Brideshead Revisited*—cited by David Watkin as the novel that had the greatest influence on the immediate postwar consciousness of architectural history—signals another, more conservative side of Rowe's affections. In his lectures, Rowe would quote ad lib from Waugh as frequently as he would from Auden. In Waugh's novel, the notion of "Et in Arcadia Ego" signifies at once the prewar idyll of life at the great house of Brideshead and its inevitable death as a boarded-up mansion requisitioned by the army. The opening line of Book I—"I have been here before"[45]— echoes throughout the emerging sense of historical heritage that was to engulf post-1945 England, the England of John Betjeman and John Piper, of Nikolaus Pevsner's county guides and Gordon Cullen's "Townscape." Waugh's narrator, an architectural artist-reader of Roger Fry's *Vision and Design* and Clive Bell's *Art*, was every artist and architect demobilized—immersed in the memories of an imaginary lost paradise and the realities of a rapidly disappearing landscape of rural rides and stately seats. Set in its "secret landscape," "prone in the sunlight, grey and gold amid a screen of boskage," Brideshead was constructed out of a veritable "collage" architecture of suspended history, with its dome said to be by Inigo Jones, its "Soanesque" library, Chinese drawing-room, Chippendale fretwork, Pompeian parlor, colonnaded terrace, and fountain "as one might expect to find in a piazza of Southern Italy."[46] Waugh's languishing prose, his close reading of every sign of the past as contrasting with the present, his continuous intimation of transience countered by a resolute facing of present and future, resonated in Britons confronted with the task of rebuilding amid the ruins.

Refusing to be trapped in arcadia and the shifting ground of customary beauty, Rowe turned to a "more specific comparison" between Palladio's Villa Foscari, or Malcontenta, and Le Corbusier's house for M. de Monzie at Garches, based on their geometrical and proportional structures: the foundation of architecture's "natural" beauty. In each of these comparisons, the influence of Wittkower is clear in Rowe's treatment of Palladio and, by association, of Le Corbusier, and is fundamental to his analysis of the plans and their geometrical properties. Drawing on Wittkower's comparison of Palladian plan types, Rowe develops what he calls "a diagrammatic comparison" to reveal the "fundamental relationships" between Garches and Malcontenta: in both, he claims, the "system is closely similar," and he proceeds to elaborate on Wittkower's identification of "six 'transverse' lines of support, rhythmically alternating double and single bays."[47] Rowe cites the quotation used by Wittkower in support of Palladio's adherence to symmetry, follows Wittkower's analysis of musical and geometrical harmonies, agrees with his teacher in seeing Palladio's study of public buildings resonate in the private realm, and picks up on Wittkower's mention of Matila Ghyka's *The Geometry of Art and Life* to the extent of reproducing a page of diagrams analyzing the Golden Section rectangle. Finally, throughout the essay, Rowe insists that the architecture of both Palladio and Le Corbusier is a result of mental energy, "an intellectual feat which reconciles the mind to the fundamental discrepancy of the programme."[48]

The debt to Wittkower is even more pronounced in Rowe's choice of illustrations. The diagrams of the "modular grid" of the plans, the first-floor plans, and the elevations of Malcontenta and Garches are ranged vertically side by side in columnar comparison (an effect lost in the republication of the essay in *Mathematics of the Ideal Villa and Other Essays*), in a direct adumbration of Wittkower's own diagrams. All of these parallels, it must be said, occur without a single reference to Wittkower or his articles. Charitably, one might argue that articles for the *Architectural Review* were regularly published without footnotes, but this fact, of course, does not preclude citing attributions in the text itself.

Inventing Modernism

After the act of Revolution, therefore—which is largely icono-clastic in character—comes the process of building anew.
—*Architectural Review*, editorial, 1947

It is significant in retrospect that Rowe's first article was published in the third number of the *Architectural Review* of 1947.

In January of that year, to celebrate the magazine's fiftieth year of publication, the editorial board joined together for the first time in many years to issue a statement of policy and to review the past fifty years of architectural development. Their "manifesto," mild enough by early twentieth-century standards, was titled "The Second Half Century," and looked toward a future both short-term and long-term in which the *Review* would play an important role in the architectural education of the profession and the general public.[49] J. M. Richards, Pevsner, Osbert Lancaster, and Hubert de Cronin Hastings pronounced themselves antirevolutionaries: their journal "does not set out to lead a political and moral or even a social revolution"; they were determined to be more open-minded than their modern movement predecessors and dedicated to "the cause of visual culture" in general, on a mission no more nor less than to "re-educate the eye" of the *Review*'s readers. In this task they were determined not only to continue the "Third Programme" pieces of high criticism ("scholar's table-talk conducted in public") and the normal process of publishing contemporary architecture, but also to open up to a wide range of cultural artifacts not necessarily high architectural in form.[50] Indeed, they had a "call" "of quite a low-class, evangelical kind," no doubt influenced by Pevsner's own Lutheranism and Hastings's populism, that was to sponsor the well-known investigations into pub architecture, townscape, and popular design that characterized the *Architectural Review* for the next two decades.[51] But this call also had an aesthetic side directed to the supposedly dogmatic modernism of the prewar years: "The obvious short-term objective must consist in getting back some of the scope and richness that the Act of Revolution discarded." This task demanded a "new humanism" for architecture, seeking "more direct contact with human aspirations," architecture "becoming more and more a vehicle for humanity's aspirations."[52]

Such a program involved discarding many of the modern movement's doctrines that in the light of experience had become "negative characteristics" and could be changed only through reactivation of the arts of expression. The editors listed: "a new richness and differentiation of character, the pursuit of differences rather than sameness, the re-emergence of monumentality, the cultivation of idiosyncracy and the development of those regional dissimilarities that people have always taken a pride in."[53] This goal perfectly matched Pevsner's call for a return to the great English tradition of the picturesque, but, as would be demonstrated by Colquhoun's stern rebuke to Pevsner in 1954, many in Rowe's circle were ready to combat the incipient "historicism" embedded in picturesque (and townscape) ideology. Yet in 1947, these "dangers" to modern movement orthodoxy were not so evident, and it is easy to trace elements of this new "freedom" announced by the editors of the *Review* in Rowe's own embrace of Pevsner's (and Wittkower's) "mannerism," as well as in his visual approach to the conceptual, intellectual "rules" of the modernist game.

For, convinced, like many of his generation—Banham and Colquhoun in Britain, Greenberg and later Leo Steinberg in the United States—that the first era of the modern avant-gardes was historically complete, Rowe saw his task with respect to the postwar practice of architecture and architectural history as defined on the one hand by the ideological and formal residue of avant-gardism, and on the other by the much longer trajectory of architectural tradition since the Renaissance. In the process, he constructed a formulation of a more or less unified "modernism" that served him as a critical armature for the rest of his life. Like Clement Greenberg, who sought to invent a similar "modernism" for painting and countered the modern movement's own myth of the "end of history," Rowe turned to history as a key to the isolation of specifically modernist moves in architecture, as well as more traditional survivals. Like Greenberg's approach to the canvas, Rowe's architectural analysis, growing out of Wölfflin, Wittkower, and Pevsner, was neo-Kantian. Whereas Greenberg sought to identify the roots and definition of modernism in the emerging "flatness" of painting after Manet, Rowe turned back further, to the Renaissance (as Manfredo Tafuri was to do later) as the touchstone of a developed architectural manner. The "modernism" thus defined by both Rowe and Greenberg, from their quite different perspectives, was parallel to that of T. S. Eliot, as Terry Eagleton has characterized it, founded on a "Janus-faced temporality, in which one turns to the resources of the pre-modern in order to move backwards into a future that has transcended modernity altogether."[54]

In this context, Rowe's initial comparison of Palladio and Le Corbusier was in no way simply the arbitrary result of applying the idea of mannerism to modernism, nor was it a fashionable conceit adopted by a few young members of Team X and the Independent Group out of a casual reading of Wittkower, or a Sunday conversation with Rowe at Banham's house. Rather, by 1930 Le Corbusier had emerged, for Rowe, as *the* Palladio of modernity. In a 1959 meditation entitled "Le Corbusier: Utopian Architect," Rowe describes Le Corbusier's influence, like Palladio's, as "principally exercised through the medium of the illustrated book; and if we wish to understand its nature, it is to his early treatise, *Towards a New Architecture,* and to the publication of his buildings and projects as his *Oeuvre Complète* that we must look. For in these books he evolves a frame of reference, persuades us to accept it, poses the problems, and answers them in his own terms; so that, like the great system makers of the Renaissance, Le Corbusier presents himself to us as a kind of living encyclopaedia of architecture, or as the index to a world where all experience is ordered and all inconsistency eradicated."[55]

In Rowe's argument, however, the comparison of Palladio and Le Cobusier remains at this level, as a comparison between architects who produced books. As filtered through Wittkower, Palladio's role is clearly as a foil through which to construct a specific form of modernism in Le Corbusier. Here, as Guido Zuliani has observed in a recent article, we should distinguish carefully between the nature and roles of the two diagrams, Wittkower's and Rowe's. The diagrams represent two different bay rhythms—Wittkower's ABCBA and Rowe's ABABA—that in turn indicate entirely divergent strategies on the part of the two historians: "Wittkower's diagram describes the structure of internal relations, that, for him, constitute the signifying content of Palladian villas, whereas Rowe's diagram is a paradigmatic configuration, a guarantor of structure, in his view, of the correct relations and hierarchies against which to evaluate the proper and improper nature of specific design choices."[56] One might go further, and state that such "design choices" would be those Rowe considered "modernist" and saw against the backdrop of a parallel set of design choices established by Palladio. In the case of Wittkower, however, the diagram is meant as an analytical reinforcement of the historian's description of Palladian spatial layout; for Rowe, the adoption of this diagram and its overlaying on the Corbusian "villa" is at once a strategy to demonstrate the shifts, inversions, and transformations of the centralized classical model, and an invitation to read, if not produce, all modern architecture according to the same method.[57] The influence of this reading method has been so strong as to inflect several generations of late modernist work, standing both as the model for design approach, as in the work of the New York Five, and as the paradigm for contemporary formalism to work against, as in the digital practices of Greg Lynn.

Mannerism

*It is perhaps inevitable that Mannerism should come to be iso-
lated and defined by historians, during those same years of
the nineteen-twenties, when modern architecture feels most
strongly the demand for inverted spatial effects.*
—Colin Rowe, "Mannerism and Modern Architecture"

Wittkower's influence is even more present in the second of
Rowe's *Architectural Review* articles, "Mannerism and Modern
Architecture," published a year after *Architectural Principles.*
Nevertheless, Wittkower's fundamental work on mannerism
in the articles on Michelangelo's Laurentian Library in the *Art
Bulletin* of 1934, and in his analysis of Palladio's Palazzo Thiene,
Palazzo Valmarana, and the Loggia del Capitanato in the first part
of "Palladio's Principles," is still unacknowledged. Indeed, the
summary of Rowe's article offered by the editors (presumably by
Pevsner, but some of it probably written by Rowe himself) mentions only Pevsner and Anthony Blunt as precedents:

> *Mannerism in architecture, using the term Mannerism as
> it was defined by art historians in the early twenties, has
> only recently received the kind of attention which used to
> be given to the Baroque. Indeed, general attempts to de-
> fine the term in relation to architecture have, in England,
> so far been limited to two—Nikolaus Pevsner's article in
> The Mint for 1946, and Anthony Blunt's lecture at the
> RIBA in 1949. Yet the conception of Mannerism is one
> which promises much for the better understanding of the
> art and architecture of more periods and places than one.
> In March Nikolaus Pevsner showed how it might be used
> to throw light on the fascinating enigma of the English*

*Elizabethan style; in this article Colin Rowe applies it to
the architecture of the Modern Movement. In doing so he
breaks completely new ground, and reaches conclusions
which may startle those who have been content to accept the Modern Movement's account of itself at its face
value.*

*The Author: C. F. Rowe, MA, architect, is at present lec-
turing at the Liverpool School of Architecture. Is convinced
that analogies between the architecture of the sixteenth
and the present century cannot be ignored in any attempt to formulate a consistent theory for contemporary
architecture.* [58]

Of the two sources mentioned here, Blunt's lecture at the
RIBA, published as "Mannerism in Architecture" in March
1949, was the most directly concerned with applying the concept
of mannerism to contemporary architecture.[59] He began with an
attempt to define the word, which he insisted for his architectural audience was no mere "affectation" but a distinct style in
itself, first noted by art historians in painting around 1900. His
prime example, following Wittkower, was Michelangelo's Laurentian Library, where "all the principles which were manifest
in Brunelleschi [were] taken and . . . simply inverted." Columns
were set into the wall, there was a visual impression of great weight
but with small consoles; columns were treated in "a wanton manner"; the wall was interrupted "with brutality."[60] Such inversions
were, he noted, "visible in even so apparently classical an architect as Palladio," illustrating the point by using Wittkower's
diagram of the facade of San Francesco della Vigna.[61]

Blunt described mannerism as more than a period style; it is,
rather, a phenomenon common to other times and places, from
the rock tombs of Petra to the watercolors of Blake and the ar-

chitecture of the late eighteenth century, from Ledoux to Soane, which is characterized by "distortion of proportions, overcrowding of the space, and the extreme exaggeration, used to produce dramatic effect. One can find corresponding elements in certain architecture of the period also, for example in the work of Frenchmen like Ledoux. . . . In his architecture we can see an arbitrary juxtaposition of elements which is strictly Mannerist, and in some cases direct borrowing from Mannerist architects like Giulio Romano."[62] In the context of Rowe's interpretation, however, it is Blunt's direct attribution of mannerist elements to Le Corbusier that resonates. For Blunt, Le Corbusier's treatment of interior space was key, "in the sense that he frequently seems deliberately to avoid any completely closed form, and allows, on the contrary, the maximum degree of interpenetration, deliberate uncertainty, if you like, in the definition of the space."[63] And he ended his lecture with a direct quotation from Le Corbusier's *Vers une architecture* praising Michelangelo's St. Peter's.[64]

The second of Rowe's acknowledged sources after Blunt's lecture was Pevsner's article "The Architecture of Mannerism" in *The Mint: A Miscellany of Literature, Art and Criticism*, edited by the critic Geoffrey Grigson and including pieces by W. H. Auden, Seán O'Casey, and Graham Greene. Written as if it were the first English exposition of the subject, this brief introduction to mannerism is also written to correct an empirically minded England that "distrusts generalizations" and leaves "the perfection and codes of law to more logical and less practical nations."[65] Pevsner argues in favor of the word "style," introduced by German and Austrian art historians, to establish a more precise understanding of the terms of the field. "Fixed terms for styles of ages," he writes, "are there to keep a host of data in reasonable order," to help in "tidying up" works of art, and to distinguish Renaissance from baroque, which would be (in his Wölfflinian terms) to separate "the static from the dynamic, the compact from the expansive, the finite from the infinite, the ideal from the over-real or over-expressive."[66] Before considering what "mannerism" might refer to in architecture, he notes the clarifying effect of its "discovery" in 1924–25, and outlines the term's first application to painting.[67] His discussion of the "formal and emotional character" of the post-Counter-Reformation buildings by Sanmicheli, Giulio Romano, Peruzzi, Michelangelo, Pirro Ligorio, Ammanati, Vignola, Palladio, and Serlio places these works and their authors in the quickly established canon of mannerism as it was received in England after the Second World War. Throughout, Pevsner uses terms like "uncomfortable balancing" (applied to the facade of Sanmicheli's Palazzo Bevilacqua); "lack of clarity," "dissonance," "precarious instability," "restlessness," "incongruous proximity" (applied to Giulio Romano's Palazzo del Te); "unstable relations" (applied to Peruzzi's Palazzo Massimi); "preciosity" (applied to Pirro Ligorio's Casino of Pius); all add up to his characterization of the style as "self-conscious," "dissenting," and "frustrated," prone to "excess within rigid boundaries"—a style "with the aim of hurting, rather than pleasing, the eye."[68]

Pevsner's article, with its range of reference, its careful formal analyses, its explanation of mannerism as a style peculiar to an age of asceticism, of the rigorism of Pius V and Loyola, a "cheerless style, aloof and austere," with "no faith in mankind and no faith in matter," evidently had a huge influence on the enlightened elite of England, and especially on Colin Rowe and his circle.[69] Pevsner's digs at English pragmatism, at "modern architects" who "suffer from . . . lack of visual discrimination" and at criticism that "suffers from it too," naturally appealed to a generation anxious to reformulate the terms of theory and criticism developed by a connoisseurial class before the war. Finally, his recognition that mannerism was not just an application of a painterly vision to facades, but rather a spatial problem, was in tune with modernist ideas of architecture in general: "Architecture is not all a matter of walls and wall patterns. It is primarily organized space," he remarked, admitting that it was "much harder to write of space than of walls," because it demanded to be "wandered through" "at least with one's eyes," in a filmic manner.[70] While he cursorily cites Wittkower on Michelangelo, Pevsner is not entirely generous to his fellow-exile and University of London colleague; he prefaces his long analysis of Michelanagelo's Laurentian Library with the flat statement that no one previously had thought of Michelangelo in the terms of mannerism as he defined it. While many scholars, from Burckhardt to Schmarsow, had noticed "incongruities" in the building, these had been interpreted as marks of "struggle," rather than the "paralysed, frozen" architecture Pevsner envisaged.[71] Not incidentally, Pevsner passes over Wittkower's in-depth analysis of the Laurenziana.

Wittkower's own idea of mannerism did not, in fact, precisely agree with those of his art historical rivals. As elaborated in his 1934 article on Michelangelo, his concept of the style was derived from a meticulous study of the reconstructed stages of design for the Laurenziana, concerned, as Margaret Wittkower noted in 1977, "with proving the existence of a 'Mannerist' style in architecture," because the term as introduced by earlier historians, such as Voss, Dvořák, Frey, and Friedländer, had emerged from a study of painting, and was not specific to architecture and its deployment of elements.[72] Reinforcing this specificity, the article was to have been prefaced by a lost section titled "Das Problem manieristischer Architektur."[73]

For Wittkower, mannerism in architecture was first and foremost to be identified in what he termed "an irreconcilable conflict, a restless fluctuation between opposite extremes." He saw this as the "governing principle of the whole building" of the Laurenziana, as supposedly load-bearing orders are recessed behind the wall they would normally articulate and support, thus reversing the usual status of wall and orders. Equally, a stair that purports to climb upward is given a cascading downward movement at its center; the stair itself fills a vestibule that properly would articulate a moment of rest for the visitor. Similarly, the details exhibit "the same theme of insoluble conflict," with inner and outer door frames given "two different and irreconcilable meanings," triglyphs hanging like "dewdrops below the pilasters," and each element neutralizing the other ad infinitum: "every attempt to work out the architecture according to one system immediately leads to the other," to the point where "ambivalence" is the dominant impression. The observer is "plunged, without being aware of it, into a situation of doubt and uncertainty."[74] As opposed to the Renaissance sense of "self-sufficiency," stability, and lack of movement, and the baroque exhibition of unequivocal, dynamic movement, mannerism subsists on a *"duality of function,"* "one of the fundamental laws of Mannerist architecture."[75]

If conflict is the first law of mannerism, then the second law Wittkower identifies is "the principle of *inversion.*"[76] As demonstrated by the facade of S. Giorgio de' Greci in Venice, with its pilasters piled on top of one another, foiling any attempts to find vertical axes, "inversion forbids an unequivocal reading of the facade; the eye is led to wander from side to side, up and down, and the movement thus provoked can again be called ambiguous." Such a principle, Wittkower claims, is entirely foreign to both the Renaissance and the baroque, demonstrating the existence of the style called mannerism, of which the Biblioteca Laurenziana is the "supreme representation."[77]

Wittkower did not confine his analysis to the historical period between 1520 and 1600 that he had identified as mannerist. Already in 1934 he was developing a tentative theory for the entire modern period, seen as an overall unity from the early fifteenth century to the mid-nineteenth century. "Mannerism" then became a generic term for architecture that was neither entirely static nor unequivocally dynamic: while art history "habitually" thought of the development of a sequence from static Renaissance to dynamic baroque, Wittkower saw the concept of mannerist ambiguity as one that could be "applied to both static and dynamic buildings," to the extent that mannerism often appears at different scales throughout the period. For Wittkower the true break was effected by the introduction in the mid-nineteenth century of modern steel construction which, like the flying buttress of the Gothic period before the Renaissance, produced structures that had no need for walls. Between the fourteenth century and the nineteenth, however, walls were the primary element, and allowed for the variegated play of the orders on and within their surfaces with no functional or structural impediment. Here, of course, Wittkower was following the general consensus, established by Giedion, that modern architecture was founded on the principles of the skeleton and the "functional" demand for honesty in its representation. Wittkower did leave one loophole for modernist criticism, however, one that Rowe would eagerly exploit, in his characterization of the Laurenziana as "the beginning of a completely new approach to architecture . . . the key to a wide area of unexplored or misinterpreted architectural history, and the explanation of much that was to happen in the next two centuries and beyond."[78] And if Wittkower himself could extend the period through to the ninteenth century, why should not an architecture dedicated no longer to the clarity of the Chicago frame, but rather to the ambiguity between surface and structure, historical tradition and modernity, be subject to analysis according to the same principles?

Rowe—despite his assertion that "the only general attempts [to apply the term 'mannerism' to architecture] in English" were those of Blunt and Pevsner, and ignoring Wittkower's magisterial essay on Michelangelo—assimilates Wittkower's entire discourse into his treatment of modern architecture. The entry facade of Le Corbusier's Villa at La Chaux-de-Fonds is compared to the facade of the Casa di Palladio in Vicenza, Zuccheri's Casino in Florence, and to a Georgian house in Suffolk Street, London. Picking up on Blunt's characterization of Soane as mannerist, Rowe even points to the reemphasis on mannerist motifs in Soane's delineation of Zuccheri for his lecture illustrations to the Royal Academy in the early nineteenth century. Rowe's reliance on Blunt reappears at the close of the essay when he quotes liberally from Le Corbusier on Michelangelo.

The center of "Mannerism and Modern Architecture," though, is an elaborate but succinct reformulation of the history of architecture since the Renaissance in terms that pit the rationalism of structure and the moral ethic of the program against the visual qualities of the eclectic and the picturesque, a tension traced through to the modern movement, split between the demands of reason and the satisfaction of the eye. Rowe finds this entire development, together with its tensions, to culminate in Le Corbusier, whose *Oeuvre complète* is framed as "a production as developed and as theoretically informed as any of the great architectural treatises of the sixteenth century."[79] But the real dilemma facing Le Corbusier—and, one supposes, Rowe and his circle, following the evident success of "Mathematics of the Ideal Villa"—was Corbusier's "incapacity to define an attitude to sensation."[80] With mathematics operating as an "absolute value," a reinforcement of "universal and comforting truths," the question arises as to the "sensuous appreciation" to be devoted to the resulting "cubes, spheres, cylinders, cones and their products."[81] In this ascription, the celebrated phrase "the masterly, correct, and magnificent play of masses brought together in light" opens up what Rowe sees as a "self-division" within Le Corbusier that was never to be closed: that between the "correctness" of an intellectual idea infusing the object from outside and the correctness of a visual attribute of the object itself. Here Rowe is set to make the parallel between the post–World War I world of Le Corbusier and the world of the Counter-Reformation, both contexts rendering balance and harmony impossible: "If, in the sixteenth century, Mannerism is the visual index of an acute spiritual crisis, the recurrence of similar attitudes at the present day should not be unexpected, and corresponding conflicts should scarcely require indication."[82]

In this way Rowe systematically compares the disturbances and exaggerations common to mannerism and to modernism: plans that are both central and peripheral, works that visually demand intellectual confirmation from the abstract perspective of the aerial view; deliberate and insoluble spatial complexities in Michelangelo and Mies alike; ambiguous spatial organizations in Vignola and Mies; and, finally, the intensity of discordant elements at different scales represented in St. Peter's and in Le Corbusier's Salvation Army Building. This comparison allows Rowe to "really measure the production of our own day": "In a composition of aggressive and profound sophistication, plastic elements of a major scale are foiled against the comparatively minor regulations of the glazed wall. Here again the complete identity of discordant elements is affirmed; and, as at St. Peter's, in this intricate and monumental conceit, there is no release and no permanent satisfaction for the eye. Disturbance is complete."[83] Rowe is, then, not so much comparing Palladio and Le Corbusier, as in the first essay, as now comparing Michelangelo and Le Corbusier. In this sense the argument is not so much about mannerism *and* modern architecture, but about Le Corbusier as "Michelangelesque" and modern architecture as "mannerist." Of course neither mannerists nor modernists were setting out with the primary goal to *be* "mannerist"—to the contrary, both envisaged themselves as the bold contrarians of their age. The supposedly blank panels of the Casa di Palladio and the Villa

Schwob were construed respectively, and respectfully, within the codes of "the architectural traditions of Renaissance humanism" and modernism.[84] What Rowe identified as "Palladio's inversion of the normal" and Le Corbusier's "formal ambiguity" were intended deliberately to "disrupt the inner core" of classical and modernist coherence, respectively. But equally, as Dvořák, Pevsner, and Wittkower had suggested, such disruption was far from classical in its historical implications; rather, it was a sign of what Rowe termed a "universal *malaise*," and of the fundamental "inner contradictions" that afflicted classicism and modernism alike.

Given such a historical sense of beginning, middle, and academic end, the slipping of modernism into neoclassicism, even as Palladianism slipped into late eighteenth-century neoclassicism, was both inevitable and a sign of decline. In this ascription it would be not Wittkower but Emil Kaufmann who, following the posthumous publication of *Architecture in the Age of Reason* in 1955, would be Rowe's guide to the eighteenth century. For Rowe viewed post-Corbusianism and post-Miesianism as moments of formal crystallization bereft of the ideological content that had (falsely but energetically) inspired modern architecture: the revolution had failed. As he concluded his review of the 1959 exhibition of Le Corbusier at the Building Center, "The success of any revolution is also its failure." Modern architecture was now ubiquitous, an "official art": rather than "the continuing *symbol* of something new, Modern architecture has recently become the *decoration* of everything existing."[85] Even as the neo-Palladian villa "at its best, became the picturesque object in the English park," so Le Corbusier, "source of innumerable pastiches and of tediously amusing exhibition techniques," is rendered empty as "le style Corbu."[86] As Rowe concluded somewhat despondently in "Mathematics of the Ideal Villa": "It is the magnificently realizable quality of the originals which one fails to find in the works of neo-Palladians and exponents of 'le style Corbu.'" But for Rowe in 1947, the distinction was clear: "The difference is that between the universal, and the decorative or merely competent; perhaps in both cases it is the adherence to rules which has lapsed."[87]

Here then, and as early as Rowe's first essays of 1947 and 1950, we can identify that sense of exhaustion, of the already seen, of the endlessly repeated formulae, that pervades his assessments of contemporary work, as if the critic/historian is, Spengler-like, already wasted by the ennui of living at the end of history. In this wasteland, as we shall see, only his former student and friend James Stirling would be exempt from criticism as having sur-mounted the transition from mannerism to neoclassicism, like some latter-day John Soane, eclectic and combinatory, abstract and symbolic, developing whatever *virtù* might be salvaged from a formalism without ideology, a rhetoric without content, from the very force of its jangled inversions in order to invent a late-modern institutional typology.

The End of Modernism

This sense of the fatigued, detached observer is confirmed when we read Colin Rowe on the subject of the New York Five. Here there is no clear sense of critical authorization of the kind offered, for example, by Giedion in support of Le Corbusier or, alterna-tively, by Pevsner against Le Corbusier, no hint of that "instru-mental" criticism so castigated by Tafuri as implicating the critic in the practice of the architect. While Tafuri himself at one point in his career was keen to engage the American five, and certainly registered (though in a fundamentally critical vein) the impact of Rossi's neorationalist typology on Krier and others, Rowe seems to have wanted to escape from any firm judgment on the issues raised. Thus, the better part of Rowe's introduction to *Five Archi-tects* (1972) is taken up more with an autopsy of modern architec-ture's failure in the face of its ubiquitous success than with any extended discussion of the contents of the book. The burden of the argument rests on the disappearance of the moral and utopian impetus in European modernism, the seemingly nonideological modern architecture of the United States, and the opening left for the recuperation of historical "meaning" through the resurrection and extension of modernist codes—in his words, Eisenman "seems to have received a revelation in Como; Hejduk seems to wish affiliation both to synthetic Cubist Paris and Constructivist Moscow," and Graves, Gwathmey, and Meier have an "obviously Corbusian orientation." His conclusion that the argument posed by the Five was "largely about the physique of building and only indirectly about its morale" avoided any confrontation with the nature of this new formalism, qua architecture as meaningful language.[88] Even in the two-paragraph erratum added as a loose page in the 1975 Oxford University Press edition, Rowe vouchsafes little more in the way of appreciation than an extremely contorted assessment of the "bourgeois," "cosmopolitan erudition" and "belligerently second hand" character of the work. Its only merit, apparently, resides in the fact that "it is what *some* people and *some* architects want," and thus difficult to fault, "in *principle*" at least.[89]

In the end, and despite the ultimate brilliance of Rowe's analytical vision, we are faced with a critic who believed that everything had already happened, one who might well be placed among those of the generation of 1945 who, fatalistically or dispassionately, found solace in the belief that the epoch of history had ended in *posthistoire* repetition and impasse.

Modernist Mannerism: Stirling

Robert Maxwell has surmised that the two essays published by James Stirling at the beginning of his career in the *Architectural Review* in 1955–56, "Garches to Jaoul" and "Ronchamp," were consciously modeled on Rowe's first two articles in the same journal.[90] Certainly Stirling, as Rowe's thesis student at Liverpool and a close member of his circle in London after 1951, was deeply influenced by Rowe in his support of the "conversion" to modernism recently effected at the Liverpool School of Architecture. But a reading of Stirling's essays reveals a strategy that goes beyond emulation and toward a fundamental reevaluation of Corbusian modernity, which was only later assumed openly by Rowe. First on Stirling's agenda is the need to shift attention from the canonical Garches to the still misunderstood Maisons Jaoul. Using the comparative method preferred by Rowe, Stirling sees the two as posed at "the extremes" of Le Corbusier's vocabulary, the "rational, urbane, programmatic" versus the "personal and anti-mechanistic."[91] Garches remained the standard, at once the "masterpiece of Neo-Palladianism" and the epitome of Le Corbusier's version of high modernism. Axial and cubic, it demands to be entered frontally, and the play of spatial movement is tightly enclosed on the interior. The Jaoul houses, by contrast, present no main facade, and are spatially active on the outside and static on the inside. Most striking, however, is the difference between the smooth, white, machine aesthetic of Garches and the rough concrete and brick construction of Jaoul: in both cases, the garden is on the roof, but one is an elegant solarium, the other an untended roof of sod and earth. One is polished, the other primitive; one a villa, the other recalling Provençal or traditional Indian farmhouses. Stirling asks: If, in some way, style is "the crystallization of an attitude," then what might account for this apparently radical shift? He answers his question in social rather than aesthetic terms, characterizing the radical, revolutionary, avant-garde, and elitist nature of Garches in contrast to the homely and potentially ubiquitous Maisons Jaoul: Garches is (properly) "Utopian" in that it anticipated "the progress of twentieth-century emancipation." This achieved, it remained for the Jaoul houses to respond to the new "status quo," to be "inhabited by any civilized family, urban or rural."[92] Two pages of photographs continue the contrast in materials and spatial organization, and directly anticipate the presentation of Stirling's own first housing project, the flats at Ham Common, a project almost literally based on the Jaoul houses, in the *Architectural Review*. The "monument, not to an age which is dead, but to a way of life which has not generally arrived" has been superseded by the livable, domestic house, constructed with traditional materials and in an informal aesthetic that is (literally and figuratively) approachable, presenting no singular and hierarchical front to the view. Reyner Banham, who would characterize this new style as the "New Brutalism" in an article published in the *Review* three months later, would similarly adopt the perambulating vision, the walk around the house, as a photographic technique for the publication of the Smithsons' school at Hunstanton.

The emergence of such a new perspective is confirmed by Stirling's second essay, "Ronchamp: Le Corbusier's Chapel and the Crisis of Rationalism." Building on the perception of a schism between Europe and the United States, as later epitomized by Rowe in his essay "The Chicago Frame,"[93] Stirling opens by contrasting the Lever House by Gordon Bunshaft of SOM and the Unité d'Habitation in Marseilles by Le Corbusier. Here the opposition is between technology and art, or the "functionalism" of industrial processes and products versus the "essentially humanist method of designing to a specific use."[94] Stirling holds that both versions were fundamentally challenged by the appearance of Ronchamp, which extends an architecture of pure space and form to an extreme "plasticity" that assumes the qualities of a "pure expression of poetry" and apparently abandons functional concerns.[95] Such plasticity can, he argues, be understood only by moving around the outside of the building: such movement is enforced by the route up the hill to the entrance, and emphasizes the semblance of a work that is both unique and personal. Art here has conquered technique.

Yet Stirling mediates the apparent divorce between aesthetics and technology by a third term, one generally refused by Rowe, of "regional" and anonymous architecture. In Le Corbusier such architecture is represented by Mediterranean references, and in Stirling by his early interest in the neoclassical docks of Liverpool. As is well known, Stirling's Fifth Year thesis, developed under the tutelage of the young Rowe, concerned the planning of a central zone of community facilities for a new town, one building of which, the community center, was developed in detail. In his thesis, Stirling documents his research: his reading (in planning and architectural sources) and his travels—to the United States, France, and through Britain, in search of an architecture for "community." He visited the Unité d'Habitation in Marseilles and the Pavillon Suisse in Paris, both by Le Corbusier; Impington Village College, Cambridgeshire, by Gropius; the Peter Cooper Union in New York; and closer to home, the East Wavertree Association in Liverpool. The overall plan for Stirling's community center evidently takes its inspiration from Le Corbusier's plan for the Mundaneum of 1929, including the "regulating lines" that proportion the siting of individual buildings. The community center is equally, on the surface, Corbusian, as it is raised up on pilotis. Critics have noted this Corbusian influence on the basis of a commonly reproduced facade drawing, and have traced it both to Rowe and to Stirling's fellow student Robert Maxwell. In his text Stirling develops an aesthetic theory for pilotis buildings, under the heading "Aesthetics of Structural Form": "The natural outcome of placing a building on stilts is to make it hover, that is if the object on the posts has direction horizontal—outwards all round. To put a box on edge (that is with greater height than breadth) on stilts is to contradict its verticality, this form should plunge into the ground like a spear. To place it on posts is against its direction. Only forms like a slab on its side, a table top, or a lying book, can be placed on posts and hover."[96] Here, Stirling, in words that not accidentally echo the speaking tone of Rowe, explains his decision to place his projected community center on pilotis, in a similar fashion to Le Corbusier at the Pavillon Suisse and Marseilles. This much is clear.

But amid a set of pages on which were glued small photographs of precedents and his own models, one page is missing a photo, which has been discovered in another folder: it is a picture of the Liverpool dock buildings, brick neoclassical structures raised up on Doric pilotis, and photographed from a perspective that is exactly similar to that of Stirling's design for his community center. Whether or not the "losing" of this photograph from the thesis book was deliberate, its first inclusion provides a clue to the foundational character of what we might call Stirling's double allegiance: to modernism on the one hand, but also to the functional roots of modernism, themselves forged out of traditional building modes—whether the Mediterranean of Le Corbusier or the more industrial forms of nineteenth-century Britain—and "classicism"—the "natural" style, so to speak, of rational architecture, whether in Le Corbusier's canon from the Parthenon to the Louvre, or in Loos's sense of a "Vitruvian" lore. In Stirling's case, the classical motifs of the British functional tradition allowed him to join these strands together, sustaining the thoroughly modern character of the thesis while giving it a classical/traditional root. In any event, the photo supports the notion that Stirling was interested in regional and regional-classical architecture from the outset and was not, as the myth would have it, drawn into it by the young Leon Krier.

From the outset, Stirling was Rowe's antidote to a more resigned Spenglerianism and nostalgic aristocratism. Indeed, Rowe's description of Stirling and Gowan's Leicester University

Engineering Laboratories (1959–1963) is equal to Waugh's description of Brideshead: a marriage of the Castle of Udolpho in *Wuthering Heights* to Decimus Burton's greenhouses, with a nod to Soane's *lumière mystérieuse*.[97] In this context, Stirling might be seen as consistently exploring all the dimensions of modernism, and pressing their implications into service as a source of invention that signaled a generalized acceptance of the modern, while simultaneously recognizing the traditional "classical" roots of locality—glass houses and docks in Britain, classical museums and historical events in Germany. Perhaps the most exemplary project demonstrating this complex dance of history and modernity, high classicism and vernacular, was the Staatsgalerie, Stuttgart. There, in a tour de force of the "collage" demanded by Rowe's historicism, Stirling transformed the precedent, Schinkel's Altes Museum, into a composition that combined a memory—the open ruin of the central "Pantheon"—with a modernity—the brightly colored steel and refractive glass lights—by means of a thoroughly traditional modern device, the *promenade architecturale*.[98] But although Rowe was able to accept the filiation between the Altes Museum and Le Corbusier's Palace of the Assembly at Chandigarh as "a conventional classical *parti* equipped with traditional *poché* and much the same *parti* distorted and made to present a competitive variety of local gestures—perhaps to be understood as compensations for traditional *poché*,"[99] he was unable, finally, to reconcile himself to Stuttgart. In the end, his overriding predilection for the classical, and by extension the classical modern, refused the absence that both Palladio's villas and Le Corbusier's Garches had in common: a facade. Without a face or facade, Rowe believed a building lost any frontality, and thus any "metaphorical plane of intersection between the eyes of the observer and what one might dare to call the *soul* of the building (its condition of internal animation)."[100] Stirling's use of the axonometric ("which will, never, yield a prime face") acts to render obsolete the one-point perspective—the revelation of facade—that, for Rowe, is the key to transparency, layering, and the animation of walls.

Stirling's double adherence to both modernism and traditional classicism was, in retrospect, not at all opposed to the main thrust of modernism itself, as delineated in the 1920s and 1930s by architects like Le Corbusier and Marcel Breuer. For, as projected by Le Corbusier and others in the 1920s, the modern movement was a double-edged machine. On the one hand, it was committed to a modernism of form, embracing all the techniques of collage, montage, and formalism in general in the service of the ideology of the avant-garde, whereby a formal strategy should serve a new social order. On the other hand, such a modernism sought a "timeless" relationship with society, based on an abstraction of traditional, nonarchitectural construction; this was seen to go hand in hand with a universalization of the inherited principles of classicism, minus their representation in the classical orders. Thus, it was not seen as a contradiction that a villa might find its *parti* in a transformation of a Palladian type, its formal language in the evocation of Mediterranean peasant houses, and its iconography in motifs taken from ships, planes, and cars. If this double vision between the new and the eternal, modern and classic, technological and traditional was not entirely clear to its protagonists in the 1920s (despite the majority of Corbusier's writings in *Vers une architecture*), it was made crystal clear to Stirling's generation by, among others, the criticism of Rowe—in the essays on "The Mathematics of the Ideal Villa" and "Mannerism and Modern Architecture"—and by the interest in local versions of the classical and functional traditions espoused by Pevsner and his colleagues in the immediate postwar issues of the *Architectural Review*.

Reyner Banham, Nikolaus Pevsner, and John Summerson at the Royal Institute of British Architects, 1961

3 FUTURIST MODERNISM
REYNER BANHAM

*Where Banham invented the immediate future, Rowe invented
the immediate past. For my generation, those two were the poles
of a debate and for some, the horns of a dilemma.*
—Robert Maxwell, introduction to Colin Rowe, "Thanks to the
RIBA—Part I"

While Colin Rowe, as architect-historian, found the answer to
a contemporary practice in the historical and modernist "mannerism" of the neo-Palladian Corbusier, Reyner Banham, the
engineer–art critic, was less convinced that modern architectural
language had been exhausted by the end of the 1920s. Banham argued in his historical account of the period 1918–1930, *Theory and
Design in the First Machine Age*, that it was precisely the formalist
and academic constraints on this language that had led it into an
impasse with the modern movement's underlying aspirations to
invent an architecture that responded to the new technological
and social conditions of the twentieth century. In this thesis,
written under the supervision of the historian Nikolaus Pevsner
at University College, London, Banham sought both to rebut the
challenge of what he regarded as the academic nostalgia of his British contemporaries and to revive the technological aspirations of
the first half of the twentieth century. The example of Pevsner was

key to his argument, just as Wittkower's historical substance and theoretical analysis had been for Rowe's initial thesis. In his formulation of the idea of the "Modern Movement" in 1936 and his complex negotiation between German modernism and English empiricism after 1940, Pevsner had established a foundation of quasi-historicist functional and technological authority that allowed Banham fully to embrace the scientific breakthroughs of the 1960s. Pevsner also influenced Banham through his reluctance to discard the aesthetic grounds of architecture and his embrace of the English picturesque as a nonacademic, "functional" aesthetic. Consequently, Banham, anti-academic throughout his career, would himself never quite relinquish his fascination with what he was to term the secret language of the "Black Box" of architecture.[1] The alliance between a renewed "picturesque" version of the architectural image and its new technological and material needs would be, for Banham, at least a contingent solution to the impasse of modernist formalism.

Modern Picturesque

The picturesque was the first, but not necessarily the ultimate, aesthetic discipline which was not based upon the grid, the axis, the module and other academic preconceptions, but rather upon free grouping of parts, free juxtaposition of different materials, upon taking things on their own merits, upon an experimental and tentative approach which is the guiding principle of the modern movement and the planner's life-line in a world of visual chaos.
—*Architectural Review*, editorial note on Pevsner's "C20 Picturesque"

The influence of the *Architectural Review* on contemporary British architecture after Nikolaus Pevsner joined the editorial staff in 1941 can hardly be overemphasized. With Pevsner's help, the journal championed modernism (not yet, if ever, to be ensconced firmly in the British context) and a belief in the vernacular roots of authentic architecture. Through his editorship and continuous contribution to its pages, Pevsner, with considerable aplomb, was able to transfer his faith in the zeitgeist from his native Germany to his adopted England, adroitly managing to combine a historical interest in the unsung Victorian, the vernacular, the "Townscape" affinities of his fellow editors, and a belief in the functionalist tradition of the modern as exemplified by the hero of his *Pioneers of the Modern Movement*.[2] These concerns were welded together by what he saw as the fundamental genius of the English for the picturesque and, more importantly, the influence of the picturesque on modern architecture itself.[3]

Pevsner outlined these propositions in a sharp rebuttal of a radio talk by Basil Taylor, who had accused the *Architectural Review* of sponsoring a "Picturesque revival."[4] Not only was Taylor wrong in his interpretation of the picturesque as a movement, Pevsner argues, but a significant heritage of the picturesque could be found in the compositional practices of the modern movement. Against Taylor's critique of the picturesque as "accidental" and "disorderly," Pevsner poses what he calls the picturesque's own terms—"varied" and "irregular"—and claims that it was precisely these qualities that lay at the basis of modernism's success. He cites as examples Gropius's Bauhaus building at Dessau and Le Corbusier's Stuttgart houses and Centrosoyuz project for Moscow. The aesthetic characteristics of these buildings included not only "cubic shapes, no moldings, large openings and so on," but more importantly, "the free grouping of the individual building, a mixture of materials, synthetic, natural, rough and smooth, and, beyond that, the free planning of the whole quarter."[5] These attributes, Pevsner concludes, are what differentiate modernism's "free exercise of the imagination stimulated by function and technique" from the "academic rule of thumb," the "strait-jacket" of which had been discarded by the modern movement.[6] For Pevsner, as for Hitchcock fifteen years earlier, "The modern revolution of the early twentieth century and the Picturesque revolution of a hundred years before had all their fundamentals in common."[7]

Taylor's radio talks had been aimed partially at the ubiquitous movement named "Townscape," sponsored by the *Architectural Review* and promoted by its art editor Gordon Cullen, a version of the picturesque revival heartily disliked by the modernist wing of British architects. Pevsner's idea of a "picturesque modernism" immediately evoked a gruff reply from the Colin Rowe circle in the form of a letter from Alan Colquhoun. Colquhoun followed Rowe in distinguishing between the eclecticism of historicism, which he called "closely connected" with the picturesque, and the search for "the secret of 'Style' itself," proper to the modern movement.[8] While it influenced modern practice, Colquhoun argued, the picturesque had to be characterized in its historical context—distinguishing, for example, between the apparent "picturesque" of a Palladio, an Edwin Lutyens, and a Le Corbusier: "All three may be equally successful from the standpoint of the Picturesque, yet, clearly, each has a content which escapes definition in those terms."[9] Central to Colquhoun's argument was the idea that any picturesque qualities, such as free grouping and a mixture of materials, were "meaningless" without other traits that offer a contrast, such as visual hierarchy, reflecting functional hierarchy. The distinction, he claimed, was between purely visual qualities, as espoused by Pevsner, and those that derive equally from didactic and mental constructs as maintained by Rowe.

Pevsner's reply to Colquhoun—asserting that he was only speaking of the aesthetic rather than the functional aspects of architecture—was, like his other critical essays for the *Review* in the early 1940s, written under the pseudonym of Peter F. R. Donner.[10] These pieces were, as the colophon stated, "frankly about the aesthetic aspect of architectural design," taking for granted modern architecture's functional basis in efficiency.[11] The first of these essays was a direct attack on Frank Lloyd Wright's recent lectures at the RIBA, delivered under the title *An Organic Architecture*, and especially on Wright's opposed categories of "Organic" and "Classic." Against this distinction, which Pevsner felt was entirely fallacious, Pevsner preferred "Dynamic" and "Static," "a more precise, more arguable and more architectural polarity . . . of real heuristic value in analyzing new as well as old building."[12] His examples were both historical—the symmetrical seventeenth-century Fenton House in Hampstead (static), versus the traditional Cotswold house (dynamic)—and modern—Joseph Frank's house for the 1927 Weissenhof exhibition in Stuttgart (static) versus Maxwell Fry's house at Kingston (dynamic). This choice of words enabled Pevsner to discriminate among varieties of these compositional qualities; but what annoyed him most about Wright's summary disposal of the classic was the inference that symmetry was equivalent to military order, "heels together, eyes front, something on the right, and something on the left."[13] To the exiled German in August 1941, this connection represented a provocation—the equivalent, as Pevsner put it, of posing the "lounge chair" against the "goose step."[14] After all, Fenton House, with its calm symmetry, could never be mistaken for a militaristic composition, for it had been built by his hosts, the English, that "balanced, quiet, self-certain race which has conceived, and chosen to live in, such houses, the only race that looks equally at ease in flannels and in white tie."[15] It was Pevsner's hope that such balance might be evolved once more—"Balanced shapes in domestic architecture, shapes to look both homely (*sit venia verbo*) and formal, neither slovenly in their homeliness, nor Prussian in their formal reserve."[16]

Such a call for "balance" indicates that Pevsner's aim was directed less at Wright, who merely served as a convenient target, and more at the English modern movement itself, represented in his argument by Maxwell Fry. Pevsner showed his continued reluctance to relinquish his support of the Gropius wing of modernism, which he had clearly demonstrated in *Pioneers* and now displayed in his eulogy of Frank's Stuttgart house. Where Fry demonstrated an "alert tension" and a "complex pattern" in his asymmetries, Frank displayed a repose, a firmness, "and a deeply satisfying finality."[17] His was the *juste milieu* of the "liberal, wise, gentle yet composed spirit" against the "single-minded concentration" of Fry, "not a manifesto . . . not self-asserting."[18] By implication, and in contrast, Fry and the English modernists presented a rather "strained countenance," some "haste in the rhythm" of their fenestration, and left "loose ends" in their compositions. No doubt their adherence to the formal principles of Le Corbusier led them to such anxious forms, for, as Pevsner noted, the rhythm of Le Corbusier was "far more pointed . . . that of the dancer seemingly independent of the weight of matter," while Gropius had the rhythm of "an accomplished machine."[19]

This implicit attack on Corbusian influences was transformed into a direct confrontation in a second article, again written under the Donner pseudonym, that October.[20] In this article, Pevsner took on Emil Kaufmann, and explicitly his *Von Ledoux bis Le Corbusier*, in order to expose the "absurdity" of pure formalism, of *l'architecture pure*, juxtaposed with the equally specious myth of the *machine à habiter*. Ledoux and Le Corbusier, conveniently brought together by Kaufmann, were to Pevsner the ultimate examples of an impossible and "inconceivable" condition—that of an "Architecture for Art's sake, architecture as a pure abstract art."[21] As examples of Ledoux's extreme "abstract formalism," Pevsner cited three of his designs taken from Kaufmann's illustrations to *Von Ledoux bis Le Corbusier*: a gate house of "surprisingly modern appearance" (the "Barrière St. Hippolyte" from Kaufmann, page 41), and the pyramidal hut of the "woodman" and spherical house for the "field-guard" (the "Haus eines Holzfällers" and "Kugelhaus für Flurwächter," from Kaufmann, page 31).[22] Following Kaufmann, Pevsner describes these "abstract cubic values" as confirming the romantic principle of "the independence and sacredness of the individual," because "each block is severed from the ground, severed from its neighbors, and severed from use." Architecture has here "become an abstract art," with "nothing left of functional soundness." Indeed, Pevsner comments, with withering bourgeois practicality, "It is unnecessary to point out that the shapes of the rooms in the spherical house are sheer lunacy from the practical point of view. No furniture can stand against its walls. Curved windows are prohibitively expensive. A curved door would prove a perplexing problem to joiner and builder."[23]

Pevsner next applies the characterization of what Ledoux himself termed "architecture puriste" to Le Corbusier. In creating an abstract art of architecture out of space, as opposed to Ledoux's volumetric projects, Corbusier had reconstrued forms that in Ledoux "strike one as barren" into "fascinating and inspiring" explorations—"even in his most alarming spatial performances."[24] Pevsner admits respect for Corbusier's "never-failing power of imagination" and "lucid and quick intellect," and describes the open plan of Le Corbusier's house for the Stuttgart Weissenhofsiedlung exhibition as possessing a "generous unity of atmosphere . . . combined with the most intriguing, most enchanting, variety of vistas in all directions"—the essence of the picturesque. Against this, however, he raises the same pedestrian critique, one that he no doubt felt would amuse and satisfy his English readers: "Is the Stuttgart house less remote from the realities of life . . . than Ledoux's spherical house? Might it not disturb the happiness of the Brown *ménage* if Mrs. Brown wants to go to bed at ten behind her low screen, the while Mr. Brown wishes to work on and smoke his pipe until 1.30? Or if Mrs. Brown has her bridge party when Mr. Brown comes home from business and goes straight to have a cold bath behind his screen? Some people like to sing in their baths. He cannot. He cannot even splash freely. And if one of them falls ill, will it not paralyze the whole house?"[25] The faintly ridiculous image of a middle-class English couple attempting to adapt their lifestyle to a Corbusian house succeeds with deadpan effect. As he ironically expresses it in conclusion, there remains for Pevsner an inexplicable contradiction between "Le Corbusier the spatial creator and Le Corbusier the writer who invented the widely used and nearly always misused theory of the *machine à habiter.*"[26]

In these early articles Pevsner laid out his strange mixture of picturesque visual criteria and a critique of functional pretense that would energize his student Reyner Banham in his embrace of the Smithsons' Hunstanton School—a work that Banham saw as an exemplar of the new brutalism, precisely formed of these two apparently discordant characteristics.

Historicism versus Functionalism

A revolt was bound to come against the formal rigidity and the uniformity of the '30s. However it is not odd and strange exterior effects which are the answer; the answer lies in planning, in siting, in landscaping, and so on. The individual building must remain rational. If you keep your buildings square, you are not therefore necessarily a square.
—Nikolaus Pevsner, "Modern Architecture and the Historian or the Return of Historicism"

In January 1961, Pevsner, one of the first historians, as Banham noted, to invent the idea of the "modern movement," sounded an alarm that has resonated ever since. In a now celebrated talk at the Royal Institute of British Architects, Pevsner registered his unease at the changing role of history and the historian for contemporary practice.[27] Whereas in the modern period, history and architecture were finally separated from collusion, now they seemed joined again as architects searched for precedents in what looked like a return of historical styles into architecture. Of course, this time architects were not returning to the Gothic or the classical so much as to modern styles themselves—creating "neo" versions of modernisms in Italy's neoliberty style, in the work of Philip Johnson, in the neo-expressionism of Le Corbusier's Ronchamp. Pevsner added "neo Art Nouveau," "neo de Stijl," "neo School of Amsterdam," and "neo Perret," all of which he saw as undermining the fundamental principles of the modern movement. From modern movement works that embraced the ethical injunction "form follows function," where the exterior is entirely transparent to the interior, Pevsner traced a historical line to the new tendency toward exteriors created not necessarily against function, but in a way that, as he put it, "does not convey a sense of confidence in their well-functioning."[28]

Pevsner's conclusion was a striking admission of the self-hating historian: "Could you not say that the Return of Historicism is all our fault, and I mean myself, personally: (a) *qua Architectural Review* and (b) *qua* historian?"[29] He thus blamed himself for the very effect of "the historian as such, and perhaps I should say, my own pitiable position in particular," through his own book *Pioneers of the Modern Movement* of 1936, and his successive articles in the *Architectural Review*, which had been "certainly misunderstood by many as an encouragement to the new historicism."[30] For Pevsner, "historicism" signified "the trend to believe in the power of history to such a degree as to choke original action and replace it by action which is inspired by period precedent."[31] As Banham later asserts in a spirited defense of his teacher, Pevsner was using the word "historicism" as it is associated with a generalized and relativistic stylistic eclecticism rather than in the various meanings attributed to the word by the German school of historical method in the late nineteenth and early twentieth century, and its resulting sense of historical determinism.[32]

A photograph of the main participants in the RIBA event at the subsequent reception shows Pevsner at the center, flanked on his left by the respondent, John Summerson, and on his right by Banham, dressed up in black tie.[33] In retrospect, this quite unconscious staging was prescient enough, as Pevsner would continue to hold the central position in determining the "Englishness" of all architecture, modern or not; Summerson would largely retreat from his support of the modernist program into a study of the eighteenth century conducted from his position as curator of the Sir John Soane Museum; while Banham would discard his formal dress in favor of longer hair and casual clothes, and embark on a pilgrimage to the United States leading from the ecologies of Los Angeles to the grain elevators of Buffalo, thence to Santa Barbara, and finally to the cathartic scenes of the western desert. The image was also prescient in another way, because it would be out of Pevsner's unfinished history of modernism, and armed with his theoretical aesthetics of the picturesque, that Banham would fabricate his own doctoral thesis; and further, it would be Summerson, in his trenchant summary of modernism's underlying functionalism, who would spur Banham to his own espousal of a functionalism beyond that of avant-garde symbolism embracing, partially at least, the latest developments in a second-industrial-revolution technology.

Functionalist Modernism

Reyner Banham once remarked that the history of a period does not always neatly coincide with the calendar. Looking back from the vantage point of 1960, mid-century architecture—that of the Festival of Britain around 1950—seemed less of a break with the past of modernism than that occurring later in the decade after the building of Ronchamp, and closer to 1957.[34] As he pointed out, Summerson, in his celebrated article of that year, "The Case for a Theory of Modern Architecture," described what he called a "Thirty-Year Rule" that measured changes in architectural taste, and duly proposed 1957 as "a year of architectural crisis."[35] In fact, the divide that both Banham and Summerson detected in the late 1950s, despite their squabbles over its chronology and architectural manifestation, was between the modern movement, universalized through the activities of CIAM and founded on the "mythology of Form and Function," and a new, freer style that Banham characterized not by the often-claimed "end of functionalism," but by the death of the slogan "Functionalism with a capital F, and its accompanying delusion that curved forms were the work of untrammeled fancy."[36] Against this "untrammeled fancy" that Pevsner was soon to characterize as a "New Historicism," both Banham and Summerson were to propose alternatives that radically reconsidered functionalism no longer in the largely symbolic guise espoused by the modern movement, but as based on "real" science. In search of what he called "une autre architecture," Banham turned to the authority of military and corporate engineers, biological researchers, and social scientists, while Summerson outlined a new concept of the program as the foundation of a "Theory of Modern Architecture."

Both were following the lead of the earlier historians and architects of the modern movement—Pevsner, Giedion, Hitchcock—who had understood modernism as fundamentally "functionalist" in character. The nature of this functionalism differed from historian to historian, but its rule over modern architecture seemed supreme: it was a way of ignoring the formal and stylistic differences of the various avant-gardes in order to provide a unifying alibi, or defining foundation, for architectural modernity. It was from this functionalist position that we have seen Pevsner criticizing Le Corbusier (formalist) and praising Walter Gropius (functionalist), and later excoriating the return of "styles" characterized as a new historicism; it was from this position too that the first generation of modern masters was criticized by Team X, among others, as not being sufficiently broad or humanist in its functionalism. And of course it was under this sign that Archigram itself was to be denounced by these historians and architects—by Giedion in the 1967 edition of *Space, Time and Architecture*, and by the Smithsons in their *Without Rhetoric* of 1973.

In his article, Summerson rejects the idea of constructing a theory of modern architecture based on the *existence* of modern buildings: to abstract formal characteristics from a select repertory of modern buildings, to provide a grammar of form, and then to illustrate how the forms embody the ideas, would only "add up to something like a Palladio of modern architecture, a pedagogical reference book" that would end up as a "hopelessly gimcrack" "ragbag of aphorisms, platitudes, and fancy jargon." Rather, a "theory" of architecture should be "a statement of related ideas resting on a philosophical conception of the nature of architecture," residing in a group of Mediterranean beliefs about reason and antiquity, continuously reformulated since the fifteenth century: "Perrault said antiquity is the thing and look how rational; Lodoli seems to have said up with *primitive* antiquity, only source of the rational; Durand said down with Laugier, rationalization means economics; Pugin said down with antiquity, up with the Gothic, and look how rational; Viollet-le-Duc said up with Gothic, prototype of the rational. Eventually a voice is heard saying down with all the styles and if it's rationalism you want, up with grain elevators and look, how beautiful!"[37]

Against this rational tradition, however, Summerson saw a new version of authority superseding the classical—that of the "biological," as advanced by László Moholy-Nagy. Moholy had stated, "Architecture will be brought to its fullest realization only when the deepest knowledge of human life as a total phenomenon in the biological whole is available."[38] For Moholy, notes Summerson, the biological was psychophysical—a demanding theory of design matching a broad idea of function that called for "the most far-reaching implications of cybernetics" to be realized "if the artist's functions were at last to be explicable in mechanistic terms."[39] In this way Summerson replaced the idea of classical and rational form with what he considered the modern conception of program—the "organic analogy" of the Renaissance, now fulfilled by science. Architectural theory had moved "from the antique (a world of form) to the program (a local fragment of social pattern)." Hence, Summerson's celebrated conclusion: "The source of unity in modern architecture is in the social sphere, in other words, the architect's program—the one new principle involved in modern architecture."[40]

Summerson defines a program as "the description of the spatial dimensions, spatial relationships, and other physical conditions required for the convenient performance of specific functions," all involving a "process in time," a rhythmically repetitive pattern that sanctions relationships different from those sanctified by the static, classical tradition.[41] The problem he identifies, similar to that of naive functionalism, is the need for a way to translate such programmatic ideas into appropriate form—a problem to which Summerson offers no direct answer. Dismissing Banham's 1955 appeal to topology in his essay on the new brutalism as "an attractive red herring (I think it's a herring)," Summerson expresses his dismay at the "unfamiliar and complex forms [that] are cropping up" in practice around him through the extension of the engineer's role.[42] Indeed, his conclusion is ultimately pessimistic. Sensing the incompatibility of a theory that holds two equal and opposite overriding principles, he remarks that any theory that posits program as the only principle leads to either "intellectual contrivances" or the unknown: "the missing language will remain missing," and our discomfort in the face of this loss would soon be simply a "scar left in the mind by the violent swing which has taken place."[43]

Banham, writing three years later, was more optimistic. While he sides with Summerson in deploring the style-mongering of the 1950s—"it has been a period when an enterprising manufacturer could have put out a do-it-yourself pundit kit in which the aspiring theorist had only to fill in the blank in the phrase *The New (. . .)-ism* and set up in business"—he finds that "most of the blanket theories that have been launched have proven fallible, and partly because most labels have concentrated on the purely formal side of what has been built and projected, and failed to take into account the fact that nearly all the new trends rely heavily on engineers or technicians of genius (or nearly so)." Banham proposes that "a new and equally compelling slogan" is needed, and suggests some of his own: "Anticipatory Design," "Une Architecture Autre," "All-in Package Design Service," and even "A More Crumbly Aesthetic."[44]

Futurism Redux

The Futurist city is back on many drawing boards, begins to be realized here and there.
—Reyner Banham, "Futurism and Modern Architecture"

Though Banham had chronicled the immersion of his contemporaries in the Palladian past, and counted Rowe within his London circle, he was nevertheless from the outset bound to a history different from that promulgated by Pevsner or Summerson, one that he would characterize later as not of the past but of the "immediate future." His affiliation with the Independent Group, his early forays into the world of pop culture and science fiction, and most of all, his work toward a PhD under Pevsner's mentorship persuaded him that the present had little to do with the mannerist or neoclassic past. Rather, in his effort to fill in the historical "gap" since 1914, where Pevsner had ended *Pioneers of the Modern Movement*, Banham became convinced that the modernists' vision of a machine-age future had been betrayed by their adherence to the remains of academic culture. More importantly, he believed a proper history of the period would unearth those architects who had truly been influential due to their lucid, unsentimental understanding of technology and its promise, those left out of the traditional histories of the modern movement. First in line were the futurists, on whom Banham delivered a lecture at the RIBA in January 1957.[45]

Tracing the meager attention paid to his heroes in previous scholarship—a footnote in Pevsner, a half-dozen paragraphs in Giedion's revised *Space, Time and Architecture* of 1953—he proclaims that as a result of his research, "this tidy and apparently settled situation has blown apart like an art-historical time-bomb."[46] Flourishing Antonio Sant'Elia's *Messaggio* and collating it with F. T. Marinetti's *Manifesto*, Banham reinstates futurism, not simply as one among the many avant-garde movements in the 1900s but as a major force, if not the major influence on the ideology of modernism. His aim was to join Sant'Elia to the futurists and to demonstrate the power of the architectural images of the Città Nuova (1914) as against, for example, the more academic and less far-sighted project for Tony Garnier's Cité Industrielle. For Banham the functionalist modernist, Marinetti's evocation of the mechanical sensibility and its translation into images by Sant'Elia represented the real roots of a vision never realized by the modernists. This vision was not of a merely symbolic order, like that of Le Corbusier, but rather of an order of technological understanding by those who knew the interiors of the racing cars they drove. Out of this vision came not only Le Corbusier's Ville Contemporaine, but the imaginary cities of the Russian constructivists, as well as the projects of Mart Stam, and, more recently, those multilevel, densely packed plans for center city renewal from the Barbican to New York. Banham ends his "time-bomb" with a sly, back-handed homage to Nikolaus Pevsner, in whose *Pioneers* he detected a truly futurist accent: "though it can find only footnote-room for Futurism as such, [Pevsner's book] is nevertheless sparked and spirited throughout by the Futurist inspiration that has bitten deep into the subconscious of Modern Architecture."[47] In this way was launched the enthusiastic search for another architecture that, in his own tribute to Pevsner, *Theory and Design in the First Machine Age*, would find its postfuturist hero in Buckminster Fuller.

Theories and Design

Early on, Banham took it to be his mission as a historian to fill in what he called the "Zone of Silence": the history of the modern movement between 1910 and 1926, between what Sigfried Giedion had taken as the subject of his *Bauen in Frankreich* (1928–29) and his later *Space, Time and Architecture* (1940–41). The common assumption of the time was that the end of the great years of the modern movement should be dated around the time of the First World War; thus, Pevsner had concluded his *Pioneers of the Modern Movement* with the industrial design exhibition of the Deutscher Werkbund in 1914, while Giedion's *Bauen in Frankreich* had stopped even earlier, with the turn of the century.

Banham, in his PhD thesis, published in 1960 as *Theory and Design in the First Machine Age*, argued otherwise.[48] Here he introduced his innovative view that the futurist movement's emphasis on technology was central to the history of modern architecture, and undertook the first close analytical interpretation in English of Le Corbusier's writings. Banham acknowledged *Vers une architecture* as "one of the most influential, widely read and least understood of all the architectural writings of the twentieth century."[49] Yet, against Rowe's reading and the prevailing climate of Le Corbusier appreciation in London, Banham found Corbusier's book without "argument in any normal sense of the word."[50] This analysis reveals more than Banham's desire to puncture what he saw as misplaced respect for Le Corbusier. As I will discuss later in this chapter, Banham's analysis of *Vers une architecture* corresponded to the underlying mission of his entire career, which would be dedicated to freeing the mechanistic from the embrace of the academic, two themes that he found in Le Corbusier. As he emphasized throughout *Theory and Design*, Banham espoused embracing science and technology in a way that would overcome the limitations of the symbolism of the modern movement. In a reprise of Le Corbusier's comparison of the sports car with the Parthenon, Banham compares Fuller's Dymaxion ground-taxiing unit to Gropius's body for the Adler Cabriolet: "Gropius' Adler, though handsome, is mechanically backward when compared with the streamlined, rear-engined harbingers of the next phase."[51]

Thus, despite his formal dress on the occasion of Pevsner's 1961 "Historicism" lecture, Banham was far from defeated by the apparent recrudescence of stylistic motifs. While understanding the complaint, and indeed shouldering some responsibility for having reintroduced historical modernism to a new generation, he was loath to give up on his own double-barreled stance—as he called himself in neofuturist tones—as a *combattero*, staunchly defending the role of the critic and historian and perhaps even that of the critic/historian, if not that of the critical historian. He opined that, far from being a regression, the new historicism, insofar as it looked to "strong" examples like Mies and Corb, was a sign of revolt against the mediocre accommodation of the

Scandinavian modern and the British picturesque: "I suppose
you can lock the cupboard and say 'You must not have any more
history, it is not good for you,' or you can add water until the stuff
is indistinguishable from anything they get elsewhere." The responsibility "lies not . . . with the historian but with the practicing architect or designer who is also a teacher: he must provoke
stronger leadership than the historian can."[52]

Banham advanced this argument in a talk that immediately
followed Pevsner's own, and served both as the student's response to the master and as a map of Banham's own future inter-
ests. Dramatically titled "The History of the Immediate Future,"
it opened with the ringing statement: "History is our only guide
to the future."[53] Banham viewed history as a social science, an
extrapolative discipline. Just as a science would plot its experimental results in a graph that would, if extended, act as a guide
to future behaviors, so "History is to the future as the observed
results of an experiment are to the plotted graph."[54] The historian then had the task of plotting a curve "beyond the last certain
point to see where it will lead." Banham's talk traced the major
trends in architectural thought since World War II, operating
on the assumption that "trends in architecture follow the strongest available influence that can fill the vacuum of architectural
theory. History filled the gap in the early 50s, imitating Corb took
over for some after that, others turned to Detroit styling and ap-
pliance affluence, others again have gone to science-fiction, or to
its historicist shadow, and at all times, of course, engineering has
been a potent source of vacuum-fillers."[55]

Reaching the current moment of the 1960s, Banham con-
tended that the human sciences had emerged as the strongest
forces: first the social studies and environmental studies of the
1950s, then the perception studies of the late fifties; and then,
logically moving from exterior to interior, the study of "how the
human being works inside": "stimulus, involuntary response,

neural and cerebral activity . . . organism and the environment."[56] In this regard, it was the new biology, in line to overhaul physics and the entire study of man, that was poised to act directly on architecture. He cited, interestingly enough in the light of our own more recent experiences in bioengineering, the work of Peter Medawar and MacFarlane Burnet, who had won the Nobel Prize in 1960 for their work in immunological reaction—the extreme disturbance of organism/environment—and the theory of clonal selection. The pair had studied the irregularities in the fleeces of hundreds of thousands of Australian sheep, working out the theory of cloning that would eventually produce Dolly in our own time, tracing fleece mosaics to somatic mutations caused by cell reproduction damage.

Banham's conclusion: "Either British and world architects will join the intellectual adventure of Human Science and transform architecture, or it will fail to make the imaginative leap, and turn introspective again."[57] His one codicil, surprising from a critic who had seemed ready to relinquish architecture in favor of science, was aesthetic: "the Human Sciences will not become architecture unless a means can be found to express them as surely as the forms of the International Style expressed the mechanistic inspiration of its Masters in the 1920s."[58]

Program, Science, and History

To deepen understanding of the conflict he saw between form and technology, Banham next introduced a series of inquiries under the title "Architecture after 1960" as a guest editor for the *Architectural Review*.[59] Printed on bright yellow paper with red accents and bold typography, these articles were launched by his now celebrated article "Stocktaking," with its parallel discussion of "Tradition" and "Design" and its obvious, design-friendly conclusion. This was followed by a group of essays on "The Science Side," by experts on weapons systems, computers, and the human sciences. The series continued with a symposium of architects chaired by Banham on "The Future of *Universal Man*," that paradigm of the traditional architectural subject. The inquiry ended with Banham's double bill on "History under Revision": a questionnaire on "Masterpieces of the Modern Movement" and a more personal critique of Pevsner in "History and Psychiatry," in which the master was put on the couch by the pupil. And to demonstrate fairness, Banham allowed the old guard back to reply, still on yellow paper, in a dyspeptic sequence of observations by the editors of the *Architectural Review*: J. M Richards, Hugh Casson, Hubert de Cronin Hastings, and Pevsner. Needless to say, Banham had the last word, adding marginal notes where he disagreed with the editors, as well as a final conclusion. His message throughout the series was clear: "Functionalism with a capital 'F'" was dead, long live functionalism, with a small "f," finally—as long promised by modernism—with a basis in real science.

Banham, as he made clear at the outset, was also replying to his immediate rival in historical criticism, John Summerson, who had proposed that the only authentic source of unity in modern architecture would be found in the *program*. It was precisely this issue of the program, and how it could be framed, that interested Banham. Unlike Summerson, who expressed skepticism that any revision of the form-function dichotomy endemic to modernism could be overcome, Banham felt that with the correct inputs—from science, technology, sociology, and the like—the program might be made pivotal once more. Further, again counter to Summerson's belief that there was no possibility of finding an architectural language to express any new programmatic aims, Banham advanced his theory of the image, joined to a hope that aesthetics might be once and for all subjected to science as a way of subsuming all relationships, including "form and function," within a broadly defined view of a new theory of the program. As he wrote of the Smithsons' school at Hunstanton, "This is not

merely a surface aesthetic of untrimmed edges and exposed surfaces, but a radical philosophy reaching back to the first conception of the building. "[60]

Using the double-column comparative technique introduced
by Rowe in "Palladio-Le Corbusier," Banham begins his own first
contribution to the series "Architecture after 1960":

> Tradition *means, not monumental Queen Anne, but the*
> *stock of general knowledge (including general scientific*
> *knowledge) which specialists assume as the ground of*
> *present practice and future progress.* Technology *repre-*
> *sents its converse, the method of exploring, by means of*
> *the instrument of science,* a potential *which may at any*
> *moment make nonsense of all existing general knowledge,*
> *and so of the ideas founded on it, even "basic" ideas like*
> house, city, building. *Philosophically it could be argued*
> *that all ideas, traditional or otherwise, are contempora-*
> *neous, since they have to be invented anew for each indi-*
> *vidual, but the practical issue is not thereby invalidated.*
> *For the first time in history, the world of* what is *is sud-*
> *denly torn by the discovery of* what could be, *is no longer*
> *dependent on* what was.[61]

In this ascription, architecture is no longer a question of "form
and function," but seriously "torn between tradition and technology," and the architect is forced to respond to the three not
entirely balanced cultural influences of science, the profession,
and history. Thus, in proposition after counterproposition,
Banham attempts to investigate the implications of architecture, understood as "the professional activity of a body of men"
and "as a service to human societies." The first might be defined
only in terms of the history of the profession and the specific
roles of those defined as architects; the second, by contrast,

could be defined only as "the provision of fit environments for human activities." The former would inevitably be confined by its definition to the design and construction of single buildings, while the latter would necessarily extend to the design of entire regions.[62]

Under the heading "Tradition," Banham traces the history of what he calls the failed "revolution" of the early twentieth century: the reaction toward "architectural" values triggered by the perceived overemphasis on sociology and technology, the demand to "*get back to architecture*," and the subsequent interest in a return to proportional systems, from the "Vitruvian Man" explicated by Wittkower to its newest iteration in Le Corbusier's "Modulor."[63] Axiality, Palladianism, and a fascination with Italian neoformalists, led by Luigi Moretti, characterized this enthusiasm for the classical principles held by architects as diverse as Gropius, Johnson, and Mies van der Rohe. Banham points to the influence of Wittkower, Rowe, and Bruno Zevi, and the dynamic teaching of Vincent Scully at Yale, as adding "a richness to the traditions of operational lore that has not been there since the deaths of Soane and Schinkel." Mies, who formerly would be analyzed in technological terms, would now be seen as an heir to the tradition of German neoclassicism.[64] This return to history was accompanied by a more local historicism known in Scandinavia as the "new empiricism" and in Italy as "neoliberty," both movements that invested value in local materials and specialized in "not putting up buildings that [the average citizen] has not seen before." All these trends toward a revisionist history and away from functionalism Banham tags as "*Formalist*"; rather than producing his desired "Architecture Autre," these trends simply reduplicated new shapes. Against an earlier image of a "smoothly-developing" modernism, Banham poses the image of a dried up pool of talent, with the old "masters" losing their way or retreating—J. J. P. Oud and Mies in isolated withdrawal, Gropius becoming "Dean of the

Formalists," and Le Corbusier building the enigma (to modernist eyes) of Ronchamp.

Banham's most important contribution in this essay lies in his conclusion, an assessment of the idea of history itself as applied to the modern movement, caught, in his terms, between the selective memory of Giedion and the will to total recall of the new historians. This latter attitude Banham blames for the "new historicism" characterized by Pevsner a year later—the "modern movement revivalism" that drew on all the eclectic sources of the early twentieth century; but he also credits it with having stimulated a new and different direction, demonstrated by the Smithsons' school at Hunstanton. In this building, a "realist" version of steel technology had taken its distance from the more abstract treatment of Mies, or the carefully calculated brick bearing walls of Stirling and Gowan's Ham Common flats; a realism more interested in structural limits than in the primitive images of Le Corbusier at the Maisons Jaoul. Only such a renewed interest in the historical basis for science and technology in architecture, Banham argues, might impel architecture out of formalism and historicism altogether, along the lines of the airform houses of John Johanssen.

Banham's second, parallel column under the heading "Technology" offers his assessment of the potential of the total environment, and its scientific ground, as a foundation for another architecture. Banham posits that architecture itself will be so transformed that it will render the contemporary profession both obsolete and unable to comprehend the radical nature of the technological revolution. Thus, though the profession can see that Buckminster Fuller has contributed to structural form with his domes, his more fundamental research into "the shelterneeds of mankind" is dismissed. Even the formulation "a house as a machine for living in" makes the mistake of presupposing "house" in such a way that, for example, a caravan is seen as a substandard house, rather than the house being seen as a substandard caravan. Instead of the fetishization of technology, as in Le Corbusier's use of the cooling tower motif for the parliament house at Chandigarh, Banham argues for the logic that lies behind the automobile, the experiments in prefabrication by Jean Prouvé and Coulon and Schein, as potential innovations that should work to create a new condition of design.

Thus the next set of articles that Banham commissioned, under the title "The Science Side: Weapons Systems, Computers, Human Science," were the first step in setting out a new theory of modern architecture based on knowledge rather than architectural precedent, whether modernist or traditional.[65] Toward this end, A. C. Brothers of General Electric outlined the approach to weapons systems developed by English Electric; M. E. Drummond of IBM sketched the emerging fields of operations research, systems simulations, linear programming, and queuing theory; and the future head of the Bartlett School of Architecture, Richard Llewelyn-Davies, wrote of the potential to mathematicize social activities.

Banham's comments in response to the three articles are critical throughout. Drummond begins by outlining the contributions that computing might make to aspects of architectural planning in four areas: operations research, systems simulation, linear programming, and queuing theory. But, he cautions, computers could add little to the aesthetic appearance of a building: "They deal in cold hard facts. They have no aesthetic sense whatsoever. Furthermore, they have no imagination. So, although I feel they may be used as aids to architecture, it is still for the human being to create that which is beautiful."[66] Banham, however, disputed this traditional separation between "mathematics" and "art" as simply replicating the old form/function divide, "not only that mathematics is part of the traditional equipment of the architect, but that aesthetics and other aspects of human psychology are no longer mysteries necessarily to be set up against 'cold hard facts.'"[67]

While Banham was clearly in favor of borrowing from technology in widespread fields—rocketry as described by Brothers, for example, offered a lesson in "total planning and teamwork"—he was as suspicious of the contemporary architectural fetishism of technology as he was of the modern movement's mystique: "Throughout the present century, architects have made fetishes of technological and scientific *concepts out of context* and been disappointed by them when they developed according to the processes of technological development, not according to the hopes of architects."[68] He concludes, with self-conscious irony, against his own enthusiasms: "A generation ago, it was 'The Machine' that let architects down—tomorrow or the day after it will be 'The Computer,' or Cybernetics or Topology."[69] Likewise, Banham responds to Drummond, electronic computing "can stand as an example of a topic on which the profession as a whole has been eager to gulp down visionary general articles of a philosophical nature, without scrutinizing either this useful tool, or their own *mathematical needs* to see just how far computers and architecture have anything to say to one another."[70] Giving the example of Charles Eames, who had spoken at the RIBA in 1959 on the "mental techniques associated with computers" important for architecture, Banham calls for a more analytical approach, examining how computers might be used, and "how far."

Banham is more generous toward his future professor at the Bartlett, claiming that the article by Llewelyn-Davies of the Nuffield Foundation had opened the way to the analysis of supposedly "soft" social and psychological facts: "*Psychological matters* can be assigned *numerical values*—and statistical techniques make it increasingly feasible to quantify them—they become susceptible to mathematical manipulation. . . . An increasing proportion of the most jealously-guarded 'professional secrets' of architecture are already quantifiable."[71] Banham interprets this as signifying that finally the gap between the unquantifiable and the quantifiable had narrowed so that all aspects of the architectural program might be assigned mathematical values. He supports this theory in his side-by-side comparison of architectural tradition and technological "progress" (tradition lost the race), and by taking on the problematic question of the historical languages of modernism in his article "History and Psychiatry."

In response to Pevsner's irritation that, throughout the series, "No architect really stood up to say that he is concerned with visual values (i.e. aesthetics) and that, if a building fails visually, we are not interested in it,"[72] Banham tartly answers: "No architect stood up to say that he was concerned with visual values because visual values are only one of six (ten? fifty?) equally important values of design." And to Pevsner's fear of Banham's scientific program that "you can have 'non-architecture' that way before you know where you are," Banham rehearses his notion of a "scientific aesthetic." Admitting that "Certainly a *fully* scientific aesthetic is impossible now—but it is a thousand-percent more possible than it was thirty years ago," he explains, "By a scientific aesthetic, I meant one that uses, as the basis and guide to design, observations (made according to the normal laws of scientific evidence) of the actual effect of certain colours, forms, symbols, spaces, lighting levels, acoustic qualities, textures, perspective effects (in isolation or in total 'gestalts') on human viewers."[73] In sum, this 1960 series seemed to support Banham's conclusion to *Theory and Design*, published in the same year: "It may well be that what we have hitherto understood as architecture, and what we are beginning to understand of technology are incompatible disciplines."[74]

This emergence of a new sensibility to the architectural program considered in its broadest terms recalls Banham and John Summerson's optimism in the late 1950s that a closer attention to science—whether of perception, information, or technology—would in the end lead to a fundamental reconception of modern movement functionalism, not in order to free architecture from observance of function, but rather to cast functionalism in a vastly expanded field—one that included, from Banham's point of view, topology, perception, biology, genetics, information theory, and technology of all kinds.

"Une Architecture Autre"

Banham had mentioned "clip-on components" for the prefabricated service rooms of a house in his 1960 "Stocktaking," but it was not until five years later that he developed a complete theory of "clip-on architecture" in an article for *Design Quarterly*, reprinted in the same year to introduce a special issue of *Architectural Design* largely devoted to the Archigram group.[75] Here he traces the genealogy of "clip-on," from the idea of "endlessness" with regard to standardization and, according to Llewelyn-Davies, from Mies to the notion of a "cell with services" introduced by the Smithsons in their plastic House of the Future of 1955, as well as by Ionel Schein in France and Monsanto in the United States. The concept of the house as a mass-produced product, mass-marketed like a Detroit car but put together on site with prefabricated components, had already inspired Banham to sketch an article on "Clip-on Philosophy" in 1961. And Cedric Price's Fun Palace, conceived for Joan Littlewood and interpreted by Price as a "giant neo-futurist machine," ran very close to the programmatic revolution for which Banham was calling in 1960: a giant "Anti-building" seen as a "zone of total probability, in which the possibility of participating in practically everything could be caused to exist."[76] Admittedly, Archigram had reversed the idea of clip-on by adopting that of "plug-in," but Banham was ready to fold this concept into his theory: "too much should not be made of this distinction between extreme forms of the two concepts: technically they are often intimately confused in the same project, and the aesthetic tradition overruns niceties of mechanical discrimination."[77] In thus returning to an "aesthetic tradition," Banham reveals his real agenda with regard to "une architecture autre": it is a call for an architecture that technologically overcomes all previous architectures, to possess an expressive form.[78] Against the way in which the "architecture of the establishment" had adopted prefabrication—"the picturesque prefabrication techniques of the tile-hung schools of the CLASP system" (a prefabricated system for building schools adopted by a consortium of local authorities in the 1960s)—he was equally opposed to the theories of "cyberneticists and O and R men" who predicted that "a computerized city might look like anything or nothing." For this reason Banham was enthusiastic about Archigram's Plug-in City, explaining "most of us want [a computerized city] to look like *something*, we don't want form to follow function into oblivion."[79]

For Banham, Archigram's projects—he characterized them as "Zoom City," "Computer City," "Off-the-Peg City," "Completely Expendable City," and "Plug-in City"—were important as much for the technology on which they were predicated as for their aesthetic qualities: "*Archigram* can't tell you for certain whether Plug-in City can be made to work, but it can tell you what it might look like." Whether their proposals are acceptable to technicians or dismissed as pop frivolity, they offer important *formal* lessons. Banham thus traces a movement from propositions about the contribution of technology to 1950s aesthetics to Archigram, in whose projects "aesthetics [offer] to give technology its marching orders."[80] As he added later: "Archigram is short on theory, long on draughtsmanship and craftsmanship. They're in the image business and they have been blessed with the power to create some of the most compelling images of our time."[81]

In this apparently dismissive characterization of Archigram as an "image business," Banham was returning to a theory developed around the mid-1950s: the notion of the "image" first posed by Ernst Gombrich in the 1950s and adopted by Banham in his characterization of brutalism. In his 1955 article "The New Brutalism," Banham had used the term "image" to escape from classical aesthetics and to refer to something that, while not conforming to traditional canons of judgment, was nevertheless "visually valuable," requiring "that the building should be an immediately apprehensible visual entity, and that the form grasped by the eye should be confirmed by experience of the building in use." For Banham, this "imageability" meant that the building in some way was "conceptual," more an idea of the relation of form to function than a reality, and without any requirement that the building be either classically formal or more abstractly topological. Whether "image" referred to a Jackson Pollock or a Cadillac, it was "something which is visually valuable, but not necessarily by the standards of classical aesthetics"; paraphrasing Thomas Aquinas, Banham further defines an "image" as "that which seen, affects the emotions."[82]

This implies that a building does not need to be "formal" in traditional terms; it could also be *aformal* and still be conceptual.[83] Thus attacking what he calls "routine Palladians" as well as routine functionalists, Banham cites the Smithsons' Golden Lane project as an example that "created a coherent visual image by non-formal means" with its visible circulation, identifiable units of habitation, and the presence of human beings as part of the total image, which was represented in perspectives with people collaged so that "the human presence almost overwhelmed the architecture."[84] In Golden Lane, as at Sheffield University, "aformalism becomes as positive a force in its composition as it does in a painting by Burri or Pollock."[85] This effect was a result of the Smithsons' general attitude toward composition, which they approached not in traditional formal terms, but with apparently casual informality: this was a compositional approach based on "an intuitive sense of topology" rather than on elementary rule-and-compass geometry. Banham concludes that the presence of topology over geometry is what marked the inception of "une autre architecture," another architecture, which displayed its qualities through the characteristics of penetration, circulation, the relations between inside and outside, and above all, the surface of apperception, which finally gave the image its force and substance: thus, beauty and geometry were supplanted by image and topology.[86] Image, for Banham, evidently related to what he was to claim in 1960 as the only aesthetic "teachable" along scientific lines: "No theory of aesthetics (except possibly Picturesque) that could be taught in schools, takes any cognizance of the memory-factor in seeing."[87]

No more than a year after the publication of "The New Brutalism," Banham, evidently straining to find an appropriate object for his image-theory in the Hunstanton School, found even the Smithsons wanting in their response to his aesthetic conditions. Reviewing the group displays in the "This Is Tomorrow" exhibition at the Whitechapel Art Gallery, Banham judged the "Patio and Pavilion" designed by the Smithsons, Nigel Henderson, and Eduardo Paolozzi—a collection of objects in a shed within a courtyard that, in the Smithsons' words, represented "the fundamental necessities of the human habitat in a series of symbols"—to be "the New Brutalists at their most submissive to traditional values . . . in an exalted sense, a confirmation of accepted values and symbols."[88] The installation by John Voelcker, Richard Hamilton, and John McHale, on the other hand, seemed more "Brutalist" in character than the brutalists, as the artists "employed optical illusions, scale reversions, oblique structures and fragmented images to disrupt stock responses, and put the viewer back on a *tabula rasa* of individual responsibility for his own atomized sensory awareness of images of only local and contemporary significance."[89] Ultimately, the authenticity of the movement lay in brutalism's refusal of abstract concepts and its use of "concrete images—images that can carry the mass of tradition and association, or the energy of novelty and technology, but resist classification by the geometrical disciplines by which most other exhibits were dominated."[90] Banham's image, then, was not only a passive symbol of everyday life or technological desire, but an active participant in the viewer's sensory perception—using all the techniques of modernist disruption, of shock and displacement, to embed its effects in experience.

Such a theory of the image, then, begins to deepen our own interpretation of what Archigram itself wanted, beyond the overtly brilliant subterfuges of advertising techniques, pop and op art, collage and montage, super graphics, and the like that rendered the actual images of Archigram so seductive and arresting. For to see an underlying commitment to topology and to the image as a confirmation of synthetic experience was to begin the process of building, out of Archigram, a "program" for architecture that went beyond its surface effects. It was in this sense, at least for Banham in 1965, and before his retreat into more conventional architectural paradigms of the "well-tempered environment," that Archigram was to provide Summerson's "missing language."

Indeed, of all those interrogating "une architecture autre" in the 1960s, the Archigram group, under the cover of what seemed to be irreverent and harmless play, had launched the most fundamental critique of the traditional architectural program. The tone was set by the first issue of the magazine *Archigram*, in May 1961, consisting of a single page with a foldout, in which David Greene polemically substituted for the "poetry of bricks" a poetry of "countdown, orbital helmets, discord of mechanical body transportation and leg walking." Eight issues followed, from 1963 to 1970, developing themes that embraced issues of expendability and consumerism at the broadest scale. In the "Living City" exhibit of 1963 at the Institute of Contemporary Arts and in its projects for Plug-in City (Peter Cook, 1964), Computer City (Dennis Crompton 1964), Underwater City, and Moving Cities (Ron Herron, 1964), Archigram explored all of the potentials for technology and social engineering to reshape the environment. Inflatables, infrastructures, pods, blobs, blebs, globs, and gloops were proposed as the engines of a culture dedicated to nomadism, social emancipation, endless exchange, interactive response systems, and, following the lead of Cedric Price, pleasure, fun, and comfort on the material and psychological level, all designed with witty technological poetics to place the total synthetic environment—human, psychological, ecological, and technological—firmly on the agenda.

The destabilizing power of these images and their evident relationship to a tradition, identified by Manfredo Tafuri as that of "Duchamp," was clear; but so was their equal commitment to technology, new and as yet uninvented, and its potential for supporting a new society, also yet to be invented. In their ironic stance toward traditional modernism and their fundamental critique of its social, psychological, and technological failings, these utopian images seemed to be dedicated to extending modernist principles to their extreme (and thereby ideal) limits. At this point, the image of science-fiction utopia joined the program of total design imagined by those who, like Tomás Maldonado at Ulm, believed that an entirely new version of the traditional *Gesamtkunstwerk* was demanded by the mass global society's complex environmental, social, and technological conditions. Here, the "psychedelic" aspirations of the utopian left met, almost seamlessly, the systematic cybernetics of the rational center.[91]

The momentary alliance between Archigram and Banham seems, however, to offer more than a historical antecedent to contemporary experiments in virtual architecture and global visions. As Mark Wigley has pointed out, Archigram was more than a "sci-fi" and pop blip on the screen of architectural history; it was embedded in the very processes of architectural practice, imaginary and real.[92] Banham himself realized this in his systematic exploration of the conditions demanded by an "autre" architecture, *The Architecture of the Well-Tempered Environment*, published in 1969. In his consideration of the newly constructed Queen Elizabeth Hall at the South Bank Centre in London (1967), he noted the conjunction of two of the major forces on design in the early sixties: Corbusian exposed concrete and the "plug-in" aesthetic of Archigram. While most commentators focused on the brutalist features of the building, Banham notes the contributions of Ron Herron, Warren Chalk, and Dennis Crompton to the design team: "In truth one could say that the Corbusian and Plug-in elements are manifest in one and the same thing, the silhouette the buildings derive from the external disposition of the main service ducts."[93] In the "romantic" silhouette of the exterior, and the concrete-enclosed air ducts that circulate on the outside of the building's volumes, Banham saw the coming together of the two main themes he had introduced in "The New Brutalism": the neopicturesque "image" that relied as much on the presence of a moving observer as it did on composition, and the technological innovations of an "autre" architecture. In this way, Banham's insistence on the role of aesthetics—of the viewer and in experience—in the promulgation of a new architecture invoked the possibility of reconceiving the notion of program in a way that might occlude the fatal modernist gap between form and function, and incorporate environmental concerns, technology, and formal invention as integral to a single discourse.

The Architecture of the Well-Tempered Environment represented a seminal stage in Banham's search for an "autre" history for an "autre" architecture. In an opening apologia, which he recognized would be entirely unwarranted "in a world more humanely disposed, and more conscious of where the prime human responsibilities of architects lie," he castigates a vision of architectural history that had divided its object of study between structures and mechanical services, privileging the former over the latter. Such a division, he argues, makes "no sense in terms of the way buildings are used and paid for by the human race."[94] At the end of his ground-breaking survey of the evolution of mechanical services and their use (or misuse) in some of the iconic buildings of the nineteenth and twentieth centuries, Banham observes that, of contemporary designers, only Buckminster Fuller and the members of Archigram had exhibited a "willingness to abandon the reassurances and psychological supports of monumental structure," citing the "threat" launched in *Archigram 7* "that 'there may be no buildings at all in *Archigram 8*.'"[95]

Beyond Architecture: Banham in LA

Historical monograph? Can such an old-world, academic, and precedent-laden concept claim to embrace so unprecedented a human phenomenon as this city of Our Lady Queen of the Angels of Porciuncula?—otherwise known as Internal Combustion City, Surfurbia, Smogville, Aerospace City, Systems Land, the Dream-factory of the Western world.
—Reyner Banham, *Los Angeles: The Architecture of Four Ecologies*

If "The New Brutalism" and his study of the "well-tempered environment" had begun Banham's search for a history of modernism that would serve the development of another architecture for the late twentieth century, it was his experience of Los Angeles between 1965 and 1971 that encouraged Banham to expand the narrow notion of "environment" as a single building into the wider frame of ecology. Los Angeles, made up of "instant architecture in an instant landscape,"[96] was a city that knew very little about "history"—especially the history of its architecture—and seemed to exist quite well without it. The unique and "extraordinary mixture of geography, climate, economics, demography, mechanics and culture" that composed Los Angeles prompted Banham to forge an entirely new kind of architectural history, one that would take architecture as equal to, if not a secondary response to, the ecological conditions of urban settlement. Further, this new history would understand "architecture" as implying the widest possible field of inquiry—from the popular restaurant and the dingbat apartment to the work of individual name architects, all set in a context that itself was taken to be "architectural" in its broadest definition. This was to be a history that went beyond the "local" histories of Pevsner in his "Buildings of England" series, or even that urban-architectural history developed by Summerson in his *Georgian London*. For Banham, the promise of scientific functionalism led inevitably to a wider program that did not simply embrace the demands of a client or translate the zeitgeist of the moment into form, but took into account the broadest set of urban geographical conditions.

Constructed from a series of radio talks for the BBC Third Programme in the summer of 1968, the book *Los Angeles: The Architecture of Four Ecologies* sketched a potential for architectural history to join with historical geography in order to explore the full implications of "ecology," a word then considered radical in art historical circles. Reviewers, ranging from those who found the very subject of Los Angeles beneath the historian's interest to those who found Banham's enthusiasm overplayed in the wake of the social turmoil of the 1960s, failed to note the more general implications of the work's scope. The book was commissioned as part of a series entitled "The Architect and Society" and edited by the British historians John Fleming and Hugh Honor (a series that included James Ackerman's elegant monographic essay on Palladio among others). Nevertheless, Banham's book certainly seemed an anomaly in the field of architectural history. Rather than a survey of the great buildings of the city—already accomplished, as Banham noted, by David Gebhard and Robert Winter[97]—the book was first and foremost intended to take a new approach by examining the whole fabric and structure of an urban region. In this attempt, Banham developed an entirely radical view of urban architecture, one that has had a major impact on the discipline of architectural history. Joining architecture to the idea of its ecology, the title immediately announces Banham's intention to pose the interrelated questions: What has architecture to do with ecology? What might be an ecology of architecture? And, even more important, what would be the nature of an architecture considered in relation to its ecology?

Taken together, Banham's answers to these three questions provided a road map for the study of urban architecture not just in its geographical, social, and historical context—this was already a common practice among the social historians of architecture in the late 1960s—but as an active and ever-changing palimpsest of the new global metropolis. Not incidentally, they also entirely redefined the architecture that scholars were used to studying, for Banham embraced all forms of human structure, from the freeway to the hotdog stand, and a plurality of forms of expression not simply confined to the aesthetic codes of high architecture. Here, of course, lay one of the problems for his early reviewers: as a critic, Banham had established himself as an apologist for pop art and pop culture, a reputation that, together with his evident fascination with technological innovation and change, made it all too easy for the book to be seen as a pop history of Los Angeles. One reviewer even bestowed the title "Schlockology" on the book.[98] The very inclusion of traditionally "nonarchitectural" structures—including even surfboards—inevitably obscured the real seriousness of Banham's intent to destabilize the entire field of architectural history by treating a subject, Los Angeles, that hardly any serious critic took seriously. But on this he was explicit from the outset. Answering his own question as to whether the city was a fit object for a "historical monograph," he wrote: "The city has a comprehensible, even consistent, quality to its built form, unified enough to rank as a fit subject for a historical monograph."[99] Hence his programmatic intent to insert the polymorphous architectures of designer houses, hamburger stands, freeway structures, and civil engineering into a "comprehensible unity" that would find its place within a total context—the whole fabric and geographic structure of the region. In this attempt to take on a whole urban region, Banham was forced by the special conditions of Los Angeles to develop an entirely radical view of urban architecture, and one that has had a major impact on the discipline of architectural history over the last thirty years.

Indeed, Los Angeles turned out to be exactly the vehicle needed to blow up what Banham had earlier called "trad" history, precisely because it defied the "trad" city as a city, and the "trad" place of architecture on the streets and squares of the "trad" city; precisely because Los Angeles was a city where the structure of the regional space was more important than individual grids or fabric; precisely because of its semi-self-conscious "pop" culture; precisely, finally, because it represented to "trad" historians everything a city should *not* be, it was possible to write the kind of history of it that was everything a history of architecture should *not* be.[100] Here it is important to approach the development of Banham's thought as a *historian* rather than as the "journalist" assumed by his reviewers, as he encountered Los Angeles, that apparently most unhistorical of cities, and to explore the effects of his complex response on the history of architecture and of cities.

It was in the summer of 1968—following radio programs dealing with the French student revolt, the "revolution" at Hornsey College of Art, the Velvet Underground's album *White Light, White Heat*, the showing of Jean-Luc Godard's *Weekend*, the assassination of Robert Kennedy, the ongoing war in Vietnam, and the Warsaw Pact invasion of Prague—that listeners to the British Broadcasting Corporation's Third Programme, the channel for intellectual discussion and cultural commentary, were treated to the decidedly better news of Reyner Banham's visit to Los Angeles in four witty talks. As published in the BBC's house organ, *The Listener*, between August 22 and September 12, they were titled respectively "Encounter with Sunset Boulevard," "Roadscape with Rusting Rails," "Beverly Hills, Too, Is a Ghetto," and "The Art of Doing Your Thing."[101]

Banham began by recounting his perplexity at the layout of the city by telling the story of his journey to Los Angeles by bus, and his mistake in assuming the downtown bus terminal would be "closer" to Sunset Boulevard and his hotel in Westwood than the station at Santa Monica. Sunset, he found, was one of those arteries that traverse the side of the Los Angeles River valley from downtown to the sea. The point of the story, it seemed, was to demonstrate to himself as much as to his audience the wonder of the rooted, Norfolk-reared, London-based, nondriving Banham feeling "at home in Los Angeles." And even more curiously, he argued that, indeed, London and Los Angeles had a lot in common, each a conglomeration of small villages, spread out in endless tracts of single-family houses, despite their vast apparent differences in terms of car travel, freeways, climate, and scale. For Banham, the structural and topographical similarities were striking.

The second talk, "Roadscape with Rusting Rails," picked up on this theme to explore the infrastructural formation of Los Angeles, and its basis not so much in freeways, as the commonplace went, but in the vast and expansive light-rail system built up between the 1860s and 1910, Pacific Electric's interurban network, which gradually, between 1924 and (extraordinarily enough) 1961, formed the backbones of Los Angeles's working and living systems. Yet this fact was merely a preface to what was to enrage critics a couple of years later, Banham's eulogy of the freeway system. This nondriver turned driver out of instant love with a city was exultant at the "automotive experience," waxing eloquent over the drive down Wilshire toward the sea at sunset, and downplaying the city's notorious smogs in comparison to those in London; his proof: "a shirt that looks grubby in London by 3 p.m. can be worn in Los Angeles for two days."[102]

Banham's third talk covered Beverly Hills, an exclusive community self-incorporated specifically to prevent the schools from being invaded by children of other classes and ethnicities, the "most defensive residential suburb in the world," an enclave of unrelieved middle-class single-family dwellings, created to send children to school without the risk of "unsuitable friends." The Listener article was illustrated by a Ralph Crane photo of a typical upper-middle-class family relaxing around the pool. Banham noted the "apparently total indifference to the needs of all communities except one's own that is one of the most continuously unnerving aspects of public life in Los Angeles," "the ugly backside of that free-swinging libertarian ethic that makes so much of Angeleno life irresistibly attractive."[103] This would be Banham's didactic method—that of contrast, "for" and "against" balancing each other, more often than not with the "for" on the winning side.

In Banham's account, Beverly Hills was a "self-contained, specialized area," and a "socio" and "functional" "monoculture."

For him it was proof that if you "insist on trying to use LA as if it were a compact European pedestrian city," you become campus-bound. Banham admits that he too nearly succumbed to this mentality: "At the University of California in Los Angeles (UCLA) you never stir out of the Rancho San José de Buenos Ayres. You live in digs in Westwood, stroll over to classes, eat in the Faculty Club or Westwood Village restaurants, go to Village bookshops and cinemas. In short you do exactly what we accuse Angelenos of doing, living restricted and parochial lives that never engage the totality of Los Angeles." But Banham was, he claims, saved by the realization that "the amount of distorted and perverted information circulating about Los Angeles in quasi-learned journals about architecture, the arts, planning, social problems and so forth," came not so much "from hasty judgments formed by lightning visitors," but rather "from visitors who may have spent a semester, a year, or even longer, in the city, but have never stirred beyond the groves of academe—eucalypts, jacarandas, bananas—planted in the 1920s on the old Wolfskill ranch that too can be a ghetto."[104]

In his last radio talk, Banham delivered his judgment on the pop culture of Los Angeles: its "doing your own thing" tradition of artistry, from the motorcycle pictures of Billy Al Bengston in the early 1960s to Von Dutch's painted crash helmets, from the ubiquitous surfboard decoration down in Venice to that monument to do-it-yourself culture, Simon Rodia's Watts Towers. These were "not, as some European critics seem to maintain in any way naive or folksy. Their structure is immensely strong, the decoration of their surfaces resourceful and imaginative."[105] The same was true of contemporary pop artists, like Ed Ruscha: his *26 Gasoline Stations*, *34 Parking Lots*, and *Every Building on the Sunset Strip* were all, to Banham's eyes, deadpan statements that were content to "do their own thing," neither judging nor criticizing.

With hindsight, these apparently random radio musings on his recent travels emerge as entirely systematic, for we realize that Banham was carefully building up three of his four final ecologies—the beach, the foothills, and the freeways—as well as beginning to treat the city's alternative architecture, that of "fantasy." Subsequent articles in *Architectural Design* (such as "LA: The Structure behind the Scene")[106] elaborated his take on the transportation network and its process of continual adjustment. By the spring of 1971, the overall plan of *Los Angeles: The Architecture of Four Ecologies* had been set, and its complicated outline developed.

And the structure of the book was indeed complicated—a number of reviewers disparaged its apparent lack of unity, and even suggested reordering the chapters. But Banham's arrangement was in fact a part of his conscious attempt to reshape not only how one looked at a city like Los Angeles—an order forced by the unique form of the city itself—but also how one wrote architectural history in a moment of widening horizons and boundaries, when the very definition of architecture was being challenged and extended to every domain of technological and popular culture, and inserted into a broad urban, social, and of course ecological context. Thus he self-consciously intersected chapters on the "ecologies" of architecture with chapters on the architecture itself, and these again with notes on the history and bibliography of the city.

The book opens with a brief history of the geographical and infrastructural formation of the city, tellingly titled "In the Rear View Mirror," as if one could, as indeed Banham did, glimpse fragments of that not-so-long history while driving the freeways and glancing back(wards) into the rear view of the city. This is followed by four chapters on each of the four "ecologies" of the title: "Surfurbia" (the beach and coastline); "Foothills" (the Santa Monica Mountains); "The Plains of Id" (the great flat central valley); and most important of all, "Autopia" (the freeway system and its correlates). These ecological studies do not form a continuous narrative but are broken in sequence by four parallel chapters on the specific "architectures" of Los Angeles: "the exotic pioneers"; "fantastic" architecture; the work of the distinguished foreign "exiles"; and a homage to the new Los Angeles modernism of the 1950s embodied in the Case Study House movement, in Banham's eyes "The Style that Nearly" but not quite became a true regional genre. These are interrupted by four thematic chapters that step out of the systematic study of ecology and architecture to add notes on the development of the transportation network, the culture of "enclaves" unique to Los Angeles, and a brief consideration of downtown. This last chapter is the most heretical with respect to traditional city guides. Whereas the latter would start with the old center and demonstrate a nostalgic sense of its "loss," in Banham's view a "note" is all that downtown deserves in the context of a city that had become an entire region, and where "downtown" seemed just a blip on a wide screen. Finally, Banham's programmatic conclusion is entitled "An Ecology for Architecture."

Such a complicated, multilayered structure was obviously Banham's attempt to irrevocably break up the normal homogeneity of architectural narratives and urban studies, insistently inserting the one into the other in a kind of montage that works against the narrative flow to instigate pauses for reflection and re-viewing, as if the historian/critic were circling around his objects of study, viewing them through different frames at different scales and from different vantage points.

On one level, this structure was entirely new, one engendered by the special conditions of Los Angeles itself; it was a freeway model of history, looking at the city through movement and as itself in movement. On another level, however, Banham the self-conscious historian of modernism, who had ten years earlier published the first full-length study of architectural theory and design between the wars, was drawing inspiration from many precedents. These included proclamations of modernism that called for the rejection of "high" architecture in favor of structures generated by functional and technological demands; alternative modernist "utopias," from the technotopias of Buckminster Fuller to the contemporary work of the Archigram group in London; appreciations of the consumer society and its modes of representation, exemplified in the discussions and exhibitions of the Independent Group in London, and notably in their "This Is Tomorrow" exhibition of 1956;[107] and scientific prognostications of the future, especially the potential effects of new biological, genetic, and chromosome research. All these paradigms and many more were formative for Banham's radical rewriting of history and theory. But, for the purpose of exemplifying the special character of *Los Angeles*, two models are particularly significant; one that had a major impact on the narrative form of the book, the other on its "ecological" content. Both, in a way that indicates Banham's polemical intention to criticize and continue the positive tendencies he detected in the first modernisms, were themselves exemplary statements of high modernist positions.

The first model was Le Corbusier's *Vers une architecture*, a precedent which might at first seem surprising, given Banham's often repeated rejection of what he called academic formalism and his critique of inadequate, modernist functionalism. Banham had already vaunted Le Corbusier's manifesto in *Theory and Design*, calling it "one of the most influential, widely read and least understood of all the architectural writings of the twentieth century."[108] Yet in analyzing the form of *Vers une architecture*, which was assembled out of individual essays from the journal *L'Esprit Nouveau*, he describes it as without "argument in any normal sense of the word": it was made up of "a series of rhetorical or rhapsodical essays on a limited number of themes, assembled side by side in such a way as to give an impression that these themes have some necessary connection."[109]

Banham identifies two main themes in his reading of Le Corbusier. The first is what he calls the "academic" approach to architecture—architecture conceived as a formal art derived from Greek and Roman models as taught in the Beaux-Arts schools of the late nineteenth century; the second are what he identifies as "mechanistic" topics—the engineer's aesthetic, ocean liners, aircraft, cars, and the like. These themes, Banham points out, alternated, chapter by chapter, through the book, with the "mechanistic" essays "firmly sandwiched" within the others. Banham further notes the rhetoric of the illustrations, the celebrated facing-page photos that point out comparisons, historical and aesthetic. This analysis, still one of the very best readings of Le Corbusier we have, is revealing in a number of ways.

First, it reveals the underlying mission of Banham's entire career, dedicated to freeing the "mechanistic" from the embrace of the academic. As he writes in the conclusion to *Theory and Design*, Banham called for "the rediscovery of science as a dynamic force, rather than the humble servant of architecture. The original idea of the early years of the century, of science as an unavoidable directive to progress and development, has been reversed by those who cheer for history, and has been watered down to a limited partnership by the mainstream. Those who have re-explored the twenties and read the Futurists for themselves feel once more the compulsion of science, the need to take a firm grip on it, and to stay with it whatever the consequences."[110] We might well imagine that in Los Angeles Banham found the solution to the modernist dream of the ubiquitous automobile, sketched with primitivist formalism by Le Corbusier in his comparison of the sports car with the Parthenon.

Secondly, Banham's description of the narrative structure of *Vers une architecture* can be applied directly to that of his own book *Los Angeles*, with its interspersed series of essays on two main themes, the ecological and the architectural. Supporting this hypothesis is the layout of the illustrations with its insistent pairing of comparative photographs on facing pages—the beach houses of Malibu from the beach side and from the road side, the Santa Monica Canyon in 1870 and in 1970, the Wayfarer's Chapel by Frank Lloyd Wright of 1949 juxtaposed against the oil rigs off Long Beach. In each case, "before" is contrasted with "after"; the architecturally designed is posed against technological form; undeveloped landscape against developed; pop against high culture, and so on, in visual comparisons that remind us immediately of Le Corbusier's temples, cars, engineering structures, and grain elevators. In this sense we might conclude that *Los Angeles* was Banham's response to, and triumph over, what he regarded as the central manifesto of 1920s modernism, and we would be reinforced in this conclusion by his sly acknowledgment to Corbusier in the last chapter, entitled not "Towards a New Architecture" but "Towards a Drive-In Bibliography"—which we might decipher as "(Driving) Towards a New Architecture."

The second major influence on *Los Angeles*, this time on its content, was perhaps more substantial and arose from Banham's discovery of a work by Anton Wagner, a German urban geographer who had chosen Los Angeles as a thesis topic between 1928 and 1933. Wagner completed his research in Santa Monica, and in 1935 published his monumental "geographical" study with the title *Los Angeles: Werden, Leben und Gestalt der Zweimillionstadt in Südkalifornien* (Los Angeles: The development, life, and form of the city of two million in southern California).[111] The subtitle of Wagner's book was calculated to evoke comparisons with that other paradigmatic modern metropolis, Berlin. Noting that Los Angeles is a "city which far exceeds Berlin in expansiveness,"[112] Wagner superimposes the plans of the two metropolises over each other to prove the point.

Wagner's research was exhaustive. He conducted numerous interviews of all types of inhabitants, and his understanding of the city was accomplished by a rigorous survey carried out, despite the distances involved, mostly on foot (unlike Banham's), as he explored and mapped its "lived space and access paths" (*Lebensraum*). At the same time (like Banham), he took his own photos: "I captured the appearance of the cities and quarters in numerous photographs which still bring to mind the details of the cityscape, despite increasing spatial and temporal distance."[113]

Interested in the play of "forces of nature" and "activities of man"—the need to study all the geographical factors and the biosphere of the region—and the urban landscape ("die städtische Landschaft"), Wagner starts the book with a detailed study of the city's geological history and structure—its "geological dynamism," as he calls it. Indeed, "dynamism" is the watchword of Los Angeles for this European observer: "A quickly evolving landscape, and a city whose formation proceeded faster than most normal urban development, thereby encompassing much larger spatial units, requires an emphasis of dramatic occurrences, movement and forces. Especially for the current form of Los Angeles, becoming is more characteristic than being. This determines the method of representation."[114] He concludes: "For Los Angeles . . . tradition means movement."[115] Present during the major Long Beach earthquake of March 10, 1933, Wagner was well aware of the kinds of movement to which Los Angeles is susceptible, and characterized the building of the city as a struggle between nature and man: "the life of so artificial an urban organism . . . depends on how much it is secured against catastrophes."[116]

Beyond this totalizing and systematic yet dynamic and processual geological "history" of the city, Wagner traces the successive development booms of Los Angeles and the growth of its communities in meticulous detail, from the establishment of the first pueblos and ranchos, which he maps, to the development of the rail transportation system, again mapped, to the aspect of every quarter in the 1930s. These maps, it should be noted, were the basis for many of those elegantly transcribed by Mary Banham for her husband's later book, as well as forming the basis of Banham's own perceptive history of transportation networks and land-ownership patterns.

Like Banham's some thirty years later, Wagner's physical survey of the "cityscape" omits nothing, however squalid; and no "architecture," however tumble-down or populist, escapes his gaze and camera. He revels in the studio lots or "stage-set cities" (*Kulissenstädte*); he speaks of the "cultural landscape" of the oil fields with their "drilling tower forests"; he examines the stylistic and plan typologies of every kind of housing, from the modest bungalow to the apartment house and Beverly Hills mansion; above all, he remarks on the eternal billboards—"a major aspect that dominates parts of the frontal view, or elevation [*Aufriss*]: the business advertisement . . . the billboard that emphasizes the incomplete [*das Unfertige*] in the landscape"—and takes two pages to describe the physiognomy of the billboard as it competes for view amid the "inelegant posts and wiring of the telephone and electric lines."[117] Wagner's final judgment of his epic study is that "It is not only architects, statisticians and economists who should draw lessons from this work of urban geography, but everyone who is a member of an urban community."[118]

It is easy to see what Banham, who called this unique work "the only comprehensive review of Los Angeles as a built environment,"[119] drew from it: the idea of a city whose history is firmly rooted in its geology and geography—a rooting that is itself as mobile as the ecological circumstances of its site; the idea of a city that is important as much for change as for permanence; the idea of the architecture of the city as less important than the totality of its constructions; the notion, finally, of taking the city as it is as opposed to any utopian, idealistic, or nostalgic vision of what it might be. As he recapitulates in the article "LA: The Structure behind the Scene," "Los Angeles represents processes of continuous adjustment, processes of apportionment of land and resources. . . . As far as Los Angeles is concerned, the land and the uses of the land are . . . the things that need to be talked about first."[120] Banham's history of the city's development, of its transportation network, of the transformation of the city from ranchos and pueblos into a single sprawling metropolis takes its cue at every moment from Wagner. Finally, Wagner's understanding that it is "movement" of every kind that characterizes Los Angeles is echoed in Banham's own sense that if there is a "local language" to be identified in Los Angeles, it is a language of "movement."[121]

In the light of such precedents, what appeared to critics as Banham's apparently light-hearted "drive-by" approach to Los Angeles emerges as a tightly constructed text, part manifesto, part new urban geography, that, joined together, form an entirely unique kind of "history." Answering Banham's own call for a posttechnological, postacademic, even postarchitectural discourse, the book resolutely sets out to engage the city as it is, refusing to lower its gaze in the face of sprawl, aesthetic chaos, or consumerist display. Rather than calling for a "new architecture," as Le Corbusier had done, Banham's manifesto asks for a new and uncompromising vision, one that might not immediately see what it wants to see, but nevertheless may be rewarded by glimpses of other, equally interesting and satisfying subjects. And, unlike Anton Wagner's call for a totalizing geo-urbanism, Banham's self-fabricated "ecology" provides him with an open framework for heterogeneity in subject matter and observation.

The city of Los Angeles, then, was both vehicle and subject for Banham, and its strange attraction allowed him to forge a new sensibility in his own work, to be fully explored, just over ten years later, in the equally misunderstood work *Scenes in America*

Deserta. Like *Los Angeles*, this book was greeted by reviewers as a "guide," an object in "a desert freak's checklist," but also like *Los Angeles*, its purpose was more serious and radical.[122] Treated as a set of personal "visions" of different deserts, it stands as a poetic evocation of landscape to be set beside all its British and American romantic precedents; yet treated, as Banham no doubt intended, as a new kind of environmental history, it is clearly the logical conclusion, the second volume, of a work, that has as its major purpose the complex examination of environmental experience as a whole. And while the "eye of the beholder" that looks in the rear-view mirror or across the Mojave is first and foremost Banham's eye, by extrapolation it stands for a sense of the meaning of objects in space that goes far beyond the architectural, the urban, the regional, to engage the phenomenology of landscape experience itself. The suppressed Pevsnerian "picturesque" that had been transformed into a theory of "image" in the 1950s is in *America Deserta* combined with the special notion of "ecology" explored in *Los Angeles* to produce a complex understanding of vision and space, observer and object, that takes the initial standpoint of "The New Brutalism"—"Introduce an observer into any field of forces, influences or communications and that field becomes distorted"[123]—and transforms it into a principle of ecological history.

Manfredo Tafuri, *Teorie e storia dell'architettura* (1970), cover

4 RENAISSANCE MODERNISM
MANFREDO TAFURI

What is commonly meant by operative criticism *is an analysis of architecture (or of the arts in general) that has as its object, not an abstract survey, but rather the "projection" of a precise poetic direction, anticipated in its structures, and originating in programmatically finalized historical analyses.*
—Manfredo Tafuri, *Teorie e storia dell'architettura*

Since the publication of his *Teorie e storia dell'architettura* in 1968, the historian Manfredo Tafuri has been characterized as a stubborn opponent of what he called "operative" history and criticism—the kind that reached back into the past in order to justify and project present practice, and in so doing distorted the historical record. "It could be said," he wrote, "that operative criticism designs past history in order to project it towards the future"; "its verification does not rely in the abstraction of principles; it measures itself each time against the results it obtains."[1] Under this rubric Tafuri included the historians Max Dvořák, Emil Kaufmann, Sigfried Giedion, and Bruno Zevi; the critics Edoardo Persico and P. Morton Shand; and the architects Adolf Behne, Bruno Taut, Le Corbusier, and Ernst May. By implication, indeed, almost none of the historians and critics of the modern movement escaped—from Pevsner to Banham, all were complicit in a mode of historical analysis that overtly or covertly pointed toward a present and future architecture. Such operative historiography was not a modern invention, however; Tafuri saw its origin in the Neoplatonic criticism of Bellori and, later, the polemical positions of academicians like François Blondel, philosophers like Marc-Antoine Laugier, and practicing architects like Pierre Patte. These critics would be followed by those historians who, like Viollet-le-Duc, James Fergusson, and Camillo Boito, "precipitate[d] the impatient demand for a new architecture in the second half of the nineteenth century."[2]

This apparently intransigent opposition to the architect-historian, or the critic-enthusiast, has been seen as a major rupture in Tafuri's work, coming at a time when, withdrawing from practice and active criticism, he joined the department of architecture at the University of Venice, to subject himself and his colleagues to a rigorous review of the history of modernity, an outcome of archival research, teamwork, and a fundamental revision of the commonplaces of modern movement ideology. But a closer reading of his prior excursions into historical research, carried on side by side with his work with planners and architects in various studies for the redevelopment of Rome and other cities, reveals a Tafuri who had not only established a mode of historical analysis before the move to Venice that exhibits many continuities with his subsequent studies, but whose training as an architect with a sensitivity to space and modulation, language and style, would continue to inform his historical reconstructions and interpretation.

Architect and Historian

Only an adequate historical preparation of the architectural stu-
dent will be able to furnish the instruments to interpret correctly
the phenomena of the past and to make them active elements
of the present without easy transpositions and anachronistic
returns.
—Manfredo Tafuri and Massimo Teodori, letter on behalf
of the Association of Students and Architects' Association of
Rome, 1960

In the last year of his studies at the University of Rome, responding to a debate in *Casabella* over the divide between education in
architecture and the profession itself, Tafuri pointed to the rigid
academicism of university education and what the editor of *Casabella*, Ernesto Rogers, had termed the "intellectual and moral
poverty of Italian university life." Tafuri and fellow-student Massimo Teodori called for the renewal of the curriculum to include
research and experiment in the urgent social, economic, and
cultural questions that would "contribute to the vast problems of
our country."[3] The curriculum they desired would coordinate between urban and architectural planning so that the division between urban and rural would be addressed, and it would end the
"pseudo-specialization of single problems." In sum, they called
for a return—or an advance—to the ideal unity of practice proposed by the modern movement but now fragmented and disin-
tegrated. As for the question of "architectural expression," Tafuri
and Teodori found that "the absence of ideological commitment
and of democratic customs and the partialization of the problem
leads architectural expression to fall back on the grammar of
the styles, whether antique, modern, or revivalist, since exclusive interest in the formal aspects of the architectural problem

disregards the fact that such forms originally expressed the reality or the aspirations of a certain period."[4] Only deep historical research could, they argued, combat what, one year later, Pevsner would illustrate as a symptom of the "return to historicism," the neoliberty movement that Banham would criticize.

Thus Tafuri, both before and immediately after graduation, was working to demonstrate the value of an integrated approach to urban and architectural problems founded on meticulous historical research. His first published articles on urbanism included studies on the post-1871 Via Nazionale in Rome;[5] a comprehensive analysis (with Giorgio Piccinato) of the plan for central Helsinki, which set the postwar schemes in the framework of the historical development of the city after the eighteenth century;[6] and his summary of a survey of the baroque extension of the medieval town of San Gregorio da Sassola, near Rome, with its long axis leading to an oval piazza.[7] Giorgio Ciucci has noted the way in which these studies, illustrated with many of Tafuri's own drawings, were from the outset concerned with the history of large-scale planning and urban structure, in contrast with the increasing tendency of intellectuals like Paolo Portoghesi, and even Tafuri's own teacher and later collaborator, Ludovico Quaroni, to look at "minor" architecture as a paradigm of popular building.[8]

In his report on the baroque expansion of Sassola, Tafuri asserts that the geometrical coherence of the facades surrounding the piazza and the standardization of the housing types along the axis made this "an exceptional intervention in planning, among the most unified examples of seventeenth-century urbanism in Lazio," carried out with such "a rigor of conception that . . . it requires a critical interpretation which will easily demonstrate the vacuity of folkloristic interpretations or romantic attitudes unfortunately so common with regard to so much architecture considered 'minor,' that, without an understanding of its innermost causes, is all too often proposed as an example, degenerating in practice into deplorable architectural populisms."[9]

Here, what Jean-Louis Cohen characterized as "the resolving power of the architect's eye [that] is different from the historian's" allowed Tafuri to investigate the history of the *"material production* of cities and buildings" (my emphasis).[10] The meticulous drawings made for this survey, reconstituting the plan, the housing typologies, and the elevations of the baroque village, share an interest in the advent of modern urbanism, its ability to cut through a medieval fabric and establish its operative geometries. Tafuri similarly prepared drawings for his articles on Helsinki and Rome, and, most importantly for his developing historical method, for his survey of the Palazzo Duca di Santo Stefano and the Badia Vecchia, or "old" abbey, in Taormina, Sicily.[11] Unlike previous historians, who had proposed various dates for the Palazzo ranging from the time of the Norman invasion to the fifteenth century, Tafuri boldly argues that it was one of a series of military constructions completed by Frederick II between his return to Sicily in 1220 and his death in 1250. Tafuri interprets the Palazzo as one of a group of typologically linked buildings, "a more or less homogeneous group of monuments, an extremely unified spatial conception; both of interior space, unified by a particular figurative expression of the rib vault, and the external space, characterized by a volumetric syncretism and a rural definition of the masses."[12] Such a typological analysis, influenced by the formal method of Giulio Carlo Argan, then professor of art history at the University of Rome, led Tafuri to posit the Palazzo as a specific architectural event that in some way precipitated a crisis, or shift, in Sicilian architecture, generated by the geometrical regularity of its plan and massing that "was antithetical to the traditional architectural taste of Norman Sicily" with its "exuberant plasticity" and "the figurative values of its structural frame." Added to this, Tafuri notes the decorative program of the Palazzo, which "inside and out, informed . . . a dualism between the two different spatial qualities, at the same time informing a not infrequent and highly expressive severity."[13] What would become a watchword of Tafuri's analytical approach—the uncovering of moments of "crisis" in history that ruptured seemingly fundamental continuities—is clearly developed here:

> *There exist, in the history of architecture and art, in general, particular moments or singular "cases" that assume a critical determining value for the comprehension of entire cultural cycles. We intend to speak of buildings, or of productions that are stylistically unified, that seem to mark a point of passage, a moment of crisis in a culture that has arrived at a high degree of maturity and that, precisely in its moment of maximum intensity, perceives in a confused way the need to go beyond itself, feels the need to verify its own historical coherence, thus giving rise to works that recapitulate in themselves, through their characteristics, the complementary horizons of diverse experiences, of cultures often distant despite their continuity.*[14]

Tafuri would bring this approach to bear on contemporary architecture in his 1963 monographic article on Ludovico Quaroni, published as a book later in the same year. In his work on Quaroni, Tafuri distinguishes between "continuity" and "crisis"—a question sharply posed in the immediate postwar period in Italy—in terms of an architect who "had recognized experimentalism as typical of the cultural adventures of these last sixteen years" and had shown himself "the most experimental," if not the "master" of experimental architecture:[15] "And in consequence he became a symbol of the tormented destiny of architecture in

Italy, a paradigmatic reference, whether as one deeply immersed in an ambience that reflected his work with extreme accuracy, or as representative or not (and this was the case more frequently), initiator of approaches, of methods, of operative models."[16] Tafuri was conscious of not wishing to publish a monograph in "the form of a *medal*," prefering to see Quaroni as a microcosmic synthesis of Italian development in general; the methodological problem was thus one of mediating "between the history of a cultural cycle and the personal history of a protagonist."[17] In a passage that was, significantly, omitted from the published book, Tafuri begins the difficult negotiation, to be resolved partially in *Teorie e storia* five years later, between "critical history" and "operative criticism"; he had tried, he explains, "to give to the research an operative dimension, not to the utopian end of annulling any distance between criticism and operation, but to establish this very criticism within an active process, in continual support of the operation, as its continuous verification and overcoming, and, in a certain way, in symbiosis with it."[18]

Tafuri's essay on Quaroni opens with a long quotation from Edoardo Persico's critical assessment of Italian art in 1930, and closes with a similarly long quotation from Giulio Carlo Argan's seminal 1957 article on architecture and ideology.[19] In this way Tafuri establishes his intellectual and architectural debts, clearing the way for a radically revised assessment of the field, historically and critically. Characteristic of his postwar moment, Quaroni the experimental eclectic is thus bracketed between Persico's disenchanted reflection on the reasons for Italian artistic decadence in the 1930s and its lack of a specific "European" historicity—its isolation from the great moral and political movements of modernism—and Argan's historical examination of the fate of the prewar avant-gardes, and their postwar effects. For Argan, the problem of the modern movement was not simply linguistic, "rational" or not, but an issue of ideology and politics.

The idea of rational architecture was in this context too simple, an attempt to solve a problem on a cultural rather than a political level. Thus, the question revolved around the definition of the "liberty" called for by the modern movement. In the epilogue to the Quaroni article, Tafuri quotes Argan: "Every liberty is always liberty *from* something; and the definition of that *from* is the most difficult moment in the road toward liberty. It is very probable that the architects of the first half of our century, in Europe and America, had defined that *from* imperfectly; and from that stems the fact that the architects of today, attempting to go beyond the experience of that architecture, overcome the limits or inhibitions that will prevent them from realizing its programs, including that which was the most authentic and vital of its moral impulses."[20] For Tafuri, Quaroni had at least recognized in his early neorealism the "cultural tragedy noted by Argan," attempting to readdress the question of architectural morality in its social context.

The question of ideology now firmly on his agenda, Tafuri began to examine historically a movement that, in its own imperfect histories from Giedion to Pevsner, had tended to repeat its own myths. In a review article of Mario Manieri-Elia's 1963 anthology of William Morris, Tafuri first took on the question of the "origin" of avant-garde ideology, locating it in the very moment where Pevsner had placed it some thirty years before.[21] The merit of Manieri-Elia's introduction and selection lay, Tafuri claims, in its reinsertion into the historical understanding of the modern movement of the ideological battles of nineteenth-century England, the contradictions between the economics of the class struggle and their cultural sublimation in the neomedieval "socialism" of a Ruskin or Morris. If the task of architectural criticism was at once to *anticipate*, testing operations and methodologies hitherto unexplored, and to "*verify the historical heredity of the modern movement*" through a "systematic reexploration of the rich and fundamental material that constitutes the theoretical foundation of the modern movement," then this anthology initiated an entire project.[22] Tafuri locates its importance not merely in the way in which Manieri-Elia revealed the complexity of such foundations, but in the anthology's reminding the present antiideological epoch of "the first great ideology of the modern movement" that held "the cause of art to be the cause of the people."[23]

Revising History

As Tafuri began his inquiry into the apparent roots of modernist ideology, he also started to push back modernity, first to the eighteenth century, with studies of the late baroque in Rome and the symbolism of the Enlightenment, and then to the period called "mannerist," a term that he questioned early on. In these articles, Tafuri moved away from the active, operative criticism of the Quaroni article and book, working simultaneously on the history of ideology and on the first of the meticulous "close readings" of architectural projects and their archival evidence that would be a continuous staple of his research. While in later essays he would bring together ideological critique and object analysis in a coherent narrative, in these preliminary studies the two domains are largely separate—although in the brief introductions and footnotes to his archival research there are indications of a future synthesis.

In a 1994 interview, Tafuri recalled the Michelangelo exhibition mounted in 1964 by Bruno Zevi and Paolo Portoghesi as confirming what had become a dominant theme of Italian historical-contemporary discourse since the publication of Argan's *L'architettura barocca in Italia* in 1956: the identification of the baroque, and especially of Michelangelo and Borromini, as "the *exemplum* for contemporary architecture."[24] But it is significant that the example Tafuri selected in a 1964 article to illustrate the fundamental idea of Roman "baroque" was concerned not with the conventional "high" baroque of Bernini but with a late survival, and one designed not by an Italian but by an architect from Lisbon: the church of the Trinity in the Largo Goldoni, designed by Emanuel Rodriguez Dos Santos, a mid-eighteenth-century work representing a "particular type of continuity with seventeenth-century baroque."[25] In this *tardo barocco*, Tafuri detected the crisis that would ultimately lead to the "revolution" of the Enlightenment; its "fire," announced in the title of his article, was precipitated by both the urban context of the church and the exacerbation of architectural language as Dos Santos drew on two centuries of post-Renaissance revivals.[26] Using the project drawings in the State Archives, Tafuri reconstructed the process of design through its different stages, the method of composition and construction, from the preexisting condition of 1733 to Dos Santos's insertion of an oval church into the existing convent complex, which was then developed in three successively more elaborate versions. This represented Dos Santos's "methodological rationalization" of the interior of the church, a rationalization that was also apparent at the exterior, with its concave entrance facade set into the solid mass of the convent. For Tafuri, the "rationalization" in plan, allied with the "flexible" handling of the architectural language, was not so far from the "rationalism" of the later eighteenth century; the analytical "furor" and linguistic fantasy were realized through a "rational principle, where mathematics and geometry were no longer instruments of control, but rather elements inherent to the imagination of [the architect's] work."[27] And in a significant nod to Emil Kaufmann, he suggests: "Whence, if you wish, if also lightly—but with enormous caution—the initiation of that investigation based on the isolation of the elements, both spatial and structural, that Kaufmann, perhaps oversimplifying, wished to see take the form of *welding together* of rule and ideation in the historical meaning of his *revolutionary architects*."[28]

A cautious reader of Kaufmann, but appreciative of his attempts to draw larger conclusions from the piecemeal evidence under study and of his pioneering work in the late eighteenth-century archive, Tafuri was to "correct" Kaufmann's theses over the next few years, first in a 1964 article on Enlightenment symbolism, and then in a ground-breaking study in 1969 of the linguistic foundations of the late seventeenth-century theories of Claude Perrault and Christopher Wren, in which he examines the confrontation between architectural values and the philosophical investigation of linguistic conventions as a function of Port Royal linguistics and the Lockean theory of knowledge.[29] More importantly, in an advance on Kaufmann's arguments for autonomy, Tafuri traced the ascendency of geometry to Wren's theories of the two foundations of beauty—natural or geometrical, and customary or social taste. Kaufmann's proposition of a "geometrical" and abstract Enlightenment was undermined, Tafuri believed, by the construction of geometry acting not as a unifying element but as the initial, and fatal, stage in the development of a stylistic eclecticism, manipulated according to taste, and instrumental in the social and cultural establishment of institutions as historical signifiers.

However, Tafuri's most significant early foray into the revision of architectural history was his investigation of mannerism, or rather—given his later refusal of the term (as well as his rejection of the book he had published on the topic in 1966)—the specificity of sixteenth-century experiments in architectural language. Again these were approached, not from a rehearsal of previous theories of mannerism from Pevsner and Wittkower to Blunt, but directly, through a comparative reading of the treatises and an equally close reading of the work of Vignola.[30] The methodological problems associated with analyzing a self-conscious and critical art were formidable; their "solution" led to Tafuri's assumption that self-criticality is a modern characteristic par excellence:

*For an artistic culture as intensely critical as that of man-
nerism, the problem of the relations between operative
practice and theoretical speculation cannot but assume
problematic aspects of the highest kind. When art, in fact,
initiates itself as a problem for itself, when through an organization of form it wishes to achieve autocritical exca-
vations, when, finally, the process of configuration tends
to substitute itself for the critical process, it is inevitable
that theory finds itself in a "difficult" if not ambiguous
situation. And this is the paradoxical event that develops
over the course of the great stage of mannerism.* [31]

Such a characterization of "mannerism" as a critical, self-
reflective culture would, over the next decades, develop into a
more totalizing thesis that would parallel Tafuri's observation
on the contemporary condition which opened his last book,
Interpreting the Renaissance: "For some time now the culture of
architecture, reflecting on itself, has sensed the presence of an
original sin that demands exculpation." [32]

The Eclipse and Rise of History

Despite Tafuri's close relations with and critical assessments of
contemporary architects and planners, the tension between his
critical review of historical evidence and his critical support of
contemporary practice inevitably developed into an intellectual
confrontation, if not self-critique. The publication in 1968 of
Teorie e storia dell'architettura has been seen as a major rupture
with his previous thought, and, largely as a result of the vagaries
of translation, this book has been taken as a starting point for the
"real" Tafuri. Yet a reading of the earlier essays and books, and
their sources, demonstrates more of a continuity than a crisis.
Tafuri's omnivorous capacity to work on the entire period from
the fifteenth century to the present continued unabated until his

death, and his patient research in the archives continued to reveal aspects of the Venetian, Mantuan, and Roman renaissances side by side with analyses of the twentieth-century avant-gardes and neo-avant-gardes, their theories, projects, and urban plans. But *Teorie e storia* was in one respect a cathartic work. Summing up the work of the previous ten years; reassessing his contemporaries, both historians and architects; reviewing the nature of modernity, and of the more ideological "modernism," it marked a moment of comprehensive articulation of half-hidden thoughts. It was also, although no doubt unconsciously, a programmatic setting-out of work for the future, one that would be gradually filled in by collective and individual research in the IUAV and by Tafuri himself over the next twenty-eight years.

In this context, it was not accidental that Tafuri began his discussion of architectural history and its relations to theory and criticism with the two events that might be posited as turning points for Anglo-American thought in the 1960s: Pevsner's 1961 lecture "Modern Architecture and the Historian, or the Return of Historicism," and its transatlantic sequel, the AIA-ACSA Teacher Seminar at the Cranbrook Academy of Art in Michigan three years later. At the Cranbrook symposium the issues latent in Pevsner's lecture came to the forefront in the confrontation between Reyner Banham and Bruno Zevi.[33] Zevi, the newly appointed chair of architectural history at the reformed University School of Architecture in Rome following the student sit-ins of 1963, struck out passionately in favor of "history as a method of teaching architecture," speaking of the techniques of abstraction, spatial analysis, model-making, and quasi-laboratory "research" that would take teaching history out of the realm of the styles and put it into the service of contemporary design as an instrument of linguistic freedom.[34] Reyner Banham was equally outspoken, accusing Colin Rowe of holding on to an academic/Beaux-Arts idea of theory and claiming that the entire category "theory of architecture" had become "vacuous, empty of formal content and devices." He traced this to the "absence of those particular reasons which cause buildings to be created and cause buildings to be the precise way they are."[35]

Those "reasons" were, for Banham as for John Summerson earlier, summed up in the general word "program." Banham's argument could be seen as the last-ditch appeal of an old-guard modernist, as was that of Pevsner, were it not for the example Banham cited. This took the form of an elaboration of a quotation from the philosopher of aesthetics Susanne Langer: "'a virtual environment, the creative space of architecture, is a symbol of functional existence.' This does not mean, however, that signs of important activities, hooks for implements, convenient benches, well-planned doors, play any part in its significance. In that thought's assumption lies the error of functionalism. Symbolic expression is something miles removed from provident planning or good arrangement."[36] For Banham, symbolic expression—especially in "pop" environments—was an integral part of what he understood as architecture. He took Langer to be referring to a kind of "Shaker" or "Norwegian" environment, and he outlined the plan of a Norwegian farmhouse, containing both ritual and functional elements. He especially stressed a tree-branch that served as a hanger for the cooking pot over the hearth, an "element of random geometry" that intruded into the otherwise rigorously geometrical interior. He ended with a "confession" that Saarinen's TWA Terminal at Idlewild (now Kennedy) Airport in New York, which had seemed to him on first sight a "grotesque" "piece of formalism," had emerged through experience and use as far superior to the endless corridors of O'Hare International, Chicago; and from here he admitted to a final acceptance of Le Corbusier's Ronchamp.[37]

For Tafuri, the debates at these events, which resumed the various strains of and between contemporary historical interpretation, all in some way "operative" in his terms, pointed to the fundamental difficulties of writing the history of "the radically *anti-historical* phenomenon" that is modern architecture.[38] Participants at the AIA conference, including Sibyl Moholy-Nagy, Bruno Zevi, and Banham, all agreed, from their very different standpoints, that the historical revivalism emerging after the collapse of the International Style—and practiced by Saarinen, Johnson, Rudolph, Kahn, Johansen, Yamasaki, and even Gropius—was a slight affair, a superficial resurrection of the styles. But Tafuri believed this was too simple a response: the architects' apparently "historical" answer to supposed "antihistorical" international modernism seemed to him to obscure the fundamentally antihistorical nature of the "new historicism"; the fundamental problem was the very antihistoricism attributed to the avant-gardes of the 1920s in the first place. Tafuri argues in *Teorie e storia*, "It would be better to trace the process of development synthetically, returning to its true origin: to the very revolution of modern art in the work of the Tuscan humanists of the fifteenth century."[39] Here, at the outset of Tafuri's career as a critical historian, was introduced the premise that would be the foundation of his modern history: that the real break came not with the eighteenth-century Enlightenment, nor with the industrial and political revolutions of the nineteenth, nor again with the avant-garde revolts of the early twentieth, but rather with those two emblematic figures of rupture with the medieval past, Brunelleschi and Alberti. Between this opening salvo in *Teorie e storia* and his last book, *Ricerca del Rinascimento*, the consistent focus of Tafuri's inquiry was to elucidate the complex filiations and deformations of an avant-garde tradition that was, in his terms, at least six centuries old.

Tafuri's strategy in returning the origins of the modern to the Renaissance was both historical, in the sense that only such a move would allow for an open reinterpretation of both the Renaissance and the modern, and polemical, in that it directly countered the critique of the 1960s "return to historicism" itself. For how could Pevsner advance all the authenticity of avant-garde modernism against historicism if modernism could be seen in the context of a fundamental "de-historicization" (*de-storicizzazione*) of architecture beginning with Brunelleschi?[40] In this strategy Brunelleschi and Alberti played, according to Tafuri, a paradigmatic role, the one breaking radically with the medieval past in order to construct a "linguistic code and a symbolic system" based on the ancients, the other attempting to construct the rational syntactic form of this system literally to "actualize" historical values. In his characterization of this revolution, Tafuri presciently (and deliberately) formulates it in such a way as to provide a radical critique of 1960s historiography, enmeshed as it was in the (false) dialectic of "historicism" versus "modernism":

> *Between a lexicon, such as that of Brunelleschi, based on the* fragments *of the classical world . . . and the philological recuperation of that classicism (as that documented by the* De re aedificatoria *of Alberti, the studies of Giuliano da Sangallo, and the complex activity of Bramante in Rome), there exists the same distance as that between those who deploy the evocative power of* citations *and* allusions *to substantiate an independent discourse in order to* construct *a new reality and those who are absorbed in recuperating the exact significance of these citations to cover the provocative delusions of reality, in order to reevoke the structures of a heroic past in their concreteness, contrasting them polemically to contemporary hypocrisies, to defend an artistic revolution that feels itself in danger, locking it up in the ivory tower of a historicism that has become an end in itself.*[41]

For Brunelleschi, Tafuri argues, the invention of a new symbolic system and its investment in autonomous objects laid open the medieval town as a site for intervention, architectural structures inserted as critical ruptures with the past and shifters of significance for the present. By contrast, Tafuri casts Alberti as a "restorer" seeking to reinvent the code of antique unity, who nevertheless compromises with the preexisting system. In this way Tafuri characterizes the double allegiance of the Renaissance as caught between two potentially opposed strategies that will resonate throughout the next three centuries:

> *On the one hand, the will to establish historically an* anti-historical code, *like the one of the revived classicism; on the other, the temptation—repressed, but continuously cropping up—to compromise and dirty one's hands with the very medieval and Gothic languages disempowered by the entire of classicism, in its apodictic declarations, inasmuch as they were guilty of betraying the givens of the* true and beautiful *of the* Antique, *elected to a* second and truer Nature.[42]

The "ghost of the Middle Ages," whether posturing as repressed history or possible revival, haunts the experimentalism of mannerism and the "bricolage" of Borromini, to the point that Tafuri can see the eclecticism of the late baroque, and the intrusion of the non- and anticlassical into the classical, as "a prophetic anticipation of the attitudes typical of the twentieth-century avant-gardes: the *collage* of *memories* extrapolated from their historical contexts [that] finds structure and a semantic location within the frame of an organic space autonomously constructed."[43] Hence the importance of Perrault, and even more of Wren, as Tafuri sought a "natural" geometric unifier for the eclecticism of his historico-political languages.

In this analysis, paradoxically enough, it is the Enlightenment, site of Kaufmann's abstract modernism, that prepared architecture for the dominance of historicism. Once separated from any remaining vestige of an "organic" classicism, and supported by the archaeological recovery of a "real" history, architecture is now open to the play of historical revival as having an absolute value in itself, calibrated according to the demands of a new civic order. Marx's celebrated analysis of the role of history in revolution is enacted here in architectural terms: the history that "weighs like an alp upon the brain of the living" now "glorified new struggles," enacting "a new historic scene in such time-honored disguise and with such borrowed language."[44] Tafuri separates architecture from history and offers two solutions: the one exemplified by the "eclecticism" of Piranesi; the other by the antisymbolism of a Durand. In both, the unity of the "classical" object is broken, either through a rejection of symbolism in favor of a desperate clinging to the signs of a lost past, or through the deliberate ignoring of history altogether in favor of a combinatorial, compositional logic based on geometry. In this way, finally, Tafuri joins the "eclipse of the *object*" to Hegel's declaration of the "death of art," and thence to the "crisis of historicity" manifested by modernism, as in the work of Mondrian, van Doesburg, Dada, and Sant'Elia.

Tafuri's semantic analysis of the contradictions inherent in historical revival since the Renaissance, setting the roots of modernist antihistoricism in the first attempts to authorize the "invention" of a new antiquity, thus formed the foundation of his research into the Renaissance, allowing him the freedom to investigate its crises and continuities as if it were an integral and, more importantly, foundational moment in the history of the avant-gardes. Against the (then) contemporary preoccupation with the post-Giedion understanding of architecture as space, Tafuri took note of the various structuralisms, from semiology to information science, that were proposing a more "scientific" observation of the architectural object. Opposing a history that, in its very narrative forms, supported a supposedly organic idea of progress and sustained "modernity" in architecture in a seamless conjunction with the ideology of capitalist development as a whole, Tafuri saw in semiology, at least, a means of cutting through the ceaseless flow of criticism in the service of architecture and of producing the outlines of an "operative" criticism that would reendow history with an objective and materialist basis. And while he was to react equally strongly against the subsequent mythologies of "architecture *as* language," the terms of semiological critique were present in his work to the end. Indeed, in *Teorie e storia* the issue of language, applied to the theorization and interpretation of architecture itself, emerges as a leitmotif of Tafuri's analysis as a "scientific" counter to either the neo-Kantian formalist tradition that culminated in Wölfflin, or the neo-Hegelian tradition that culminated in Riegl.

Tafuri found support on this point in Sergio Bettini's analysis of architectural history as semantic criticism. Bettini, in an article published in 1958 in the second volume of *Zodiac*, titled "Semantic Criticism and the Historical Continuity of European Architecture," had written: "Whoever exercises the practice of criticism of art or architecture sooner or later recognizes the opportunity for an attentive semantic control of the language adopted: that is to say, of the instrument which serves them to practice their own criticism."[45] Tafuri cites this article in *Teorie e storia* to confirm his belief that architecture might in fact be a language, subject to its laws and its critical examination: "Art is not representation but it is, itself, the formal structure of history. This is true even if we assume art is a language: we can then say that the language of art is the morphology of culture."[46] He also cites Bettini's introduction to the prescient 1953 Italian translation of Alois Riegl's *Spätrömische Kunstindustrie* (Late Roman art industry), in which

Bettini suggests that the "language" of architecture is not simply a symbolic or iconographic system in the terms of Panofsky, but rather a language in its own right; and more importantly, is, as far as history was concerned, *the* language:

> In Bettini's fundamental introduction to the Italian translation (1953) of Riegl's Spätrömische Kunstindustrie, the structuralist tone takes on the aspect of a precisely calibrated critical method. Bettini (and not only in this essay) demonstrates his assimilation—almost alone in the Italian cultural scene of this time—of the contributions of the Anglo-Saxon semantic schools, from Tarski to Carnap, and to the Meaning of Meaning by Ogden and Richards, but has explicitly recognized the linguistic character of artistic production, linking the problem of criticism to what he terms the "paradox of metalanguage."[47]

That language is the internal explication of architecture, and that this language is in turn "history" as construed by society, might well be seen as the intellectual premise of Tafuri's formal analysis of architecture for the rest of his career.

But *Teorie e storia*—the combined result of having punctured the balloon of "history in the service of architecture" and the mediated assessments of the ruling "scientific" methodologies—while preparing the ground for Tafuri's preferred "instrumental criticism," does not necessarily provide a clear picture of what a nonoperative history might be, in either narrative or subjective terms. Indeed, the obvious influence of structuralist and poststructuralist theories on history seems, for Tafuri, to lead to a kind of stasis where the rejection of the overarching narrative leaves no narrative in its place. Caught, like Nietzsche, in the endless relays between "monumental," "antiquarian," and "critical" history, Tafuri embraces the third, but at the same time inherits its dangers—as Nietzsche put it, while bringing the past "before the tribunal [of history], scrupulously examining it and finally condemning it," unmitigated critique "takes the knife to its roots."[48] The gradual resolution of this tension, or rather its empirical and conceptual testing over many years and in different contexts at diverse scales, is the subsequent history of Tafuri's own practice.

Ideology and Utopia

Just as it is not possible to establish a Political Economy based on class, but only a class critique of Political Economy, so it is not given to "anticipate" a class architecture (an architecture "for a liberated society") but only possible to introduce a class critique of architecture. *Nothing beyond this from the—sectarian and partial—point of view of a rigorous Marxism.*

—Manfredo Tafuri, *Teorie e storia*

In the late 1960s and 1970s in Italy and from the 1980s in the United States, it became commonplace to believe that Tafuri was a Marxist, and to see his contributions to history as a model of a rigorous "Marxist" historiography, albeit of the special kind understood as Marxist in post-1968 Italy. This view of Tafuri emerged most strongly after the publication of his seminal essay "Per una critica dell'ideologia architettonica" in 1969, and was reinforced in his preface to the second edition of *Teorie e storia* a year later.[49] Through his implied reference to Marx's *Critique of Political Economy* and *German Ideology* in the essay's title, Tafuri evidently wished to reinforce his claims for a "scientific" and therefore critical history as against the operative criticism that tended to support architectural production, and further to encourage the idea of a critical, or even revolutionary, architecture. As he remarks, "Any attempt to overthrow the institution [of architecture], the discipline, leading us into the most heightened negations or the most paradoxical ironies—as the case of Dada and surrealism teaches us—is destined to see itself overturned into a positive contribution, into a 'constructive' avantgarde, into an ideology all the more positive because all the more dramatically critical and self-critical."[50] But in this passage we can understand architecture not simply as a case of the design of buildings or the planning of towns, but rather as an institution. And as an institution, as a "discipline," subject to all the regulations of bourgeois society and the capitalist state, "architecture" is a fundamentally modern phenomenon, one born with, and in support of, all the advanced institutions of developed capitalist societies. In this sense, "architecture"—the totality of structures, systems, ideas, practices that are bound up with buildings designed and built by architects—is an ideology. It takes its place beside law, religion, and the rest as the mystification of material practice. In this assertion, as he wrote in the preface to the English translation of *Progetto e utopia* in 1976, Tafuri thought he would have avoided subsequent claims that he had produced "an apocalyptic prophecy, 'the expression of renunciation,'" leading to "the ultimate pronouncement of the 'death of architecture.'"[51] In his mind, from the Marxist position of the journal *Contropiano*, all this was evident. But his readers in architecture, separating his essay from this context, simply found him to be "against" architecture purely and simply.

Tafuri also made it clear that as a work of ideological criticism, "Per una critica dell'ideologia architettonica" had to be placed within the wider context of political theory in Marxist thought from 1960 to 1969: the studies of Fortini (*Verifica dei poteri*), Tronti, and above all of his friends Alberto Asor Rosa and Massimo Cacciari. From the standpoint of 1969, then, Tafuri was proclaiming not a death of architecture but a conscious recognition of "architecture's" role as an ideology, and with this a recognition of the fading of this role, its developing uselessness for capitalist development. What interested him was not any revolutionary role for a new or radical architecture, but "the precise identification of those tasks which capitalist development [had] taken away from architecture." The drama of contemporary architecture, rather than being located in its search for a new ideological, reformist, utopian, or developmental role, lay in its "sublime uselessness," leading to its recourse in "form without utopia." For this uselessness Tafuri had no nostalgia or regret ("because when the role of a discipline ceases to exist, to try and stop the course of things is only regressive utopia, and of the worst kind"), nor was he making a prophecy ("because the process is actually taking place daily before our very eyes"). And neither capitalism nor any existing postrevolutionary society had yet found a replacement—an "institutionally defined role for the technicians charged with building activity."[52]

What Tafuri is calling "architectural ideology" is that definition of architecture, current since at least the late eighteenth century, as something above and beyond mere building. The philosopher d'Alembert had said it in his introduction to the *Encyclopédie:* "Architecture in the eyes of a philosopher is but the embellished mask of one of man's greatest needs."[53] That is, in the eyes of a philosopher dedicated to the eradication of masks and embellishment in favor of naked truth, architecture is a rhetorical cover for what later architects were to call function. Ruskin repeated this definition in a more idealist sense when he distinguished between building as shelter and a work of architecture that raised the soul; or Pevsner in his notorious "Lincoln cathedral is a work of architecture; a bicycle shed is a building."[54] Hence the "ideology" of architecture is precisely what distinguishes itself from its own material practice. In this sense, Tafuri logically calls for a scientific analysis of building practices as a preliminary for establishing what might emerge as a role for the "technicians of building activity" after the revolution. The role of the historian is then to trace the complicated evolution of architecture as an ideology from the Renaissance on, in Tafuri's time frame, and to demonstrate all the contradictions embodied and exploded along the way. And first in line were the contradictions of so-called radical or avant-garde experiments to invent "other" architectures, which had turned so quickly into regressive utopias or new forms of ideology.

Anxiety

To dispel anxiety by understanding and internalizing its causes: this would seem to be one of the principal ethical imperatives of bourgeois art.
—Manfredo Tafuri, "Toward a Critique of Architectural Ideology"

The words "anxiety" and "anguish" recur throughout Tafuri's writing. "To dispel anxiety by understanding and internalizing its causes," ran the opening lines of *Progetto e utopia* as of the essay "Per una critica dell'ideologia architettonica": "this would seem to be one of the principal ethical imperatives of bourgeois art" (*Allontare l'angoscia comprendendone e introiettandone le cause: questo sembra essere uno dei principali imperativi etivi dell'arte borghese*).[55] Later in the same essay, Tafuri, as if citing himself in quotation marks, will use the same phrase—"dispelling anxiety by internalizing its causes"—with reference to Le Corbusier's Obus project for Algiers.[56] The same preoccupation reappears in mature form in the foreword to *Ricerca del Rinascimento:* "The theoretical anxieties [*ansie*] of the nineteenth century already expressed a sort of anguish [*angoscia*] when confronted by an architecture that was becoming increasingly self-referential." Tafuri asks: "If the origins of the aforementioned 'anguish' [*agonia*] are to be located in the humanist affirmation of the subject, how can one hope for a recovery based on subjective volition?"[57] What is being registered in these quasi-nostalgic terms—anguish and decline—is, according to Tafuri, no less than the crumbling of the a priori foundations of referentiality seen to have been established so firmly in Renaissance and baroque art—the era of the "triumph of linear perspective" and "naturalism." In his argument, the "anguish" already being exhibited during the nineteenth century was seen by the twentieth-century avantgardes as a form of liberation, even as their opponents were casting the notion of "loss" and "decline" in terms that, as Tafuri remarks, seemed to register the "aesthetic equivalent of a homicide or a mass catastrophe."[58] Yet, considered from the point of view of a historian rather than that of a nostalgic memory artist, such terms would seem to "exhibit a surfeit of meaning." Instead, Tafuri suggests that one replace the term "anguish" with the more neutral term "accomplishment": thus the "accomplishment" of the "referent"—the very triumph of the so-called Renaissance would also be accompanied by its successive displacement. Modernism, then, would be a displacement of referentiality, rather than a loss.

In this way, Tafuri counters the "foundationalist nostalgia" common to modernists—who would celebrate this "loss"—and their opponents. The commonplaces of postmodernism—such as the "compulsion to quote" that results in the fragmentation of language—are seen to be only part of a more general reflection on the "eclipse" of totality and plenitude that was the object also of high modernism: and thus Le Corbusier's and Mies van der Rohe's "interrogations of the very principles of European rationality" join James Stirling's "ironies" as symptoms of the same "displacement" of the referent.[59]

Against this "horizon," Tafuri situates his researches on the Renaissance: "Formulated in the space where the present finds its problems, they attempt a dialogue with the 'era of representation.'"[60] But, in distinction to former historians of the Renaissance from Wölfflin to Wittkower, themselves largely taken up with the myth of "decline" and "eclipse," of "anguish" and "loss," Tafuri offers no preconceived version of this "representation" nor of the "Renaissance" that previously characterized this period. What he does offer is a series of investigations of considerable narrative complexity into the debates that swirled around referentiality at the moment when they were not yet conscious of being debates in a postconceived "humanism" or "perspectivity." Their politics and aesthetics are presented, so to speak, in the raw; their shifts and turns of individual and group position analyzed in terms that at once join them to economic, opportunistic, and intellectual power struggles. History in this sense, and compared to the grand universal historicisms of the nineteenth and twentieth centuries, is seen as a "weak power" that, rather than resolving the problems of the past in a momentarily satisfying solution, leaves them "living and unresolved, unsettling our present."[61]

This is the question Tafuri addresses in the foreword to the *Ricerca*, where the question of "perspectivity" becomes activated not simply as an analogue to the historian's method, but in terms of its own history: precisely, the relations between perspective theory and practice and the question of referentiality. Tafuri's meditation on perspective is set in a dense, two-page summary of the "project" that had marked his entire career, which he attempts to bind to the contents of the *Ricerca*. On the surface, it is at once a diagnosis of contemporary and modern architectural culture and a hypothesis for its historical reformulation. For Tafuri, in 1992 as in 1968, the problem is signaled by a "culture of architecture reflecting on itself," an internalized discourse of meaning that continuously identifies a "crisis" but fails to comprehend the way in which the nature of this so-called crisis is linked to culture as a whole, and equally refuses to acknowledge the unoriginality of its call to arms. But where in 1968 this crisis was characterized under the semiotic sign of "meaning," in 1992 the question is raised in the context of the postmodern (what Tafuri calls the "hypermodern"). Tafuri argues that "the current theoretical *habitus* does not differ considerably from others that have determined twentieth-century aesthetic choices; in fact, it reproduces the familiar compulsion to overturn the dominant order"[62]—replicating the sense of crisis felt by the historical avant-gardes as a function of a break from history itself, accompanied by a critical awareness of an "anguish of the referent," or, in Walter Benjamin's terms, the "decline of the aura."

Certainly in the *Ricerca* Tafuri seems to "accomplish" what he had set out as the historical project in *Teorie e storia*—to counter the avant-garde "myth is against history" (as Barthes put it) with history against myth, to "rescue historicity from the web of the past," where modernism "from the very beginning, in the European avant-garde movements [presented itself] as a true challenge to history."[63] Uniting Dada and de Stijl, Kahn and Rietveld, under this antihistorical umbrella—all movements that attempted to substitute the "myth of Order" for historicism—Tafuri acted to reinstate history, to resist the "eclipse" of history that had been the dream of modernism. In this way the studies in *Venezia e il Rinascimento* (1985) and *Ricerca del Rinascimento* work toward a redefinition of architectural history on multiple levels: interdisciplinary and interinstitutional, they study "the nodes where events, times, and mentalities intersect," calibrating the ways in which "political decisions, religious anxieties, the arts and sciences, and the *res aedificatoria* become irrevocably interwoven."[64]

Disenchantments

Total disenchantment produces great historians. And Manfredo Tafuri was a great historian of this kind.

—Alberto Asor Rosa, "Critique of Ideology and Historical Practice"

Despite Tafuri's apparent accomplishment of his historical project, embedded in his examination of the notion of "loss" and consequent "anguish" is a sense that the historian too is implicated; that the "loss" spoken of with such rhetorical surfeit also haunts him in such a way as to raise difficult questions of interpretation and historical distance. While in his early works, such as *Progetto e utopia*, Tafuri makes it clear that the "loss" or "disenchantment" he speaks of is one construed by bourgeois ideology, and stems from what social scientists like Max Weber understood as the *Wertfreiheit* or value-free liberal ideal, in the foreword to *Ricerca* his historical perspective has shifted somewhat. In 1968, to take one example, Tafuri claimed Walter Benjamin, in his recognition of Baudelaire's experience of the city as "shock," to be a companion in the struggle to define the historical parameters of modernity and the modernism that was its representation. In 1992, however, Tafuri groups Benjamin with other nostalgic bourgeois theorists of loss, including some who seem ideologically opposed. Thus in his discussion of the myths that have surrounded modernity and its "decline," Tafuri states: "Fortunately for us, the reception of specific moments in the history of modern criticism permits a 'bracketing off' of the ideological sign originally stamped on them. For example, it is difficult indeed not to sense the close affinity between Sedlmayr's intuition of loss, Walter Benjamin's concept of the 'decline of the aura,' and Robert Klein's reflections on the 'anguish of the referent.'"[65] Such a "bracketing off" certainly allows Tafuri to construe a more generalized version of the modern anguish complex, even to trace it to the Renaissance; but in a deliberately shocking way, it also ignores historical distinctions of an "ideological" nature that are not as simple as the quoted "slogans" imply. In relation to the received history of political ideas, Tafuri's "bracketing" begs the question: Is it indeed possible, or intellectually responsible, to bring together, except on a purely linguistic level, the nostalgic despair of a National Socialist ideologue, the resigned modernism of a German Jewish Marxist, and the phenomenological disquiet of a Romanian Jewish exile in Paris—the first, a melancholic survivor but unrepentant conservative; the second, an exile on the run from the Nazis; the third, a survivor of, in his own words, "compulsory labor for Jews," and a refugee from dictatorship after the war? Or, for that matter, can one join the sense of Sedlmayr's "loss of center," which is tied to a prognosis of doom, to that of Benjamin's loss of "aura," tied to a materialist understanding of the media and its political potential, and that of Klein's perspective theory, which traced the "agony" of the disappearance of reference (in the emergence of abstract art) to the problems raised by a subject with a fixed point of view? It is interesting in this regard that Tafuri himself, perhaps for reasons of rhetorical symmetry, translates what Klein actually calls an "agony of reference" into an "anguish of the referent," thus shifting the entire argument from the subjective process of referentiality to the object of signification and historically reifying what in Klein's terms was a living process activated by human subjects.

The pervasive sense of anguish that Tafuri descries in modern bourgeois society is, as he makes explicit, intimately connected to what Max Weber termed the "disenchantment" of the world as experienced by the modern intellectual. Pervasive throughout all of Weber's writing, this theme was summarized succinctly in his late lecture "Wissenschaft als Beruf" (Science as a vocation) of 1919: "The fate of our times is characterized by rationalization and, above all, by the 'disenchantment of the world'" (*Entzauberung der Welt*).[66] This disenchantment—a consequence of the stripping away of the "mythical" in the modern, a mythical that for Weber gave the human condition a "genuine plasticity"—was, as Tafuri illustrates in the third chapter of *Architecture and Utopia*, a logical result of the triumph of rationalism, the "freedom from values" inherent in the acceptance of science as the dominating force in the world. Tafuri's historical project, on this level, was to reveal this disenchantment for what it was, and to see, with all the veils of ideology stripped away, the various avant-garde attempts to mirror this crisis of values as so many buffers against the anguish and shock of their disappearance. "Disenchantment," whether Weberian or later, thence became a leitmotif of Tafuri's analysis. To take only one example from *Theories and History*, Tafuri labels the late work of Paul Rudolph as disenchanted: "the 'signs' used by Rudolph . . . [are] disquieting for their skeptical disenchantment."[67] Tafuri here seems to be echoing Weber's observation that "disenchantment" had produced a situation, for better or for worse, where "our greatest art is intimate rather than monumental," leading to Weber's conclusion that "if we try to compel and to 'invent' a monumental sense of art, lamentable monstrosities will be produced."[68]

But the "disenchantment"—literally "demythologization"—described by Tafuri seems also to have had deeper roots; if, as Weber remarked, a world without myths was the common inheritance of postrationalist intellectuals, Tafuri himself can hardly be exempted from the group. As he revealed in an interview with Françoise Véry in 1976, reflecting on the writing of *Theories and History*, he was far from having a critical distance from his own version of disenchantment. At the time of writing, he states: "We were locked in a castle under a spell, the keys were lost, in a linguistic maze—the more we looked for a direction, the more we entered magic halls full of tortured dreams. . . . Once you entered the maze, Ariadne's thread was broken, and to go on from there you simply had to ignore Ariadne's thread."[69] The book was written in the space of what Tafuri called "magic halls full of tortured dreams," where Sade and Piranesi conjured their visions against those of Enlightenment reason, in a contemporary context that seemed to echo that of the late eighteenth century—Tafuri cites Godard's *Une femme est une femme* and Peter Weiss's *Marat/Sade*. Indeed, disenchantment was, as Asor Rosa points out, a fundamental characteristic of Tafuri's stance as historian:

> *Once the phase of the "critique of architectural ideology" came to a close, this left behind in the mind of its theoretician a sense of total disenchantment, as if he had become a total stranger from the mechanism of values, procedures and connivance embedded in any discipline with an academic status. . . . Leaving the "critique of ideology" behind did not mean returning to architectural ideology, not even to the discipline closer to architectural historiography; rather it meant understanding that in this field too one should come as close as possible to the certainty of the datum, resisting both for the present and the past, all ideological seductions. . . . There is a link between the . . . inexorable demolition of all present and past structures of self-illusion and self-mystification—and the full revelation of a . . . political vocation. . . . Once no veil any longer exists, all that remains is to study, understand, and represent the mechanisms of reality [with the instruments of objective inquiries]. Total disenchantment produces great historians.*[70]

The historian of disenchantment, himself disenchanted, thus is enabled to enter the disenchanted realm of history without ideology. Perhaps it is here, imbricated with the stance of the historian without ideology, that Tafuri finds himself on the interior of a discourse for which he stands not only as its historian but as its exemplary figure. In this sense, within the "bracketing" of the anguish and loss of a Sedlmayr, a Benjamin, and a Klein, and despite his understandable desire to restrain the "surfeit" of meaning they disclose, might we not now include Tafuri himself?

And by the time Tafuri wrote the foreword to *Ricerca* in 1992, the historian of disenchantment was sufficiently identified with the disenchanted historian to enable these strange combinations, the result, it seems, of Tafuri's sense of a more urgent and general purpose that called for a consideration of the century's disenchantment "as a whole," and no longer concerned with small discrimination on behalf of a "good" or a "bad" kind. Thus Benjamin is paired with his apparent opposite, Sedlmayr, and Tafuri is enabled to push back to the Renaissance what had seemed to him in the first place the provisional origins of the crisis of modernity. The "long Renaissance" is given an overarching position above the successive "modernisms" that it houses; the collapse of perspective certainty as a guarantee of the central position of the humanist subject is identified as a direct outcome of, and contemporaneous with, the verification of the perspective rule itself.

Thus, in the first chapter of the *Ricerca*, the fiction of the "humanist" Brunelleschi is unmasked in the retelling of the "cruel and unreal comedy" that reveals the architect-perspectivist as an unscrupulous manipulator of human "identities" in the service of destabilizing identity itself. Similarly we realize, in Tafuri's early essays on Alberti, that it is the troubled, nightmare-ridden figure of a sociopath attempting to use architecture to steer his way through imminent chaos that takes hold over the serene mathematical and harmonious visions of a Wittkowerian analysis. In this unnerving vision of architecture as experiment conceived as a metaphoric game with human subjects (and for Tafuri, all designs are experiments in the real, scientific sense), the calculated "shocks" of the modernist avant-garde, the ruptures of Piranesian space, and the anamorphoses of the late baroque take their place within the same frame and as symptomatic events in the same systemic history of perspectivism. On these grounds, it is true that, whatever the motives or conclusions of the analyses, Sedlmayr, Benjamin, and Klein agree, as pathologists studying the same corpse may agree on the symptoms but vehemently reject the others' diagnoses. Tafuri's historical "bracketing," then, does not refuse political or ideological distinctions, but rather understands all such distinctions as pertinent to an autopsy of the age as a whole. For such a task, a Weber has to be accompanied by his Spengler; a Sedlmayr by his Benjamin; a Klein by his Tafuri.

5 POSTMODERN OR *POSTHISTOIRE?*

Now there is no longer any internal development within art!
It is all up with art history based upon the logic of meaning,
and even with any consistency of absurdities. The process of
development has been completed, and what comes now is al-
ready in existence: the confused syncretism of all styles and
possibilities—posthistory.
—Arnold Gehlen, *Zeit-Bilder,* 1961

The history traced in this book, one of a consistent desire to re-
negotiate the terms with which postwar architecture treated its
own and previous history, was on one level a simple product of
modernism itself. Modernism, as the story goes, refused history in favor of abstraction; its functional promises and technological fetishism were nothing but failed utopias of progress; its
ideology was out of touch with the people, if not antihumanis-
tic. Its formal vocabularies were sterile and uncommunicative,
which is why the verities of so-called postmodernism seemed
appealing, insofar as they were apparently in direct opposition.
In the myth of the postmodernists, history was welcomed back
as a counter to abstraction; any pretense to functional program
was abandoned as overdeterministic and controlling; its language, drawn from the roots of humanistic architecture or the

explicit iconography of advertising, was popular, if not populist. At its most extreme, as supported by a scion of the British
royal family, it sought to return us to a more comfortable past
rendered out of the whole cloth of classical (or better, village)
style. Postmodernism was, it claimed, finally in touch with the
people. In this formulation, modernism appears to have been
out of history and against history, and, in its strident, avant-
garde attempts to break with history, was nothing but a failed
utopia of escape from history. Postmodernism, on the other
hand, seemed to accept history as value and speech, and insisted on the fundamental continuity of history, a history that
comfortably ties us back to our humanistic roots and thereby
renders us, once again, more human.

And yet a closer inspection of the historical stances of the
moderns and their postwar supporters has revealed the discon-
certing fact that, far from rejecting "history" as such, modernism
perhaps respected it too much. In asserting the need to break with
the past, whether in futurist, neoplasticist, purist, or constructivist terms, the modernist avant-gardes in fact understood history
as a fundamental force, an engine of the social world. Whether
conceived in Hegelian or Marxist terms, as transcendentalist or
dialectical, history *moved*, and society moved along with it. If the
avant-gardes had any illusions, they were founded on the belief
that this movement might be anticipated, its force applied to new
and anticipated ends. Even the abstraction of modernist vocabulary was derived from the deep respect modernism evinced for
history—a history that, from Heinrich Wölfflin to Bruno Zevi,
searched for essences and structures rather than stylistic affects.
Indeed, it would be true to say that never was history more alive
than in its so-called modernist rejection.

In this vein, however, postmodernism might be said to have
demonstrated a profound disdain for history in favor of an ahis-

torical *myth*. Its ascriptions of "humanism" to the Renaissance were, after all, little more than the worn-out shards of mandarin connoisseurs, from Bernard Berenson to Geoffrey Scott, the very endgame of the Renaissance revival, with the Renaissance itself a fabrication based on mid-nineteenth-century myths of glorious Italy from Jules Michelet to Jacob Burckhardt. Postmodernism's willingness to ransack history, as well as billboards, for its vocabulary revealed it indeed as fundamentally disrespectful of history, and even more disrespectful of the present. For a prince to imagine a restored country village and his architect to imagine a restored classical Atlantis were two sides of an aristocratic illusion founded on an antidemocratic, if not antisocial, ideology of the postromantic period. Whether peasants in cloaks or intellectuals in togas, society was imagined as stable and in place, with no untidy disruptions forced by industrial or political conflict. In fact, conflict was surprisingly absent from postmodern models of society and culture; its "history" was, as Manfredo Tafuri suspected, a history "without tears," where the opposition bluntly stated by Le Corbusier as "Architecture or Revolution" was finally resolved in favor of architecture.

To think as a modernist, then, would be to think of history as an active and profoundly disturbing force; to take history on its own terms; realistically or idealistically to tangle with history and wrestle it into shape. It would be, indeed, to think historically. To think as a postmodernist, by contrast, would be to ignore everything that makes history history, and selectively to pick and choose whatever authorizing sign fits the moment. History is used and abused in postmodernism; it is feared and confronted in modernism.

But the historical field after 1945 is more complex than such an oversimplified binary opposition might imply. For, starting with Kaufmann and continuing with Rowe, Banham, and Tafuri, the effort to overcome the polemics of modernism's willed break with history was itself a profoundly counterhistorical move. To imply, as Kaufmann did, that the Enlightenment and its geometries of reason were forms of the eternal modern, or as Rowe did, that the ambiguities of mannerism were in some way reemergent in modernism, or as Banham did, that history constructed a trajectory for itself that might be graphed into its "future," or finally as Tafuri did, that modernism was simply the end result of an epistemological break between the medieval and Renaissance worlds, was to imply that history had in some sense come to completion. If the end might be predicted, or indeed had arrived, then the future was to be bereft of all but repetition.

Here, postwar "histories" of modernism join with the commonly understood phenomena of "postmodernism" within a long-established tradition of what has been called *posthistoire* thought. Invented as an idea if not as a term (historians disagree as to whether the word can be found in his voluminous works) by the mathematician Antoine-Augustin Cournot, "posthistoire" was applied to the moment when a human creation (whether an institution or an object) reached the stage when there was no possibility of its further development—when all that could be done was its endless perfecting. The "posthistorical" phase, as Cournot called it, followed the prehistorical and the historical, and was an inevitable endpoint of all cultures, already demonstrated by the static nature of Chinese bureaucratic society over the last millennium.[1] For Cournot—and it is not impossible that he, or an account of his theories, was known to Le Corbusier—all cultural and social objects, from institutions to buildings and artworks, developed into types and type forms in posthistorical periods. In this sense, the idea of *posthistoire* was conceived at the height of historicism's own apparent dominance: it was, in fact, a profoundly historicist conception, the inevitable result of historical thought.

As it was to be received in the twentieth century, however, *posthistoire* was less a historical than a counterhistorical idea, representing for the disenchanted intellectuals of the 1930s and 1940s a kind of finalism akin to that already developed in post-Darwinian biology. It stood for an ending, a conclusion of all movement, and thus for an end to any hope. As the Belgian philosopher Hendrick de Man described it, writing after the Second World War: "The term posthistorical seems adequate to describe what happens when an institution or a cultural achievement ceases to be historically active and productive of new qualities, and becomes purely receptive or eclectically imitative. Thus understood Cournot's notion of the posthistorical would . . . fit the cultural phase that, following a 'fulfillment of sense,' has become 'devoid of sense.' The alternative then is, in biological terms, either death or mutation."[2] From Hendrick de Man (and, we might hazard, his nephew Paul De Man) to Arnold Gehlen and Gianni Vattimo, the concept evidently contained the potential to destabilize and criticize the dominant historicist tendencies of the late nineteenth century from within. And it was a concept especially suited for the characterization of the history of art, which is, in a way, a history of things that, through stylistic or functional development, readily become thought of as "perfected." Thus, for Gehlen and de Man, *posthistoire* represented a kind of endgame toward which everything they looked at seemed to be tending. They saw a relentless stasis, an endless return of the same, an impossibility of breaking out of the iron frame of bureaucracy and politics, and a corresponding search for charisma—the leader or the event that would break open the possibility of a different and more active future; thence their fascination with both mass movements of workers on the one hand and with Hitler's program on the other.

If, in the post-Nietzschean terms of Gianni Vattimo, *posthistoire* is simply a recognition of the modern world as it is—a

world of change without change, mutability without mutability—
then "posthistoire" is a concept that allows the description of "the
experience of the end of history." Taking his cue from Gehlen,
who found the term useful to sum up the mentality that followed
postmodern disillusionment in the great nineteenth-century
narratives of historical progress—the moment, as Gehlen says,
"when progress becomes routine"—Vattimo sees such routiniza-
tion in the developments of technology and consumerism that,
while continuously renewed, nevertheless stay the same:

> There is a profound "immobility" in the technological
> world which science fiction writers have often portrayed
> as the reduction of every experience of reality to an ex-
> perience of images (no one ever really meets anyone else;
> instead, everyone watches everything on a television
> screen while alone at home). This same phenomenon can
> already be sensed in the air-conditioned, muffled silence
> in which computers work.

> Flattened out, simultaneous, the world appears de-
> historicized. What made us "modern"—i.e. the experience
> of living every day in a narrative history of progress and
> development reinforced by the daily newspaper—now
> comes to a halt. The "master" narrative, once a secu-
> larization of religious salvation, now fails, and multiple
> other possible narratives rise up.[3]

In the context of our argument, it is significant that Vattimo
goes beyond other *posthistoire* thinkers in order to join the end-
of-history argument to the emergence of postmodernism. He
specifies: "What legitimates postmodernist theories and makes
them worthy of discussion is the fact that their claim of a radical
'break' with modernity does not seem unfounded as long as these

observations on the posthistorical character of contemporary existence are valid."[4]

———

Thus we are presented with the end of modernity and the end of architectural history, respectively, as the immediate corollary of a postmodern condition. In this way we might see postmodernism as a special moment in *posthistoire* thought or, better, as a special case of *posthistoire* thought in architectural terms. Indeed, seen in this context, (architectural) postmodernism has had a continuous presence in the modern world since the late nineteenth century. From the Hampstead Garden Suburb to Prince Charles's village of Poundbury; from the nostalgic *Heimat* style of the 1920s to the New Urbanist settlements of the 1980s; from the Queen Anne and Renaissance revivals of Edwardian England to the mock Italian piazzas of New Orleans; from the streets of Camillo Sitte to the Strada Nuovissima of Portoghesi: all these countermodernisms and antimodernisms take their logical place in a world conceived as, finally, without history, where all history has been transformed into an empty sign of itself, deprived of its force and discomforting violence, combined in a luminous vision of a world without change. The addition of advertising, of the world of Las Vegas, to this iconographic soup was then a simple step entirely consistent with a view of the world as an image of its past and an illusion without future.

This understanding of *posthistoire* thought in architecture does not, however, exclude a great deal of work that, while it may *look* modern enough, nevertheless corresponds to a counterhistorical trend. After all, *posthistoire* already understands "modernity" itself as a closed and completed historical field, and the different styles of the modern have often enough been evoked in the same way that postmodernism evoked classical motifs. Thus, "constructivism" can easily enough be resurrected under the guise of "deconstructivism," while we have seen ample evidence recently of a neoexpressionism, drawn from the languages of Taut, Scharoun, and the sets of movies like *Das Cabinet des Dr. Caligari.* We might suspect that even "hi-tech" itself, seemingly so innocent in its unabashed "modernity," would fall into this category as well. In much of this work, which seems on the surface to represent a continuity of the modern, we can detect stylistic conceit and historical reference as repetition rather than an inner understanding of the transformational dynamics of historical thought and practice.

Which opens the question: What, then, outside the politically regressive and image-filled frame of the *posthistoire,* is left for historical thought, and thence for a modernity conceived of historically? In the first place, it is not difficult to agree with Jürgen Habermas and others that we are still, in some way, deeply involved in the modern, as historically defined. Whether we place the emergence of this tendency in the scientific and aesthetic academies of the seventeenth century, the philosophic thought of the eighteenth, the political and industrial revolutions of the nineteenth, or the scientific breakthroughs of the twentieth, it is clear that our *historical* response to these phenomena is one of fundamental recognition, of affinity rather than estrangement. A recent example would be that cited by the Harvard historian of science Peter Gallison, who has found important lessons for contemporary global positioning systems in the temporal conundrums of Einstein and Poincaré. Secondly, if this is the case, it is equally clear that "modernity" is a continuing project of reevaluation and innovation, based on experiment and internal investigation.

In architectural terms, such a project would involve not the outward citation of an already formed language, but the internal study and development of architectural language in itself, or, alternatively or in conjunction, a similarly rigorous and productive approach to the fundamental program of the work. It is in such a way that, for example, architects from van Doesburg to Peter Eisenman have understood the nature of the formal language of architecture, and others from Le Corbusier to Rem Koolhaas have understood the radicality of the program. We might, indeed, begin to characterize the qualities of the modern in this way, thus bypassing the vexed question of style (itself a *posthistoire* concept) in order to construe historically and dynamically a sense of our own modernity. Such a task would involve an approach to modern history that refuses closure and neofinalism, and rather sees all questions posed by modernity as still open. In this formulation, the history of modern architecture would not seek to classify style or movement, even if this were a part of the historical record itself, but would look for places where the uncomfortable questions of form and program with respect to society and its political formation were asked; where irresolution rather than resolution was assumed; where projects were started but left unfinished, not as failures but as active and unresolved challenges; where disruptions from outside the field inconveniently questioned the verities of established practices; where the very forms in which we conceive of history itself have been put into question. We would need to reassess disruptive moments and figures, not as curiosities and embarrassments, nor as washed-up utopias (utopia, after all, is a *posthistoire* concept), but as openings into the process, rather than the appearance, of modernity; we would also need to seriously reevaluate the sacred cows of modernity, whose work has become, too quickly, canonical, in order to detect the internal inconsistencies, the still-open questions lurking behind their monographical facades; finally, we would need to open up those ideas of "modernism" so prevalent after the Second World

War that were proposed in order to tidy up the erratic field of the early avant-gardes and to provide rules for being modern in the era of reconstruction.

In this context, historians of the modern movement might then be seen not only as contributing to our historical knowledge of earlier phases of the modern, although this is important, but equally as instances of the processes of modernity's self-reflection, themselves to be opened up as unanswered questions. Thus Kaufmann's formal definitions of "autonomy" that resonated so powerfully in the practice of architects from Johnson and Rossi to Eisenman; Rowe's condensation of all history into a set of figure-ground elements ready to be collaged together in the simulacrum of a "city for all seasons"; Pevsner's already nervous identification of the "return of historicism" in 1960 (a phenomenon that might lead us to question the apparent newness of the postmodern irruption in the 1980s); Banham's interrogation of the "program" as calling for a new relationship between science and aesthetics, which gave so strong an impetus to the experiments of Cedric Price; and Tafuri's reinscription of modernity as constituted by the initial gesture of the Renaissance, thereby opening up the perceived nature of modernity itself—all these "histories" should be conceived as so many modernist projects in and for themselves, and used to challenge the preconceptions of our own historical consciousness.

NOTES

INTRODUCTION

1. Fredric Jameson, *A Singular Modernity: Essay on the Ontology of the Present* (London: Verso, 2002), 169. Jameson characterizes Greenberg as "that theoretician who more than any other can be credited as having invented the ideology of modernism full-blown and out of whole cloth" (ibid.).

2. Reyner Banham, "The New Brutalism," *Architectural Review* 118, no. 708 (December 1955): 355.

3. Adolf Behne, *Der moderne Zweckbau* (Munich: Drei Masken Verlag, 1926); Gustav Adolf Platz, *Die Baukunst der neuesten Zeit* (Berlin: Propyläen Verlag, 1927); Sigfried Giedion, *Bauen in Frankreich, Bauen in Eisen, Bauen in Eisenbeton* (Leipzig: Klinkhardt & Biermann, 1928); Bruno Taut, *Modern Architecture* (London: The Studio, 1929); Walter Curt Behrendt, *Modern Building: Its Nature, Problems, and Forms* (London: Martin Hopkinson, 1937); Henry-Russell Hitchcock, *Modern Architecture: Romanticism and Reintegration* (New York: Payson and Clarke, 1929); Nikolaus Pevsner, *Pioneers of the Modern Movement from William Morris to Walter Gropius* (London: Faber and Faber, 1936); Sigfried Giedion, *Space, Time and Architecture: The Growth of a New Tradition* (Cambridge: Harvard University Press, 1941).

4. See the excellent analysis by Panayotis Tournikiotis, *The Historiography of Modern Architecture* (Cambridge: MIT Press, 1999), which must form the basis of any serious study of the works of Pevsner, Zevi, Benevolo, Hitchcock, Collins, and Tafuri. Influenced by the semiotic structuralism of his thesis advisor Françoise Choay, Tournikiotis restricts his analysis to the structural comparison of key texts, deliberately removing any discussion of context or authors, in the belief that "the context . . . and the personalities . . . have nothing to tell us about the nature of the *written discourse per se*" (5–6). The present work, however, studies these relations specifically, understanding the writing of history, whether or not under the guise of objectivity, to form a practice immersed in the theory

and design of architecture at any one moment, within a comprehensive practice that, as it embraces all aspects of the architectural field, might properly be called its "discourse." A less "structuralist" and analytical introduction to the field is Demetri Porphyrios, ed., "On the Methodology of Architectural History," special issue of *Architectural Design* 51, no. 7 (1981), which, in its range of critical essays by historians on historians, represents an important snapshot of the field in the late 1970s.

5. The first book to use "history" in its title was in fact Bruno Zevi's *Storia dell'architettura moderna* (Turin: Einaudi, 1950); the first in English was Jürgen Joedicke's *A History of Modern Architecture*, translated by James Palmes (London: Architectural Press, 1959) from his *Geschichte der modernen Architektur: Synthese aus Form, Funktion und Konstruktion* (Stuttgart: Gerd Hatje, 1958). It is interesting to consider that both are postwar reflections on a modernity already in the past and subject to serious critique, the one written in exile in the United States, and at Harvard, where the International Style was already academicized, the other in Germany on the wreckage of modernity's darker follies; but both are by authors who sought to rescue the ideals and formal premises of modernism and set them on new democratic bases.

6. Alois Riegl, *Stilfragen: Grundlegungen zu einer Geschichte der Ornamentik* (Berlin: G. Siemens, 1893), and *Die spätrömische Kunst-Industrie nach den Funden in Österreich-Ungarn im Zusammenhange mit der Gesammtentwicklung der bildenden Künste bei den Mittelmeervölkern* (Vienna: K. K. Hof- und Staats-druckerei, 1901); Heinrich Wölfflin, *Prolegomena zu einer Psychologie des Architektur* (Munich: Dr. C. Wolf & Sohn, 1886), and *Renaissance und Barock: Eine Untersuchung über Wesen und Entstehung des Barockstils in Italien* (Munich: Theodor Ackermann, 1888); August Schmarsow, *Das Wesen des architektonischen Schöpfung* (Leipzig: Karl W. Hiersemann, 1894).

7. Adolf von Hildebrand, *Das Problem der Form in der bildenden Kunst* (Strasbourg: Heitz and Mündel, 1893), trans. Max Meyer and Robert Morris Ogden as *The Problem of Form in Painting and Sculpture* (New York: G. E. Stechert, 1907); retranslated in Harry Francis Mallgrave and Eleftherios Ikonomou, eds., *Empathy, Form, and Space: Problems in German Aesthetics, 1873–1893* (Santa Monica: Getty Center for the History of Art and the Humanities, 1994), 227–279.

8. Paul Frankl, *Die Entwicklungsphasen der neueren Baukunst* (Stuttgart: Verlag B. G. Teubner, 1914).

9. Robert Vischer, *Über das optische Formgefühl: Ein Beitrag zur Aesthetik* (Leipzig: Hermann Credner, 1873).

10. See Mallgrave and Ikonomou, introduction to *Empathy, Form, and Space*, 1–85; and Michael Podro, *The Critical Historians of Art* (New Haven: Yale University Press, 1982).

11. Paul Frankl, *Principles of Architectural History: The Four Phases of Architectural Style, 1420–1900*, trans. and ed. James F. O'Gorman, foreword by James Ackerman (Cambridge: MIT Press, 1968). The new title is an evident reference to the English translation of Wölfflin's *Kunstgeschichtliche Grundbegriffe* as *Principles of Art History*.

12. Heinrich Wölfflin, *Renaissance and Baroque*, trans. Kathrin Simon, introduction by Peter Murray (Ithaca: Cornell University Press, 1964), 87.

13. Nikolaus Pevsner, *Leipziger Barock: Die Baukunst der Barockzeit in Leipzig* (Dresden: Wolfgang Jess, 1928). In the foreword, Pevsner thanks "Wilhelm Pinder und Franz Studniczka, Rudolf Kautzsch und Leo Bruhns, denen ich vielleicht, wenn auch nicht mehr auf Grund persönlich genossener Ausbildung, so doch auf Grund seiner für die ganze wissenschaftliche Methode dieses Buches vorbildlichen Arbeiten über das Wesen des Barockstiles, August Schmarsow anfügen darf," and refers to August Schmarsow's *Barock und Rokoko: Eine kritische Auseinandersetzung über das malerische in der Architektur* (Leipzig: S. Hirzel, 1897), vol. II of Schmarsow's *Beiträge zur Aesthetik der bildenden Künste*.

14. Manfredo Tafuri, *Teorie e storia dell'architettura* (Rome and Bari: Edizioni Laterza, 1968; 3rd ed., 1973).

15. Ibid. (1973), 266; my translation. The English translation of the fourth (1976) edition of *Teorie e storia*, translated by Giorgio Verrecchia with a foreword by Dennis Sharp (London: Granada Publishing, 1980), is thoroughly unreliable and filled with omissions and mistakes. The present citation is an example, where "esperienzi 'informali,'" referring to avant-garde experiments in the *informe* or "nonformal" as they had been tied back to prehistoric architectures, is rendered meaningless by the phrase "some abstract experiences."

1 NEOCLASSICAL MODERNISM: EMIL KAUFMANN

This chapter grew out of three invitations: to present a paper at the conference "The Last Things before the Last," organized by the PhD students in the School of Architecture at Columbia University; to respond to a paper by Barbara Johnson at a conference organized by T. J. Clark at Berkeley and the San Francisco MOMA under the title "What Was Modernism and Why Won't It Go Away"; and to present a paper at the conference in Paris organized by the Anyone Project in 1999. A more developed account was read at a Getty conference on architectural history and art history in the spring of 2000, and at a symposium on the "Culture of Disenchantment" hosted by the Center for Modern and Contemporary Studies at UCLA in 2001. I have benefited from the responses, conversations, and debates at all these conferences. Preliminary versions of this chapter were published as "Any mores," in Cynthia Davidson, ed., *Anymore* (Cambridge: MIT Press, 2000), 244–248, and as "The Ledoux Effect: Emil Kaufmann and the Claims of Kantian Autonomy," *Perspecta: The Yale Architectural Journal* 33 (2002): 16–29.

1. For a sympathetic but brief summary of Kaufmann's life, see Meyer Schapiro's obituary, "Emil Kaufmann (1891–1953)," *College Art Journal* (Winter 1954): 144; and James Grote van Derpol, "Emil Kaufmann, 1891–1953," *Journal of the Society of Architectural Historians* 12, no. 3 (1953): 32. For contemporary assessments of Kaufmann, see Georges Teyssot, "Neoclassic and 'Autonomous' Architecture: The Formalism of Emil Kaufmann 1891–1953," in Demetri Porphyrios, ed., "On the Methodology of Architectural History," special issue of *Architectural Design* 51 (1981): 24–29; and Gilbert Erouart, "Situation d'Emil Kaufmann," in Emil Kaufmann, *Trois architectes révolutionnaires: Boullée, Ledoux, Lequeu,* ed. Gilbert Erouart and Georges Teyssot (Paris: Éditions de SADG, 1978), 5–11. See also Monique Mosser, "Situation d'Emil K.," in *De Ledoux à Le Corbusier: Origines de l'architecture moderne* (Arc-et-Senans: Edition Fondation C. N. Ledoux, 1987), 84–89; Daniel Rabreau, "Critique d'Emil Kaufmann, 'Trois architectes révolutionnaires,'" *Bulletin Monumental* (1979): 78–81.

2. Emil Kaufmann, *Von Ledoux bis Le Corbusier: Ursprung und Entwicklung der autonomen Architektur* (Vienna and Leipzig: Rolf Passer, 1933). Translations in the text from this work are mine.

3. For responses to Kaufmann in the 1930s, see Meyer Schapiro, "The New Viennese School," *Art Bulletin* 17 (1936): 258–266; Edoardo Persico, *Scritti critici e polemici,* ed. Alfonso Gatto (Milan: Rosa e Ballo, 1947), 210–211; Hans Sedlmayr, *Verlust der Mitte—Die bildende Kunst des 19. und 20. Jahrhunderts als Symptom und Symbol der Zeit* (Salzburg: Otto Müller Verlag, 1948), trans. Brian Battershaw as *Art in Crisis: The Lost Centre* (London: Hollis and Carter, 1957). For a general review of Kaufmann's reception and a comparison with that of Sigfried Giedion, see the excellent thesis by Detlef Mertins, "Transparencies Yet to Come: Sigfried Giedion and the Prehistory of Architectural Modernity" (PhD diss., Princeton University, 1996), 170–180.

4. Allan Braham, *The Architecture of the French Enlightenment* (Berkeley: University of California Press, 1980), 7; David Watkin, *The Rise of Architectural History* (Chicago: University of Chicago Press, 1980), 180.

5. See especially Frederic J. Schwartz, *Blind Spots: Critical Theory and the History of Art in Twentieth-Century Germany* (New Haven: Yale University Press, 2005), for a refreshing analysis of the work of Hans Sedlmayr.

6. Christopher S. Wood, ed., *The Vienna School Reader: Politics and Art Historical Method in the 1930s* (New York: Zone Books, 2000), 69.

7. Schapiro, "The New Viennese School"; Walter Benjamin, *Das Passagen-Werk,* ed. Rolf Tiedemann, in *Gesammelte Schriften,* vol. 5 (1982), trans. Howard Eiland and Kevin McLaughlin as *The Arcades Project* (Cambridge: Harvard University Press, 1999).

8. Emil Kaufmann, "Three Revolutionary Architects, Boullée, Ledoux, and Lequeu," *Transactions of the American Philosophical Society* 42, part 3 (October 1952): 431–564.

9. Emil Kaufmann, *Architecture in the Age of Reason: Baroque and Post-Baroque in England, Italy, and France* (Cambridge: Harvard University Press, 1955).

10. Hubert Damisch, "Ledoux avec Kant," introduction to the French translation of Emil Kaufmann, *De Ledoux à Le Corbusier: Origine et développement de l'architecture moderne* (Paris: L'Equerre, 1981), 11–21.

11. See Franz Schulze, *Philip Johnson: Life and Work* (New York: Knopf, 1994), 157–158, 194–196, 216.

12. Aldo Rossi, "Emil Kaufmann e l'architettura dell'Illuminismo," *Casabella Continuità* 222 (1958), reprinted in Rossi, *Scritti scelti sull'architettura e la città,*

1956–1972, ed. Rosaldo Bonicalzi (Milan: CLUP, 1975), 62–71. Kaufmann's influence is seen also in Rossi's "Introduzione a Boullée" (1967) and "L'architettura dell'Illuminismo" (1973), in *Scritti scelti*, 346–364, 454–473.

13. This according to the brief biography published in the *Journal of the American Society of Architectural Historians* 3, no. 3 (July 1943): 12, and evidently provided by Kaufmann himself: "Dr. Kaufmann, a pupil in art history of Max Dvořák, Joseph Strzygowski, and Hans Semper, in classical archaeology of Emanuel Loewy, and in general history of Ludwig von Pastor, received his Doctor of Philosophy degree from the University of Vienna in 1920." Emanuel Loewy's *Die Naturwiedergabe in der älteren griechischen Kunst* was published in Rome in 1900 and translated by John Fothergill into English in 1907 as *The Rendering of Nature in Early Greek Art*. See Ernst Gombrich, *Art and Illusion: A Study in the Psychology of Pictorial Representation* (Princeton: Princeton University Press, 1960), 22–23. Loewy's theories of style were resumed by Meyer Schapiro in "Style," in A. L. Kroeber, ed., *Anthropology Today: An Encyclopedic Inventory* (Chicago: University of Chicago Press, 1953), 301.

14. Max Dvořák, *Katechismus der Denkmalpflege* (Vienna, 1916). Schapiro summarizes Kaufmann's career: "Among his teachers were Strzygowski and Dvořák; the latter, especially, helped to form his thinking about art and was very dear to him. Unable to obtain a teaching position, Dr. Kaufmann became a bank employee, devoting himself to his studies in his leisure hours. As a result of the Nazi occupation of Austria, he lost his position and left the country. He came to the United States in 1940. Without regular employment, he lived in extremely poor circumstances, but dedicated himself with extraordinary single-mindedness and scruple to researches of which his only reward was his satisfaction in revealing hidden aspects of the history of architecture and in scholarly work well done. . . . He died on July 3, 1953, in Cheyenne, Wyoming, while en route to Los Angeles" ("Emil Kaufmann [1891–1953]," 144).

15. Emil Kaufmann, "Die Architekturtheorie der französischen Klassik und der Klassizismus," *Repertorium für Kunstwissenschaft* 44 (1924): 197–237. Kaufmann elaborated his account of "neoclassicism" in the review article "Klassizismus als Tendenz und als Epoche," *Kritische Berichte zur kunstgeschichtlichen Literatur* (1933): 201–214, which considered concepts of "Klassizismus" from Alois Riegl,

August Schmarsow, Paul Zucker, Paul Frankl, A. E. Brinckmann, Sigfried Giedion, Wilhelm Pinder, and Wolfgang Herrmann.

16. Teyssot, "Neoclassic and 'Autonomous' Architecture." Teyssot concisely analyzes the debates over this stylistic and periodic ascription, noting in Giedion's 1922 thesis *Spätbarocker und romantischer Klassizismus* the terms "late baroque neoclassicism" and "romantic neoclassicism," which took off directly from Riegl's own attempt to revise the characterization of another neglected period, that of the *Spätrömische*.

17. Emil Kaufmann, *Der Kunst der Stadt Baden* (Vienna: Österreichischer Bundesverlag, 1925).

18. Emil Kaufmann, "C. N. Ledoux," *Künstlerlexikon Thieme Becker* 22 (1928): 536–537; "Die Wandlungen der Bildform bei Ferdinand Georg Waldmueller," *Zeitschrift für bildende Kunst* 64 (1930–1931): 209–216.

19. Emil Kaufmann, "Architektonische Entwürfe aus der zeit der französichen Revolution," *Zeitschrift für bildende Kunst* 62 (1929–1930): 45.

20. Emil Kaufmann, "C. N. Ledoux und der klassizistische Kirchenbau," *Kirchenkunst* 3 (1931): 62.

21. Ibid.

22. Emil Kaufmann, "Die Stadt des Architekten Ledoux: Zur Erkenntnis der autonomen Architektur," *Kunstwissenschaftliche Forschungen* 2 (Berlin, 1933): 131–160.

23. Ibid., 133.

24. Ibid., 138.

25. Ibid., 142.

26. Claude-Nicolas Ledoux, *L'architecture considérée sous le rapport de l'art, des moeurs et de la législation* (Paris: chez l'auteur, 1804), 185, 115.

27. Kaufmann did not provide a note to this source until the publication of his *Three Revolutionary Architects*.

28. Kaufmann, "Die Stadt," 146.

29. Ledoux, *L'architecture*, 234.

30. Kaufmann, "Die Stadt," 152–153.

31. Ibid., 153; cited in Teyssot, "Neoclassic and 'Autonomous' Architecture," 28.

32. Kaufmann, *Von Ledoux*, 3.

33. Paul Klopfer, *Von Palladio bis Schinkel: Eine Charakteristik der Baukunst des Klassizismus* (Eszlingen: Paul Neff, 1911). Director of the Grand Duke's building union and trade school in Weimar, Klopfer also wrote a handbook on architectural styles, *Die Baustile* (Leipzig: E. U. Seemann, 1912), and several studies of the German private house: *Die deutsche Bürgerwohnung* (Freiburg: Paul Waetzel, 1905), *Die Gestaltung des Wohnhauses* (Stuttgart: Konrad Wittwer, 1912), *Das deutsche Bauern- und Bürgerhaus* (Leipzig: Alfred Kröner, 1915), and *Wie baue ich mein Haus und wie beschaffe ich mir eine gediegene Wohnungseinrichtung?* (Stuttgart: Wilhelm Meyer-Ilschen, n.d.). In a coincidental, reversed symmetry to Kaufmann's *Von Ledoux bis Le Corbusier*, Klopfer's *Von Palladio bis Schinkel* is almost entirely taken up with tracing the development from the baroque to neoclassicism, and mentions Palladio only at the very beginning.

34. Kaufmann, *Von Ledoux*, 5–6.

35. Ibid., 12.

36. Ledoux, *L'architecture*, 30; cited in Kaufmann, *Von Ledoux*, 12.

37. Central to Kaufmann's analysis of Ledoux was the treatise that Ledoux had published two years before his death, the magisterial first volume of a planned five-volume work, *L'architecture considérée sous le rapport de l'art, des moeurs et de la législation*. This work, with 416 folio pages of text and 125 engraved plates of Ledoux's built and ideal projects, constituted the main evidence for what was known of Ledoux in the 1920s; indeed, despite subsequent discoveries of original drawings for specific projects and archival verification of the dates of certain commissions, *L'architecture*, with all its amphibological excesses and architectural hubris, still remains central to any interpretation of Ledoux. The two central post-Kaufmann studies of Ledoux remain Michel Gallet, *Claude-Nicolas Ledoux, 1736–1806* (Paris: Picard, 1985), and Anthony Vidler, *Claude-Nicolas Ledoux: Architecture and Social Reform at the End of the Ancien Régime* (Cambridge: MIT Press, 1989).

38. Kaufmann, *Von Ledoux*, 16–17.

39. Ibid., 19.

40. Ibid.

41. Ibid., 20.

42. Ibid., 30.

43. Ibid., 32.

44. Ibid., 33.
45. Ibid., 34.
46. Ledoux, *L'architecture*, 90; cited in Kaufmann, *Von Ledoux*, 43.
47. Kaufmann, *Von Ledoux*, 36.
48. Hannes Meyer, "La realidad soviética: Los arquitectos," *Arquitectura* 9 (1942); in English in *Task Magazine* 3 (1942). Reprinted in Hannes Meyer, *Scritti 1921–1942: Architettura o rivoluzione*, ed. Francesco Dal Co (Padua: Marsilio, 1969), 214–215.
49. Immanuel Kant, *Critique of Pure Reason*, trans. Paul Guyer and Allen Wood (Cambridge: Cambridge University Press, 1997), 100–101 (Axi–Axii).
50. Theodor W. Adorno, *Kant's Critique of Pure Reason* (Stanford: Stanford University Press, 2001), 54–55.
51. Ibid., 54.
52. Ernst Cassirer, *Kant's Life and Thought*, trans. James Haden (New Haven: Yale University Press, 1981), 243; originally published as *Kants Leben und Lehre*, 1918.
53. Theodor W. Adorno, *Kant's Critique of Pure Reason*, ed. Rolf Tiedemann, trans. Rodney Livingstone (Stanford: Stanford University Press, 2001), 54–55.
54. Ernst Cassirer, "Das Problem Jean-Jacques Rousseau," *Archiv für Geschichte der Philosophie* 41 (1932): 177–213, 479–513. The intertwined histories of Kaufmann and Cassirer were again to intersect with the publication much later of the English edition of Cassirer's *Philosophy of the Enlightenment* and Kaufmann's posthumously published *Architecture in the Age of Reason* (1955).
55. Kaufmann, *Von Ledoux*, 61.
56. Kaufmann, "Die Stadt," 41.
57. Ledoux, *L'architecture*: "Le sentiment apprécié d'un plan est à l'abri de toute domination. Il émane du sujet, il doit adapter à la nature des lieux et des besoins" (65); "Tout détail est inutile, je dis plus, nuisible, quand il devise les surfaces par des additions mesquines ou mensongères" (91); "Toutes les formes que l'on décrit d'un seul trait de compas sont avouées par le goût. Le cercle, le carré, voilà les lettres alphabétiques que les auteurs emploient dans la texture des meilleurs ouvrages" (135).
58. Kaufmann, *Von Ledoux*, 42.
59. Ibid., 48.
60. Ibid., 61.

61. Ibid., 62; quoting Richard J. Neutra, *Wie baut Amerika?* (1927).

62. Kaufmann, *Von Ledoux*, 62; quoting Stonorov and Boesiger, *Le Corbusier et Pierre Jeanneret* (Zurich: Girsberger, 1930), 27, 23. See also Ledoux, *L'architecture*, 135.

63. Kaufmann, *Von Ledoux*, 62.

64. Ibid., 63.

65. Schapiro, "The New Viennese School," 258–267.

66. Ibid., 265.

67. Ibid.

68. Sedlmayr had written his dissertation on the Viennese architect and early architectural historian Fischer von Erlach and gained his *Habilitation* in 1933 with a thesis on Bruegel. After the war, he joined the editorial board of the Catholic review *Wort und Wahrheit* and, rehabilitated in 1951, took up the position of professor at Ludwig Maximilian University, Munich, the chair once held by Wölfflin and Pinder, finally to teach in Austria between 1964 and 1969 at Salzburg.

69. Wood, *The Vienna School Reader*, 25.

70. Sedlmayr, *Art in Crisis*, 117.

71. Ibid., 4.

72. Ibid., 107.

73. Ibid., 101.

74. Ibid., 256.

75. Ibid., 256.

76. Kaufmann, *Architecture in the Age of Reason*, 266, n. 439.

77. Emil Kaufmann, review of Marcel Raval and J.-Ch. Moreux, *Claude-Nicolas Ledoux* (Paris, 1945), *Art Bulletin* 30, no. 4 (1948): 289, n. 3. Following a long list of phrases from his earlier articles compared with those in Raval and Moreux, Kaufmann concludes: "Whereas Horst Riemer copied a large part of my 1929 essay word by word (cf. *Zeitschrift für Kunstgeschichte*, 1935, p. 189), Raval and Moreux (and likewise Gertrude Rosenthal in the *News of the Baltimore Museum of Art*, November 1947) have appropriated a large part of my concepts." Kaufmann's review details how a new work should have remedied the deficits of the 1934 biography by G. Levallet-Haug. The authors, he states, "knew that they had to avoid the gravest shortcomings of the Levallet biography; that they had to deal with Ledoux's historical position and to interpret his performances. They are apparently not up to their task" (288).

78. Kaufmann, *Architecture in the Age of Reason*, 265, n. 481: "the Lequeu documents of the Bibliothèque Nationale escaped her attention, so she could discuss Lequeu merely in a general way."

79. Philipp Fehl, review of *Das Menschenbild in unserer Zeit* by Hans Sedlmayr (Darmstadt: Neue Darmstaedter Verlagsanstalt, 1951), *College Art Journal* 13, no. 4 (Winter 1954): 145–147.

80. Emil Kaufmann, "Claude-Nicolas Ledoux, Inaugurator of a New Architectural System," *Journal of the American Society of Architectural Historians* 3, no. 3 (July 1943): 13.

81. Ibid.

82. Kaufmann, review of Raval and Moreux, 289.

83. Kaufmann, "Claude-Nicolas Ledoux, Inaugurator," 17–18.

84. Ibid., 18.

85. Emil Kaufmann, "Nils G. Wollin: 'Desprez en Suède,'" *Art Bulletin* 28 (1946): 283.

86. Ibid., 284.

87. Kaufmann, *Architecture in the Age of Reason*, x.

88. I outlined the connection between Kaufmann and Johnson in "From Ledoux to Le Corbusier to Johnson, to . . . ," *Progressive Architecture* (May 1991): 109–110. Since then the argument has been significantly elaborated by Detlef Mertins in "System and Freedom: Sigfried Giedion, Emil Kaufmann, and the Constitution of Architectural Modernity," in Robert E. Somol, ed., *Autonomy and Ideology: Positioning an Avant-Garde in America* (New York: Monacelli Press, 1997), 212–231.

89. Kaufmann, "Claude-Nicolas Ledoux, Inaugurator," 12–20. Published along with John Coolidge's call for "The New History of Architecture," *Journal of the American Society of Architectural Historians* 3, no. 3 (July 1943): 3–11, Kaufmann's text was both a summary of his ground-breaking work on Ledoux and a methodological polemic on behalf of his personal interpretation of the concept of "system" developed in the Vienna school and applied to architecture in the "abstract" work of the late eighteenth century.

90. Kaufmann, "Claude-Nicolas Ledoux, Inaugurator," 12.

91. Ibid., 18.

92. Philip Johnson, "House at New Canaan, Connecticut," *Architectural Review* 108, no. 645 (September 1950): 153.

93. Damisch, "Ledoux avec Kant," 20

94. See Somol, ed., *Autonomy and Ideology.*

95. Whereas Kaufmann gave credit due to Ledoux for exploring Kant's concept of autonomy and Johnson and Rossi elaborated the premise, it is perhaps only Le Corbusier who remains unexamined as the modernist neo-Kantian architect par excellence. In the spirit of the idea "from Ledoux to Le Corbusier," I hope soon to complete research on Le Corbusier in terms that construe his aesthetic politics within the neo-Kantian revival of the first quarter of the twentieth century between Victor Basch, Elie Faure, and Henri Focillon.

2 MANNERIST MODERNISM: COLIN ROWE

This chapter was originally developed in response to an invitation to speak on the relations between Peter Eisenman and Leon Krier at the Yale University School of Architecture in November 2002. A shorter version was published as "Colin Rowe," in Cynthia Davidson, ed., *Eisenman/Krier: Two Ideologies: A Conference at the Yale School of Architecture* (New York: Monacelli Press, 2004), 52–61.

1. Colin Rowe, "Addendum 1973" to "The Mathematics of the Ideal Villa," in *The Mathematics of the Ideal Villa and Other Essays* (Cambridge: MIT Press, 1976), 16.

2. Ibid.

3. Colin Rowe, *As I Was Saying: Recollections and Miscellaneous Essays,* ed. Alexander Caragonne, vol. 1 (Cambridge: MIT Press, 1996), 2.

4. Ibid.

5. Rudolf Wittkower, "Inigo Jones, Architect and Man of Letters," *Journal of the Royal Institute of British Architects* 60 (1953); reprinted in Wittkower, *Palladio and English Palladianism* (London: Thames and Hudson, 1974), 60.

6. Colin F. Rowe, "The Theoretical Drawings of Inigo Jones: Their Sources and Scope" (M.A. thesis in the History of Art, University of London, November 1947). This thesis is also referred to by Margaret Whinney, "Inigo Jones: A Revaluation," *Journal of the Royal Institute of British Architects* 59, no. 8 (June 1952): 288: "It has recently been shown that Jones meant to do more than instruct by example alone, for a careful example by Mr Colin Rowe, of the great number of drawings not related to executed buildings has revealed that a treatise on architecture was in preparation though the book may never have been written. [Note 6. I am very grateful to Mr. Rowe for permission to refer to his unpublished thesis, *The*

Theoretical Drawings of Inigo Jones, their sources, and scope. University of London, 1947.]"

7. Rowe, *As I Was saying,* 1: 2.

8. Fritz Saxl and Rudolf Wittkower, *England and the Mediterranean Tradition,* exh. cat. (London: Warburg and Courtauld Institutes, 1945). This was later reissued as Saxl and Wittkower, *British Art and the Mediterranean* (London: Oxford University Press, 1948). Wittkower contributed the second part of the book, which emphasized the eighteenth century. In his consideration of Lord Burlington's house at Chiswick, for example, he stressed the free adaptation of the Palladian model by the English architect, who drew equally on Scamozzi and Inigo Jones. See Wittkower, "The English Interpretation of Palladio," *England and the Mediterranean,* 54.

9. Rowe, "Theoretical Drawings," 2.

10. Colin Rowe, "The Mathematics of the Ideal Villa: Palladio and Le Corbusier Compared," *Architectural Review* 101, no. 603 (March 1947): 101–104; "Mannerism and Modern Architecture," *Architectural Review* 107, no. 641 (May 1950): 289–300.

11. Rowe, "Theoretical Drawings," 17.

12. Ibid.

13. Ibid., 18.

14. Ibid., 64–65.

15. Ibid., 65–66.

16. Ibid., 27.

17. Ibid.

18. Ibid., 45.

19. Reyner Banham, "The New Brutalism," *Architectural Review* 118, no. 708 (December 1955): 354–361.

20. Ibid., 358–361.

21. Ibid., 361.

22. Reyner Banham, *The New Brutalism* (London: Architectural Press, 1966), 14–15.

23. Ibid., 15.

24. Peter D. Smithson, response "Against the Motion" to Nikolaus Pevsner in "Report of a Debate on the Motion 'that Systems of Proportion Make Good Design Easier and Bad Design More Difficult,' Held at the R.I.B.A., 18 June, 1957," *RIBA Journal* 64, no. 11 (September 1957): 461.

25. Rudolf Wittkower, *Architectural Principles in the Age of Humanism* (London: Warburg Institute, 1949). The text was made up of articles previously published in the *Journal of the Warburg and Courtauld Institutes:* "Alberti's Approach to Antiquity in Architecture," *Journal of the Warburg and Courtauld Institutes* 4 (1940–1941): 1–18; "Principles of Palladio's Architecture," part I, *Journal of the Warburg and Courtauld Institutes* 7 (1944): 102–122, and part II, *Journal of the Warburg and Courtauld Institutes* 8 (1945): 68–106. As noted by Alina A. Payne, Wittkower added chapter 1, "The Centrally Planned Church in the Renaissance," and a section on Palladio's optical and psychological concepts for publication in the book: Payne, "Rudolf Wittkower and Architectural Principles in the Age of Modernism," *Journal of the Society of Architectural Historians* 53 (September 1994): 322–342.

26. Peter Smithson, letter, *RIBA Journal* 59 (1952): 140–141, cited in Henry Millon, "Rudolph Wittkower, *Architectural Principles in the Age of Humanism:* Its Influence on the Development and Interpretation of Modern Architecture," *Journal of the Society of Architectural Historians* 31 (1972): 89.

27. Wittkower, "Principles of Palladio's Architecture," II, 103. For a full discussion of Wittkower's analytical method in the context of modernist art theory, see Payne, "Rudolf Wittkower," and for an account of the reception of *Architectural Principles,* see Millon, "Rudolph Wittkower."

28. Payne, "Rudolf Wittkower," 325.

29. Wittkower, "Principles of Palladio's Architecture," I, 108–109, citing Palladio, *Quattro libri,* I, chapter 20, 48.

30. Wittkower, "Principles of Palladio's Architecture," I, 109.

31. Ibid., 109–110.

32. Ibid., 111.

33. Ibid.

34. Ibid.

35. Ibid., II, 103.

36. Wittkower, *Architectural Principles,* 135.

37. Quoted in Rowe, *As I Was Saying,* 1: 47.

38. Rudolf Wittkower, "Safety in Numbers," review of R. W. Gardner, *A Primer of Proportion in the Arts of Form and Music* (New York: William Helburn, 1945), *Architectural Review* 100, no. 596 (August 1946): 53.

39. Editors' note, *Architectural Review* 101, no. 603 (March 1947); the cover illustration was taken from Fredrik Macody Lund's *Ad Quadratum: A Study of the Geometrical Bases of Classic and Medieval Religious Architecture* (London: Batsford, 1921).

40. Colin Rowe, "The Mathematics of the Ideal Villa: Palladio and Le Corbusier Compared," *Architectural Review* 101, no. 603 (March 1947): 101; citing Christopher Wren, *Tract I*, on architecture, in Christopher Wren, Jr., *Parentalia: or Memoirs of the Family of the Wrens* (London, 1750), 351–352. As transcribed by Lydia Soo, the full text (I have added Rowe's excisions in square brackets) reads:

> There are two causes of Beauty, natural and customary. Natural is from Geometry, consisting in Uniformity (that is Equality) and Proportion. Customary Beauty is begotten by the Use [of our Senses to those Objects which are usually pleasing to us for other Causes,] as Familiarity [or particular Inclination] breeds a Love to Things not in themselves lovely. Here lies the great occasion of errors[; here is tried the Architect's Judgment:] but always the [true] Test is natural or geometrical Beauty. Geometrical Figures are naturally more beautiful than [other] irregular[; in this all consent as to a Law of Nature. Of geometrical Figures,] the Square and the Circle are most beautiful; next the Parallelogram and the Oval. [Strait Lines are more beautiful than curve; next to strait Lines, equal and geometrical Flextures; an Object elevated in the Middle is more beautiful than depressed. Position is necessary for perfecting Beauty.] There are only two [beautiful] Positions of strait lines, perpendicular and horizontal: this is from Nature, and consequently Necessity, no other than upright being firm. [Oblique Positions are Discord to the Eye, unless answered in Pairs as in the Sides of an equicrural triangle.]

See *Wren's "Tracts" on Architecture and Other Writings*, ed. Lydia M. Soo (New York: Cambridge University Press, 1998), "Tract 1," 154.

41. Wren, "Tract 1," 153.

42. Rowe, "Mathematics," 103–104.

43. Ibid., 100.

44. Erwin Panofsky, "'Et in Arcadia Ego': On the Conception of Transience in Poussin and Watteau," in Raymond Klibansky and H. J. Paton, eds., *Philosophy and History: Essays Presented to Ernst Cassirer* (Oxford: Clarendon Press, 1936), 223–254.

45. Evelyn Waugh, *Brideshead Revisited: The Sacred and Profane Memories of Captain Charles Ryder* (New York: Little, Brown, 1999), 21.

46. Ibid., 35, 80.

47. Rowe, "Mathematics," 101.

48. Ibid., 104; the illustration "Harmonic decompositions of the φ rectangle" is taken from Matila Ghyka, *The Geometry of Art and Life* (London: Sheed and Ward, 1946), 132.

49. J. M. Richards, Nikolaus Pevsner, Osbert Lancaster, and Hubert de Cronin Hastings, editorial, *Architectural Review* 101, no. 601 (January 1947): 36.

50. Ibid., 22–23. For a detailed study of this period of the *Architectural Review*'s policies toward planning and popular culture, see the excellent thesis by Erdem Erten, "Shaping 'The Second Half Century': *Architectural Review*, 1947–1971" (PhD diss., Massachusetts Institute of Technology, 2004).

51. Richards et al., editorial, 23.

52. Ibid., 36.

53. Ibid.

54. Eliot was, of course, a central reference for both Rowe and Greenberg. For Rowe he represented a position dedicated to the essential roots of talent in tradition, and was a champion of the virtues and values of the ambiguous and the difficult; for Greenberg; Eliot was an opponent worthy of Greenberg's most lucid and extended essay from the 1950s, "The Plight of Our Culture," yet Eliot's essay "Definition of Culture," however elitist and conservative, tested the limits of Greenberg's own definition of modern cultural production as "kitsch."

55. Rowe, *As I Was Saying*, 1: 137.

56. Guido Zuliani, "Evidence of Things Unseen," in Cynthia Davidson, ed., *Tracing Eisenman* (New York: Rizzoli International, 2006), 319–348.

57. And this method is indeed seductive—as a student, I carefully traced each and every Corbusian house plan, finding the hidden Palladian structure that would reveal its modernist mechanisms, and finally applying the approach to my diploma written thesis on the specifically modern classicism of McKim, Mead and White in the late nineteenth century. Unpublished Cambridge diploma thesis, 1965.

58. Editor's comment, *Architectural Review* 107, no. 641 (May 1950), contents page. Pevsner understandably wishes to point to his own publications on mannerism and refers to his article "Double Profile: A Reconsideration of the Elizabethan Style as Seen at Wollaton," *Architectural Review* 107, no. 639 (March 1950): 147–153, where he develops the themes "Mannerism and Mediaevalism," and "Mannerism and the Elizabethans." The phrase opening with "Is convinced" is pure Rowe, however, and suggests that he wrote the copy for this summary.

59. Anthony Blunt, "Mannerism in Architecture," *Journal of the Royal Institute of British Architects* 56, no. 5 (March 1949): 195–200.

60. Ibid., 197.

61. With so much of his material drawn from Wittkower without direct attribution, it is not surprising that in the discussion following the lecture, and after a comment from Wittkower himself in the audience, Blunt confesses: "I think I ought to reveal what an embarrassment it has been to find Dr. Wittkower here, because after all he invented, or as he puts it, discovered Mannerism! Therefore it has been extremely embarrassing to speak in front of such an expert on the subject" ("Mannerism," 200).

62. Ibid., 198–199.

63. Ibid., 199.

64. Among the responses to Blunt's talk, Wittkower, generously enough in the circumstances, tried to allay the questions of skeptics who might see mannerism as simply degeneration. John Summerson protested the characterization of Soane as a mannerist, and Peter Smithson wondered whether those with academic training who then inverted the system nevertheless retained something of their original academicism. This last remark, anticipating Banham's tracing of the academic origins of modernism ten years later, also seems to prefigure Rowe's sense of the academic nature of mannerism in Le Corbusier.

65. Nikolaus Pevsner, "The Architecture of Mannerism," in Geoffrey Grigson, ed., *The Mint: A Miscellany of Literature, Art and Criticism* (London: Routledge and Sons, 1946), 116.

66. Ibid., 117.

67. On mannerism in painting Pevsner cites Dvořák, Friedländer, Panofksy, and, of course, himself, writing between 1920 and 1926, and in architecture Panofsky, Gombrich, Coolidge, and Wittkower between 1930 and 1943.

68. Pevsner, "The Architecture of Mannerism," 120–132.

69. Ibid., 135.

70. Ibid., 126.

71. Ibid., 125.

72. Rudolf Wittkower, "Michelangelo's Biblioteca Laurenziana," *Art Bulletin* 16 (1934), republished in Wittkower, *Idea and Image: Studies in the Italian Renaissance* (London: Thames and Hudson, 1978), 10–71.

73. Margaret Wittkower, foreword to Wittkower, *Idea and Image*, 8. The lost manuscript is listed in "The Writings of Rudolf Wittkower," in Douglas Fraser, Howard Hibberd, and Milton J. Lewine, eds., *Essays in the History of Architecture Presented to Rudolf Wittkower* (London: Phaidon Press, 1967), 378, as "'Das Problem der Bewegung innerhalb der manieristischen Architetktur,' *Festschrift für Walter Friedländer zum 60. Geburtstag am 10.3.1933* (unpublished typescript), 192 ff."

74. Wittkower, *Idea and Image*, 60–61.

75. Ibid., 63.

76. Ibid., 65.

77. Ibid., 66.

78. Ibid., 67.

79. Rowe, "Mannerism," 295.

80. Ibid.

81. Ibid., 296.

82. Ibid.

83. Ibid., 299.

84. Ibid., 290.

85. Rowe, *As I Was Saying*, 1: 136.

86. Rowe, "Mathematics," 104.

87. Ibid., 104.

88. Colin Rowe, introduction to Arthur Drexler, ed., *Five Architects: Eisenman, Graves, Gwathmey, Hejduk, Meier* (New York: Oxford University Press, 1972), 5.

89. Colin Rowe, erratum to introduction to *Five Architects*, reprint (New York: Oxford University Press, 1975), n.p.

90. Robert Maxwell, "James Stirling: Writings," introduction to *Stirling: Writings on Architecture*, ed. Robert Maxwell (Milan: Skira, 1998), 26. The two articles by James Stirling are "Garches to Jaoul: Le Corbusier as Domestic Architect in

1927 and 1953," *Architectural Review* 118, no. 705 (September 1955): 145–151, and "Ronchamp: Le Corbusier's Chapel and the Crisis of Rationalism," *Architectural Review* 119, no. 711 (March 1956): 155–161.

91. Stirling, "Garches to Jaoul," 145.

92. Ibid., 151.

93. Colin Rowe, "Chicago Frame," *Architectural Review* 120, no. 718 (November 1956): 285–289.

94. Stirling, "Ronchamp," 155.

95. Ibid., 161. It is interesting in the light of Rowe's influence that Stirling sees Ronchamp as an example of "the initial ideology of the modern movement . . . being mannerized" (ibid.).

96. James Stirling, "Thesis for the Liverpool School of Architecture" (1950), 1.

97. Colin Rowe, "James Stirling: A Highly Personal and Highly Disjointed Memoir," in Peter Arnell and Ted Bickford, eds., *James Stirling: Buildings and Projects* (New York: Rizzoli, 1984), 15.

98. This comparison was also belatedly admitted by Rowe in his reprinting of "The Mathematics of the Ideal Villa" in 1974.

99. Rowe, "Addendum 1973."

100. Rowe, "James Stirling," 23.

3 FUTURIST MODERNISM: REYNER BANHAM

Preliminary versions of sections of chapter 3 were published as "Toward a Theory of the Architectural Program," *October* 106 (Fall 2003): 59–74; "Still Wired after All These Years?" *Log*, no. 1 (Fall 2003): 59–63; and as part of the introduction to the reprint of Reyner Banham, *Los Angeles: The Architecture of Four Ecologies* (Berkeley and Los Angeles: University of California Press, 2000), xvii–xxxiii.

1. Reyner Banham, "A Black Box: The Secret Profession of Architecture," *New Statesman and Society* (12 October 1990): 22–25. In this article, published two years after his death, Banham came to the conclusion, always implicit in his criticism, that there was indeed a distinction to be drawn between what Le Corbusier had described as the "Engineer's Aesthetic" and "Architecture." The distinction was "between fundamental modes of designing," between Wren and Hawksmoor, for example; and he issued a deeply felt plea to architects to recognize the limits and nature of "architecture" in the Western tradition, in order then to open it

to the demands of a more extensive practice toward "a more habitable environment." This last essay by Banham deserves serious scrutiny, as both an admission of defeat in changing "architecture" at all during his polemical career, and an expression of respect for such a tenacious tradition.

2. Nikolaus Pevsner, *Pioneers of the Modern Movement from William Morris to Walter Gropius* (London: Faber and Faber, 1936); 2nd ed. titled *Pioneers of Modern Design from William Morris to Walter Gropius* (New York: Museum of Modern Art, 1949).

3. In tracing Pevsner's relationship with the *Architectural Review*, I have been helped by the doctoral dissertation of Erdem Erten, "Shaping 'The Second Half Century': The *Architectural Review* 1947–1971" (PhD diss., History and Theory of Architecture, MIT, 2004). The first part of the thesis is devoted to the Townscape program developed by the editors under Hubert de Cronin Hastings, J. M. Richards, and Nikolaus Pevsner; the second half charts the positions of the *Architectural Review* with respect to the "humanization" of modern architecture.

4. Nikolaus Pevsner, "C20 Picturesque," *Architectural Review* 115, no. 688 (April 1954): 227–229. Pevsner was replying to the third of three BBC Third Programme talks on "English Art and the Picturesque," broadcast by the art critic Basil Taylor, that indicted the influence of what Taylor called "this imperfect vision" on the last twenty years of English architecture.

5. Ibid., 228.

6. Ibid., 229.

7. Ibid.

8. A. I. T. Colquhoun, letter to the editors, *Architectural Review* 116, no. 691 (July 1954): 2.

9. Ibid.

10. The pseudonym was used several times by Pevsner in the 1940s, no doubt to disguise the "auteur" nature of the journal in these years; between July and December 1941 alone, five articles, one review, and a letter were signed "Donner," which, of course, means "thunder" in German. One of the more interesting, given later accusations against Pevsner of pro-Nazi sympathies, is a trenchant and unambiguous critique of Hitler's architectural aesthetics for its inhuman uniformity and scale of the buildings, whether modernist, medievalizing, or neoclassical: "With the Nazis, architects as well as painters, it is all a surreptitious gratification of vulgar instincts concealing themselves to secure outward dignity under

a Neo-Classical disguise. Hence these diluted Greek motifs, this over-obvious symbolism, these hackneyed compositions—all dodges to achieve an easy appeal with the masses (and the Führer) and hide the Beast in View." Peter F. R. Donner [pseudonym for Nikolaus Pevsner], "Criticism," *Architectural Review* 90, no. 539 (November 1941): 178.

11. The editors' note stated: "These monthly articles are frankly about the aesthetic aspect of architectural design. They are written in the belief that we cannot take the practical basis of modern architecture for granted. They claim . . . there is now room, in criticism, as in actual design, for study of the aesthetic basis that the art of architecture postulates." Editors' note, *Architectural Review* 90, no. 536 (August 1941): 68.

12. Peter F. R. Donner [Nikolaus Pevsner], "Criticism," *Architectural Review* 90, no. 536 (August 1941): 69.

13. Ibid., 68.

14. Ibid., 69

15. Ibid., 70.

16. Ibid.

17. Ibid.

18. Ibid.

19. Ibid., 69.

20. Peter F. R. Donner [Nikolaus Pevsner], "Criticism," *Architectural Review* 90, no. 538 (October 1941): 124–126.

21. Ibid., 124.

22. Ibid., citing Kaufmann's *Von Ledoux bis Le Corbusier*.

23. Ibid., 125.

24. Ibid.

25. Ibid.

26. Ibid.

27. Published as Nikolaus Pevsner, "Modern Architecture and the Historian or the Return of Historicism," *Journal of the Royal Institute of British Architects* 68, no. 6 (April 1961): 230–260. The talk had been given at the RIBA on 10 January 1961, and was later adapted for a BBC radio program, broadcast on 11 February 1961, "The Return of Historicism," BBC Third Programme, and printed in Nikolaus

Pevsner, *Pevsner on Art and Architecture: The Radio Talks*, ed. Stephen Games (London: Methuen, 2002), 271–278.

28. Pevsner, "Modern Architecture and the Historian," 230.

29. Ibid., 234.

30. Ibid.

31. Ibid., 230.

32. Reyner Banham, "Pevsner's Progress," *Times Literary Supplement* (17 February 1978): 191–192. Banham was reviewing David Watkin's *Morality and Architecture*, which had aroused his ire by the gratuitous comparisons of Pevsner to Goebbels, and the inferences Watkin drew from Pevsner's use of the word "totalitarian" in the conclusion of *Pioneers of Modern Design*. Banham is equally blunt in his refutation of Watkin's attempt to apply a rigid definition derived from Karl Popper to the word "historicism": "It has always been perfectly clear what Pevsner means by the word, and it is difficult to find a more convenient label to describe what he is discussing when he uses it, and it nowhere impinges on its other meanings, including those used in describing historiographical techniques" (191).

33. Pevsner, "Modern Architecture and the Historian," 238.

34. Reyner Banham, "Architecture after 1960," *Architectural Review* 127, no. 755 (January 1960): 9.

35. John Summerson, "The Case for a Theory of Modern Architecture," *Journal of the Royal Institute of British Architects* 64, no. 8 (June 1957): 307–310.

36. Banham, "Architecture after 1960," 9.

37. Summerson, "The Case for a Theory," 308.

38. Quoted in ibid., 309.

39. Ibid.

40. Ibid.

41. Ibid.

42. Ibid., 310.

43. Ibid.

44. Banham, "Architecture after 1960," 9.

45. Reyner Banham, "Futurism and Modern Architecture," *Journal of the Royal Institute of British Architects* 64, no. 4 (February 1957): 133.

46. Ibid., 129.

47. Ibid., 135.

48. Reyner Banham, *Theory and Design in the First Machine Age* (London: Architectural Press, 1960).

49. Ibid., 220.

50. Ibid., 222.

51. Ibid., 304.

52. Banham, response to Pevsner, "Modern Architecture and the Historian," 238.

53. Reyner Banham, "The History of the Immediate Future," *Journal of the Royal Institute of British Architects* 68, no. 7 (May 1961): 252. The talk was delivered at the RIBA on 7 February 1961, less than a month after Pevsner's talk.

54. Banham, "The History of the Immediate Future," 252.

55. Ibid., 255.

56. Ibid., 256.

57. Ibid., 257.

58. Ibid.

59. The *Architectural Review* series "Architecture after 1960" included Reyner Banham, "Architecture after 1960," *Architectural Review* 127, no. 755 (January 1960): 9–10; Reyner Banham, "Stocktaking," 127, no. 756 (February 1960); A. C. Brothers, M. E. Drummond, and R. Llewelyn-Davies, "The Science Side: Weapons Systems, Computers, Human Sciences," 127, no. 757 (March 1960): 188–190; "The Future of *Universal Man* Symposium with Anthony Cox, Gordon Graham, Lawrence Alloway," 127, no. 758 (April 1960): 253–260; Reyner Banham, ed., "History under Revision," with "Questionnaire, Masterpieces of the Modern Movement," and Reyner Banham, "History and Psychiatry," 127, no. 759 (May 1960): 325–332; "Propositions," with J. M. Richards, Nikolaus Pevsner, Hugh Casson, and H. de C. Hastings, sidebar notes by Banham, 127, no. 760 (June 1960): 381–388.

60. Reyner Banham, "School at Hunstanton," *Architectural Review* 116, no. 693 (August 1954): 153.

61. Banham, "Stocktaking," 93. Emphasis his.

62. Ibid.

63. Ibid., 94.

64. Ibid., 95–96.

65. Brothers, Drummond, and Llewelyn-Davies, "The Science Side."

66. Ibid., 188.

67. Banham, editorial comments in ibid., 188.

68. Banham, in ibid., 184.

69. Banham, in ibid.

70. Banham, in ibid., 185–186.

71. Banham, in ibid., 188. Banham concluded: "A very large part of the psychophysiological relationship between man and environment is likely to fall to the mathematician, not—as heretofore—the mystic."

72. Pevsner, "Propositions," 383.

73. Ibid., 386–387.

74. Banham, *Theory and Design*, 329.

75. Reyner Banham, "A Clip-on Architecture," *Architectural Design* 35, no. 11 (November 1965): 534–535.

76. Ibid., 535.

77. Ibid.

78. Banham first used the term *"une architecture autre"* in his essay "The New Brutalism," *Architectural Review* 118, no. 708 (December 1955): 361. For a review of the possible sources of the term, see Nigel Whiteley, *Reyner Banham: Historian of the Immediate Future* (Cambridge: MIT Press, 2002), 118–122.

79. Banham, "Clip-on," 535.

80. Ibid.

81. Reyner Banham, "A Comment from Peter Reyner Banham," in Peter Cook, ed., *Archigram* (Basel: Birkhäuser, 1972), 5.

82. Banham, "The New Brutalism," 358. The best analysis of Banham's image theory in relation to his technological futurism is Jonathan Farnham, "Vero pop per gente d'oggi: Reyner Banham, storia e fantascienza / Pure Pop for Now People: Reyner Banham, Science Fiction and History," *Lotus* 104 (1977): 111–131. Farnham studies Banham's idea of a "history of the immediate future" with respect to the science-fiction novels and comics of the 1950s.

83. Banham, "The New Brutalism," 358.

84. Ibid., 361.

85. Ibid.

86. Ibid.

87. Reyner Banham, *A Critic Writes: Essays by Reyner Banham*, selected by Mary Banham, Paul Barker, Sutherland Lyall, and Cedric Price (Berkeley: University of California Press, 1996), 382–383.

88. Reyner Banham, "This Is Tomorrow Exhibit," *Architectural Review* 120, no. 716 (September 1956): 188.

89. Ibid.

90. Ibid.

91. As Manfredo Tafuri noted, these two were in fact soon to come together literally in public presentation: "Their designs conquered a market that had remained closed to the products of Neoliberty; their desecrations, justified by appeals to Duchamp, finally gained international recognition at an exhibition organized by Emilio Ambasz at the Museum of Modern Art in 1972: 'Italy. The New Domestic Landscape.'" Manfredo Tafuri, *History of Italian Architecture, 1944–1985*, trans. Jessica Levine (Cambridge: MIT Press, 1989), 99.

92. Mark Wigley in conversation with the author.

93. Reyner Banham, *The Architecture of the Well-Tempered Environment* (London: Architectural Press, 1969), 257.

94. Ibid., 11.

95. Ibid., 265.

96. Reyner Banham, *Los Angeles: The Architecture of Four Ecologies* (London: Penguin Books, 1971), 21.

97. David Gebhard and Robert Winter, *A Guide to Architecture in Southern California* (Los Angeles: Los Angeles County Museum of Art, 1965). Banham called this work a "model version of the classical type of architectural gazetteer—erudite, accurate, clear, well-mapped, pocket-sized" (*Los Angeles*, 21).

98. Francis Carney, "Schlockology," review of *Los Angeles: The Architecture of Four Ecologies*, by Reyner Banham, *New York Review of Books*, 1 June 1972.

99. Banham, *Los Angeles*, 21.

100. The consideration of architecture as "trad" or "non-trad" was drawn by Banham in his critique of Sir Basil Spence's rebuilt Coventry Cathedral, in "Coventry Cathedral—Strictly 'Trad, Dad,'" *New Statesman* 63 (25 May 1962): 768–769. The argument over tradition was taken up by Stanford Anderson in a lecture of 1963 at the Architectural Association, London. See Stanford Anderson, "Architecture and Tradition that Isn't 'Trad, Dad,'" in Marcus Whiffen, ed., *The History, Theory and Criticism of Architecture* (Cambridge: MIT Press, 1964).

101. The four pieces in *The Listener* were Reyner Banham, "Encounter with Sunset Boulevard," *The Listener* 80 (22 August 1968): 235–236; "Roadscape with Rusting Rails" (29 August 1968): 267–268; "Beverly Hills, Too, Is a Ghetto" (5 September 1968): 296–298; "The Art of Doing Your Thing" (12 September 1968): 330–331.

102. Banham, "Roadscape with Rusting Rails," 268.

103. Banham, "Beverly Hills, Too, Is a Ghetto," 296.

104. Ibid., 298.

105. Banham, "The Art of Doing Your Thing," 331.

106. Reyner Banham, "LA: The Structure behind the Scene," *Architectural Design* 41 (April 1971): 227–230.

107. For an account of this exhibition and the pop movement in general, see Lawrence Alloway et al., *Modern Dreams: The Rise and Fall of Pop* (London: Institute of Contemporary Art, 1988).

108. Banham, *Theory and Design*, 220.

109. Ibid., 222–223.

110. Ibid., 13.

111. Anton Wagner, *Los Angeles: Werden, Leben und Gestalt de Zweimillionstadt in Südkalifornien* (Leipzig: Bibliographisches Institut, 1935). A manuscript translation of this work by Gavriel O. Rosenfeld, entitled *Los Angeles: The Development, Life, and Form of the Southern Californian Metropolis*, was commissioned by the Getty Research Institute in the History of Art and the Humanities, Los Angeles, 1997. Quotations are from this translation. Wagner, whose uncle had settled in Santa Monica in 1878, had been guided in his search for a topic by his advisor at the University of Leipzig, the urban geographer O. Schneider, who had himself published a work on "Traces of Spanish Colonization in the American Landscape" (*Spuren spanischer Kolonisieren in US-amerikanischen Landschaften* [Berlin, 1928]).

112. Wagner, *Los Angeles: The Development, Life, and Form of the Southern California Metropolis*, 1.

113. Ibid., 7.

114. Ibid., 6.

115. Ibid., 207.

116. Ibid., 166.

117. Ibid., 168, 169, 172.

118. Ibid., 207.

119. Banham, *Los Angeles*, 247.

120. Banham, "LA: The Structure behind the Scene," 227.

121. Banham, *Los Angeles*, 23.

122. Reyner Banham, *Scenes in America Deserta* (Salt Lake City: Gibbs M. Smith, 1982).

123. Banham, "The New Brutalism," 355.

4 RENAISSANCE MODERNISM: MANFREDO TAFURI

A first version of part of chapter 4 was published as "Disenchanted Histories: The Legacies of Manfredo Tafuri," *ANY* 25/26 (2000): 29–36.

1. Manfredo Tafuri, *Teorie e storia dell'architettura*, 2d ed. (1968; Bari: Edizioni Laterza, 1970), 165. Translation slightly emended from Manfredo Tafuri, *Theories and History of Architecture*, ed. Dennis Sharp, trans. Giorgio Verrecchia (London: Granada, 1980), 141.

2. Tafuri, *Theories and History*, 149.

3. Manfredo Tafuri and Massimo Teodori, letter in "Un dibattito sull'architettura e l'urbanistica italiane: Lettere di studenti," *Casabella* 214 (July 1960), 56.

4. Ibid.

5. Manfredo Tafuri, "La prima strada di Roma moderna: Via Nazionale," *Urbanistica* 27 (June 1959): 95–109.

6. Giorgio Piccinato and Manfredo Tafuri, "Helsinki," *Urbanistica* 33 (April 1961): 88–104.

7. Manfredo Tafuri, with Salvatore Dierna, Lidia Soprani, Giorgio Testa, and Alessandro Urbani, "L'ampliamento barocco del commune di S. Gregorio da Sassola," *Quaderni dell'Istituto di Storia dell'Architettura* (Facoltà di Architettura, Università di Roma) 31 (1961): 360–380.

8. Giorgio Ciucci, "The Formative Years," in "The Historical Project of Manfredo Tafuri," special issue, *Casabella* 619/620 (January–February 1995): 13–25 This article, the best of all those making up this special double issue of *Casabella* on Tafuri, traces his intellectual career and influences in detail from the 1950s to 1968. Tafuri's articles on the planning of Rome—"Il problema dei parchi pubblici in Roma e l'azione di 'Italia Nostra,'" *Urbanistica* 34 (Summer 1961): 105–111;

"Studi e ipotesi di lavoro per il sistema direzionale di Roma," *Casabella* 264 (June 1962): 27–35; "Un'ipotesi per la città-territorio di Roma. Strutture produttive e direzionali nel comprensorio Pontino" (with Enrico Fattinnanzi for the studio AUA), *Casabella* 274 (April 1963): 26–37—all share this analytical approach to large-scale planning. Tafuri wrote, "The present historical moment of the modern movement is certainly characterized by an effort to widen its critical and operative themes: toward the definition of a new dimension of urban space, which corresponds to a new dimension in the very methods of planning." Tafuri, "Studi e ipotesi," 27.

9. Tafuri et al., "L'ampliamento barocco," 369.

10. Jean-Louis Cohen, "Ceci n'est pas une histoire," special issue on Tafuri, *Casabella* 619–620 (1995): 53.

11. Manfredo Tafuri with Lidia Sopriani, "Problemi di critica e problemi di datazione in due monumenti taorminesi: Il Palazzo dei Duchi di S. Stefano e la 'Badia Vecchia,'" *Quaderni dell'Istituto di Storia dell'Architettura* 51 (1962): 1–13.

12. Ibid., 4.

13. Ibid.

14. Ibid., 1; also cited in English in Ciucci, "The Formative Years," 17; translation slightly altered.

15. Manfredo Tafuri, *Ludovico Quaroni e lo sviluppo dell'architettura moderna in Italia* (Milan: Edizioni di Comunità, 1963).

16. Manfredo Tafuri, "Ludovico Quaroni e la cultura architettonica italiana," *Zodiac* 11 (1963): 133. This article served as the introduction to the book published in the same year: Tafuri, *Ludovico Quaroni*.

17. Tafuri, "Ludovico Quaroni," 137.

18. Ibid.

19. Tafuri cites the polemical fragment of Edoardo Persico, "Sull'arte italiana," first published in 1930, and republished in Persico, *Scritti critici e polemici*, ed. Alfonso Gatto (Milan: Rosa e Ballo, 1947), 311–313; and Giulio Carlo Argan, "Architettura e ideologia," *Zodiac* 1 (1957): 49–51, reprinted in Argan, *Progetto e destino* (Milan: Mondadori, 1965), 82–90.

20. Argan, "Architettura e ideologia," cited by Tafuri in "Ludovico Quaroni," 144; also in *Progetto e destino*, 90.

21. Manfredo Tafuri, "Architettura e socialismo nel pensiero di William Morris," *Casabella* 280 (October 1963): 35–39.

22. Ibid., 35; italics in source.

23. Ibid.

24. Manfredo Tafuri, "For a Historical History," interview with Pietro Corsi, special issue on Tafuri, *Casabella* 619/620 (1995): 147; reprinted from *La Rivista dei Libri* (April 1994).

25. Manfredo Tafuri, "Un 'fuoco' urbano della Roma barocca," *Quaderni dell'Istituto di Storia dell'Architettura* 61 (1964): 1–20.

26. Tafuri would develop this analysis of the interaction of urban context and architectural language in "Borromini in Palazzo Carpegna: Documenti inediti e ipotesi critiche," *Quaderni dell'Istituto di Storia dell'Architettura* (1967): 85–107.

27. Tafuri, "Un 'fuoco,'" 16.

28. Ibid., 17.

29. Manfredo Tafuri, "Simbolo e ideologia nell'architettura dell'Illuminismo," *Comunità* 124/125 (November–December 1964): 68–80; "'Architectura artificialis': Claude Perrault, Sir Christopher Wren e il dibatto sul linguaggio architettonico," in *Barocco europeo, barocco italiano, barocco salentino (Atti del Congresso Internazionale sul Barocco, Lecce, 21–24 settembre, 1969)* (Lecce: L'Orsa Maggiore, 1969), 374–398.

30. Manfredo Tafuri, "L'idea di architettura nella letteratura teorica del manierismo," and "J. Barozzi da Vignola e la crisi del manierismo a Roma," *Bollettino del C.I.S.A Andrea Palladio* 9 (1967): 369–384, 385–399. Tafuri's *L'architettura del manierismo nel '500 europeo* (Rome: Officina, 1966) resumed these theses in a book he would later repudiate for what he felt was its oversimplified analysis and conclusions.

31. Tafuri, "L'idea di architettura," 369.

32. Manfredo Tafuri, *Interpreting the Renaissance: Princes, Cities, Architects*, trans. Daniel Sherer, foreword by K. Michael Hays (New Haven: Yale University Press, 2006), xxvii.

33. The proceedings of the AIA-ACSA Teacher Seminar on "The History, Theory and Criticism of Architecture," held at the Cranbrook Academy of Art in 1964, were published in Marcus Whiffen, ed., *The History, Theory and Criticism of Architecture* (Cambridge: MIT Press, 1965).

34. Bruno Zevi, "History as a Method of Teaching Architecture," in Whiffen, ed., *The History, Theory and Criticism of Architecture*, 11–21.

35. Reyner Banham, "Convenient Benches and Handy Hooks: Functional Considerations in the Criticism of the Art of Architecture," in Whiffen, ed., *The History, Theory and Criticism of Architecture*, 93.

36. Cited in ibid., 96.

37. Ibid., 96–97.

38. Tafuri, *Teorie e storia*, 19, my translation.

39. Ibid., 24.

40. Ibid.

41. Ibid., 25. The English translation, *Theories and History of Architecture* (London: Granada, 1980), is consistently unreliable; a single example among many would be this passage, which translates *ipocrasie* as "disappointments."

42. Ibid., 27.

43. Ibid., 34.

44. Karl Marx, *The Eighteenth Brumaire of Louis Bonaparte*, cited in Tafuri, *Teorie e storia*, 39.

45. Sergio Bettini, "Critica semantica e continuità storica dell'architettura europea," *Zodiac* 2 (1958): 7.

46. Ibid., 12; cited in Tafuri, *Teorie e storia*, 209.

47. Tafuri, *Teorie e storia*, 208.

48. Friedrich Nietzsche, *Untimely Meditations*, trans. R. J. Hollingdale (Cambridge: Cambridge University Press, 1983), 76.

49. Manfredo Tafuri, "Per una critica dell'ideologia architettonica," *Contropiano* 1 (January–April 1969): 31–79; translated by Stephen Sartorelli as "Toward a Critique of Architectural Ideology," in K. Michael Hays, ed., *Architecture Theory since 1968* (Cambridge: MIT Press, 1998), 6–35.

50. Tafuri, *Teorie e storia*, preface to the second edition, 3.

51. Manfredo Tafuri, *Architecture and Utopia: Design and Capitalist Development* (Cambridge: MIT Press, 1976), viii.

52. Ibid., ix–x.

53. Jean Le Rond d'Alembert, *Discours préliminaire de L' 'Encyclopédie'* (1750) (Paris: Editions Gonthier, 1965), 39.

54. Nikolaus Pevsner, *An Outline of European Architecture* (1943; New York: Charles Scribner's Sons, 1948), xix.

55. Tafuri, "Per una critica dell'ideologia architettonica," *Contropiano* 1, cited in *Casabella* 619/620, 31. This phrasing did not change in the book *Progetto e utopia* (Bari: Laterza, 1973).

56. Tafuri, "Toward a Critique of Architectural Ideology," 27. See also Tafuri, *Architecture and Utopia: Design and Capitalist Development*, trans. Barbara Luigia La Penta (Cambridge: MIT Press, 1976), 131. Here, and in *Theories and History, angoscia* is translated as "anguish," intimating a more "romantic" and individualistic emotionalism than Tafuri's "anxiety," which is deliberately related to the Marxist concept of alienation, and to Freud's construction of anxiety as a modern neurosis.

57. Tafuri, *Interpreting the Renaissance*, xxviii. I have inserted the significant terms from the Italian edition, *Ricerca del Rinascimento* (Turin: Einaudi, 1992).

58. Ibid.

59. Ibid., xxix.

60. Ibid.

61. Ibid.

62. Manfredo Tafuri, "A Search for Paradigms: Project, Truth, Artifice," trans. Daniel Sherer, *Assemblage* 28 (December 1995): 47. This is the first version of Sherer's translation of the foreword to *Ricerca*, and is closer to the original Italian than that translated in *Interpreting the Renaissance*, xxvii.

63. Tafuri, *Theories and History of Architecture*, 7–8.

64. Manfredo Tafuri, *Venice and the Renaissance* (Cambridge: MIT Press, 1989), x.

65. Tafuri, *Interpreting the Renaissance*, xxviii.

66. Max Weber, cited in Lawrence A. Scaff, *Fleeing the Iron Cage: Culture, Politics, and Modernity in the Thought of Max Weber* (Berkeley: University of California Press, 1989), 224.

67. Tafuri, *Theories and History*, 156.

68. Max Weber, "Science as a Vocation," in Peter Lassman and Irving Velody, eds., *Max Weber's 'Science as a Vocation'* (London: Unwin Hyman, 1989), 30.

69. Manfredo Tafuri, "Entretien avec Françoise Véry," *Architecture, Mouvement, Continuité* 39 (June 1976): 37.

70. Alberto Asor Rosa, "Critique of Ideology and Historical Practice," special issue on Tafuri, *Casabella* 619/620 (1995): 33. He notes, "the work of Tafuri in the

Contropiano period produced with the sense of 'total disenchantment' an estrangement still more total [*un totale disincanto, una estranità ancora più totale*] regarding the mechanism of values and connivance [*omertà*] that are the bases of any humanistic discipline academically understood." Ibid.

EPILOGUE: POSTMODERN OR *POSTHISTOIRE?*

1. See Antoine-Augustin Cournot, *Traité de l'enchainement des idées fondamentales dans les sciences et dans l'histoire*, 2 vols. (Paris: Hachette, 1861). For a clear description of Cournot's historical theories, see Raphaël Lévêque, *L' "Elément historique" dans la connaissance humaine d'après Cournot* (Paris: Les Belles Lettres, 1938). Lévêque was, with Raymond Ruyer (who had written his dissertation on Cournot, *L 'humanité de l'avenir d'après Cournot* [Paris: Félix Alcan, 1930]), one of many "neovitalists" before the Second World War whose work influenced Arnold Gehlen, and Hendrick de Man after 1945.

2. Hendrick de Man, unpublished manuscript, "The Age of Doom" (1950), published in Peter Dodge, *A Documentary Study of Hendrick de Man, Socialist Critic of Marxism* (Princeton: Princeton University Press, 1979), 345.

3. Gianni Vattimo, *End of Modernity: Nihilism and Hermeneutics in Postmodern Culture* (Baltimore: Johns Hopkins University Press, 1991), 7–8.

4. Ibid., 11.

INDEX